Karen Brown's
FRANCE B&B

2009

Chateau de Messey
Ozenay

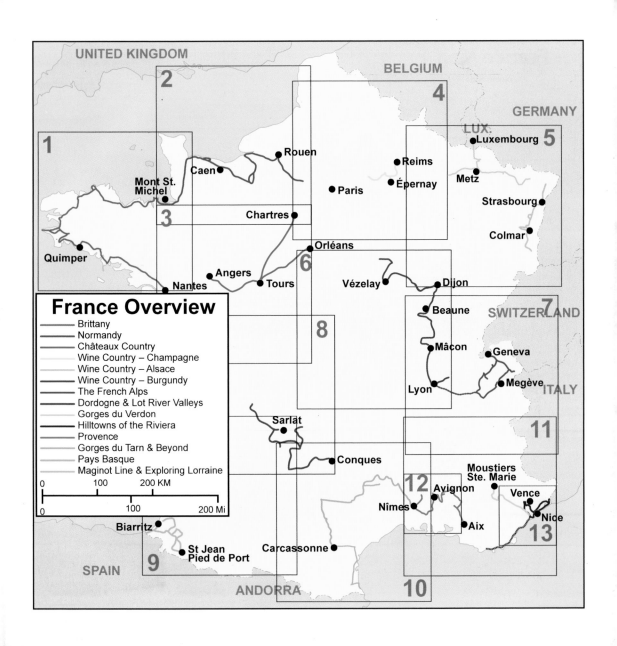

France Overview

- Brittany
- Normandy
- Châteaux Country
- Wine Country – Champagne
- Wine Country – Alsace
- Wine Country – Burgundy
- The French Alps
- Dordogne & Lot River Valleys
- Gorges du Verdon
- Hilltowns of the Riviera
- Provence
- Gorges du Tarn & Beyond
- Pays Basque
- Maginot Line & Exploring Lorraine

0   100   200 KM

0   100   200 Mi

UNITED KINGDOM

BELGIUM

GERMANY

LUX.

SWITZERLAND

ITALY

SPAIN

ANDORRA

Rouen
Caen
Mont St. Michel
Chartres
Orléans
Angers
Tours
Nantes
Quimper
Paris
Reims
Épernay
Metz
Luxembourg
Strasbourg
Colmar
Vézelay
Dijon
Beaune
Mâcon
Geneva
Lyon
Megève
Sarlat
Conques
Nîmes
Avignon
Aix
Moustiers Ste. Marie
Vence
Nice
Biarritz
St Jean Pied de Port
Carcassonne

1 2 3 4 5 6 7 8 9 10 11 12 13

France Map 2

- ● Places to Stay
- Brittany
- Normandy
- Châteaux Country

0   25   50 KM
0   25   50 Mi

UNITED KINGDOM

English Channel

Boulogne -sur-Mer

Guide to Normandy Beaches

Cherbourg

Utah Beach
Omaha Beach
Gold Beach
Juno Beach
Sword Beach

Dieppe

Le Havre

Dieppe

Cherbourg

Pointe du Hoc

St Laurent sur Mer

Colleville sur Mer

Port en Bessin

Longues sur Mer

Le Havre

Trouville

Pont Audemer

Rouen

N14

Grandcamp Maisy

Arromanches

Crépon

St Germain du Pert

Vouilly

Deauville

Appeville

Seine

Bayeux

Le Breuil-en-Bessin

Caen

N13 Lisieux

Bernay

Evreux

Giverny

A13

St Lô

Livarot

Crouttes

Vimoutiers

Villiers le Mahieu

Falaise

N138

Servon

Argentan

Haras National du Pin

N12

Mont St Michel

Vergoncey

N158

Moulicent

St Pierre de Plesguen

Alençon

Chartres

N10

N175

N12

St Leonard des Bois

A11

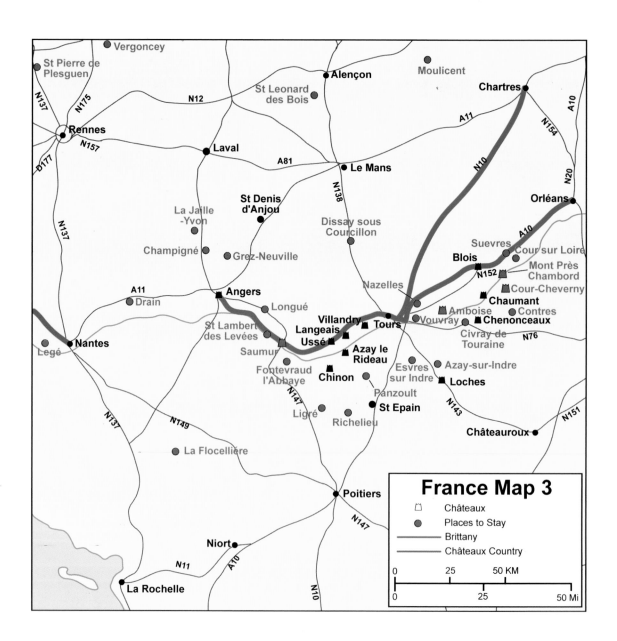

France Map 3

Châteaux

● Places to Stay

Brittany

Châteaux Country

| 0 | 25 | 50 KM |

| 0 | 25 | 50 Mi |

Vergoncey

St Pierre de Plesguen

Moulicent

Alençon

Chartres

St Leonard des Bois

N137

N175

A11

A10

N154

Rennes

N157

N12

N10

N20

Laval

A81

Le Mans

D177

Orléans

La Jaille -Yvon

St Denis d'Anjou

A10

N137

Champigné

Grez-Neuville

Dissay sous Courcillon

N138

Suevres

Cour sur Loire

Blois

Mont Près Chambord

N152

Cour-Cheverny

A11

Drain

Longué

Nazelles

Chaumant

Angers

Villandry

Amboise

Contres

St Lambert des Levées

Langeais

Tours

Vouvray

Chenonceaux

Nantes

Ussé

Saumur

Azay le Rideau

Civray-de Touraine

N76

Legé

Fontevraud l'Abbaye

Chinon

Esvres sur Indre

Azay-sur-Indre

St Lambert

Panzoult

Loches

N137

N149

Ligré

St Epain

Richelieu

N143

N151

La Flocellière

Châteauroux

N147

Poitiers

N137

N147

Niort

N11

A10

N10

La Rochelle

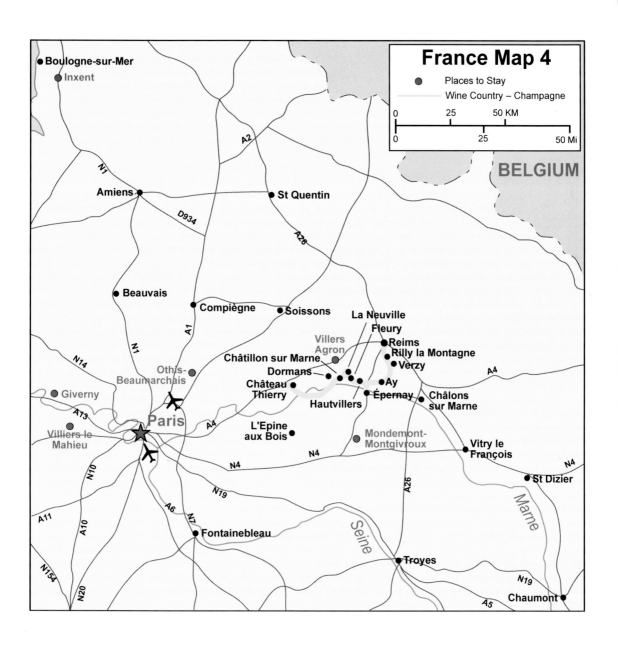

France Map 4

- Places to Stay
- Wine Country – Champagne

0   25   50 KM
0   25   50 Mi

BELGIUM

Boulogne-sur-Mer
Inxent

A2

N1

Amiens

St Quentin

D934

A26

Beauvais

Compiègne

Soissons

La Neuville
Fleury

Villers
Agron

Reims
Rilly la Montagne

N14

Châtillon sur Marne

Verzy

A1

Dormans

Ay

A4

N1

Othis-
Beaumarchais

Château
Thierry

Épernay

Châlons
sur Marne

Giverny

Hautvillers

A13

Paris

A4

Villiers le
Mahieu

L'Epine
aux Bois

Mondemont-
Montgivroux

Vitry le
François

N10

N4

N4

A26

St Dizier

N4

N19

Marne

A6

N7

A11

A10

Fontainebleau

Seine

N154

N20

Troyes

N19

Chaumont

A5

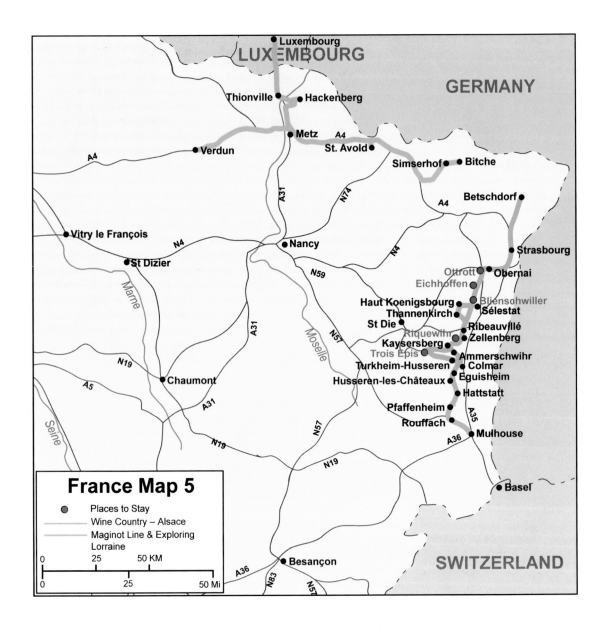

France Map 5

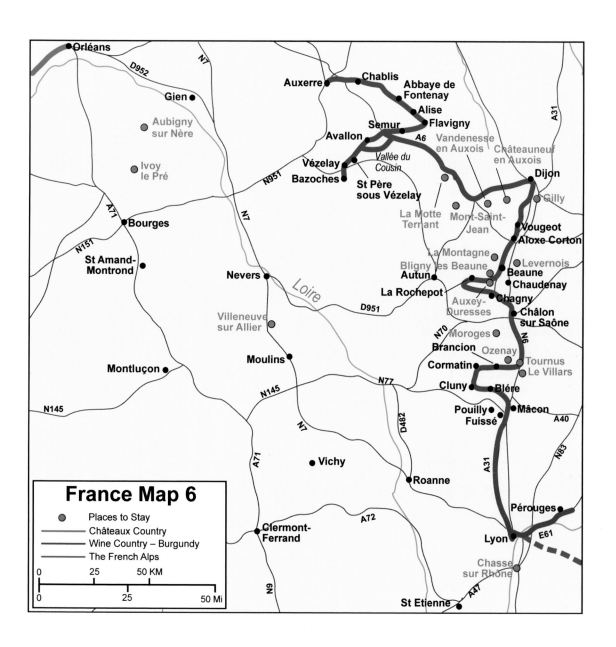

France Map 6

- ⬤ Places to Stay
- — Châteaux Country
- — Wine Country – Burgundy
- — The French Alps

0   25   50 KM
0   25   50 Mi

Orléans
Gien
Aubigny sur Nère
Ivoy le Pré
Bourges
St Amand-Montrond
Nevers
Moulins
Montluçon
Vichy
Roanne
Clermont-Ferrand
Villeneuve sur Allier

Auxerre
Chablis
Abbaye de Fontenay
Alise
Flavigny
Semur
Avallon
Vézelay
Bazoches
St Père sous Vézelay
Vallée du Cousin
Vandenesse en Auxois
Châteauneuf en Auxois
Dijon
Gilly
La Motte Ternant
Mont-Saint-Jean
Vougeot
Aloxe Corton
La Montagne
Levernois
Bligny les Beaune
Autun
La Rochepot
Beaune
Chaudenay
Chagny
Auxey-Duresses
Châlon sur Saône
Moroges
Brancion
Ozenay
Tournus
Le Villars
Cormatin
Cluny
Bléré
Pouilly Fuissé
Mâcon
Pérouges
Lyon
Chasse sur Rhône
St Etienne

Loire

N7
D952
A31
A6
N951
A71
N151
D951
N70
N6
N77
D482
N145
N145
N7
A71
N9
A72
A31
A40
N83
E61
A47

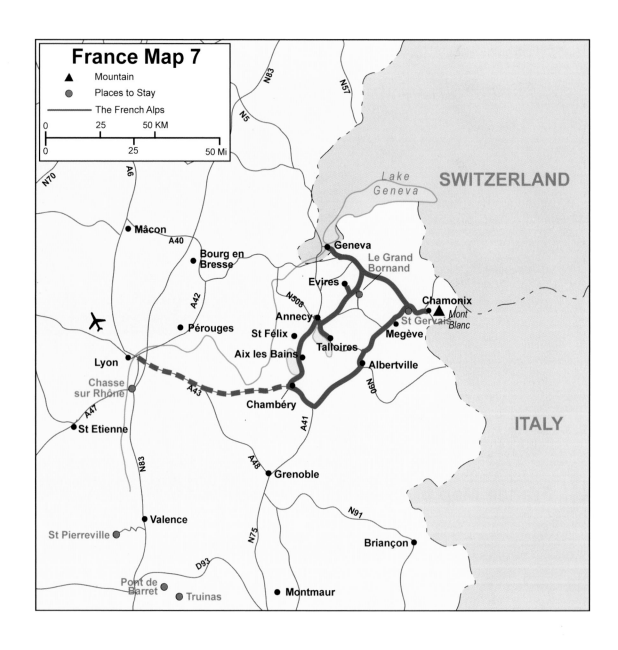

France Map 7

▲ Mountain

● Places to Stay

— The French Alps

0   25   50 KM

0   25   50 Mi

SWITZERLAND

ITALY

Lake Geneva

N83

N57

N5

N70

A6

A40

A42

N508

A47

A43

N83

A48

N75

D93

A41

N90

N91

Mâcon

Bourg en Bresse

Pérouges

Lyon

Chasse sur Rhône

St Etienne

St Pierreville

Valence

Pont de Barret

Truinas

Montmaur

Grenoble

Chambéry

Aix les Bains

St Félix

Annecy

Talloires

Evires

Geneva

Le Grand Bornand

St Gervais

Chamonix

Mont Blanc

Megève

Albertville

Briançon

France Map 8

Places to Stay

Dordogne & Lot River Valleys

0   25   50 KM

0   25   50 Mi

La Flocellière

Chantonnay

Poitiers

N137

N149

Niort

N11

A10

N10

N147

N145

N20

La Rochelle

N137

Saintes

Cognac

N141

Angoulême

N10

D674

Limoges

N21

N20

Pauillac

Brantôme

Hautefort

N89

Castelnau de Médoc

Périgueux

N89

Lascaux

Brive la Gaillarde

Collanges la Rouge

La Roque St Christophe

Les Eyzies

Carennac

Castelnau

N89

Bordeaux

St Emilion

Bergerac

Paunat

Sarlat

Montal

Aurillac

Beynac

Loubressac

Le Coux

Padirac

Dordogne

Domme

Rocamadour

Gramat

N122

St Vivien

D710

Duravel

Mercuès

Tour de Faure

Conques

N140

Figeac

N20

N21

Lot

Villeneuve

Cahors

St Cirq Lapopie

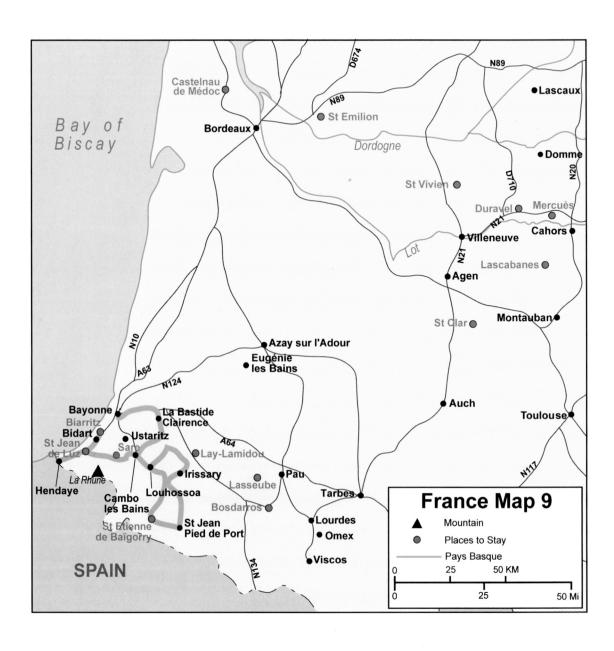

France Map 9

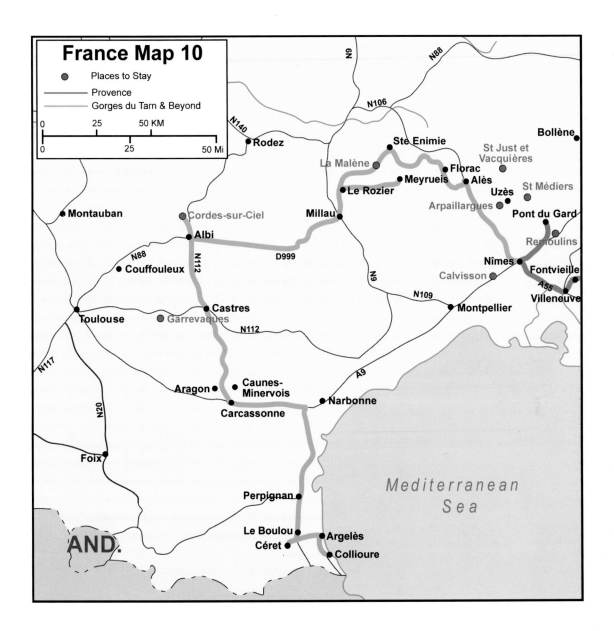

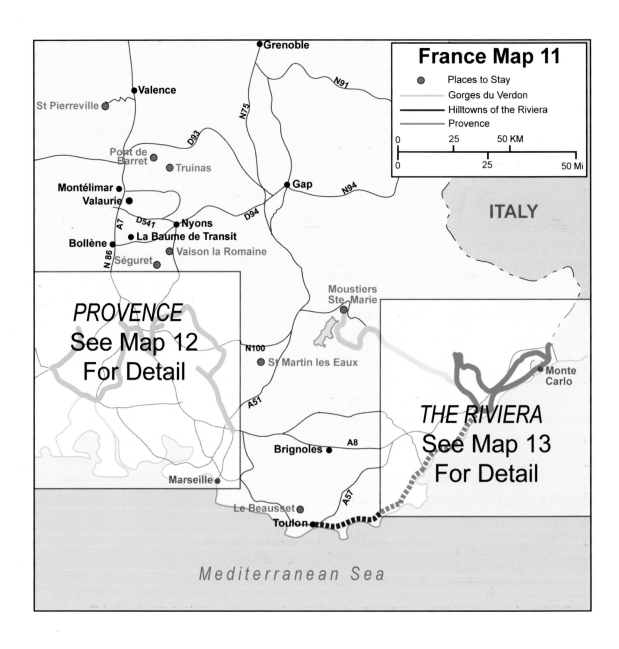

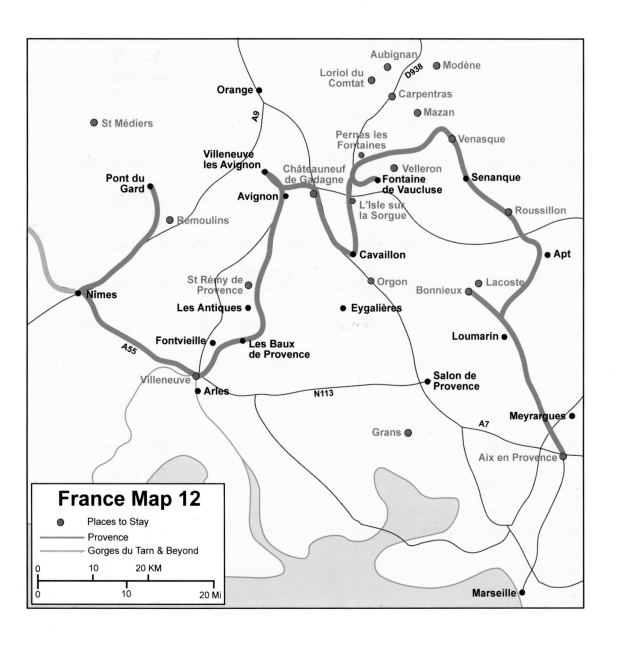

France Map 12

- ● Places to Stay
- ── Provence
- ── Gorges du Tarn & Beyond

0   10   20 KM
0   10   20 Mi

Aubignan
Modène
Loriol du Comtat
Orange
St Médiers
Carpentras
Mazan
Pernès les Fontaines
Venasque
Villeneuve les Avignon
Châteauneuf de Gadagne
Velleron
Fontaine de Vaucluse
Senanque
Pont du Gard
Avignon
L'Isle sur la Sorgue
Roussillon
Rémoulins
Cavaillon
Apt
St Rémy de Provence
Orgon
Lacoste
Nîmes
Bonnieux
Les Antiques
Eygalières
Loumarin
Fontvieille
Les Baux de Provence
Villeneuve
Salon de Provence
Meyrargues
Arles
Grans
Aix en Provence
Marseille

A9
D938
A55
N113
A7

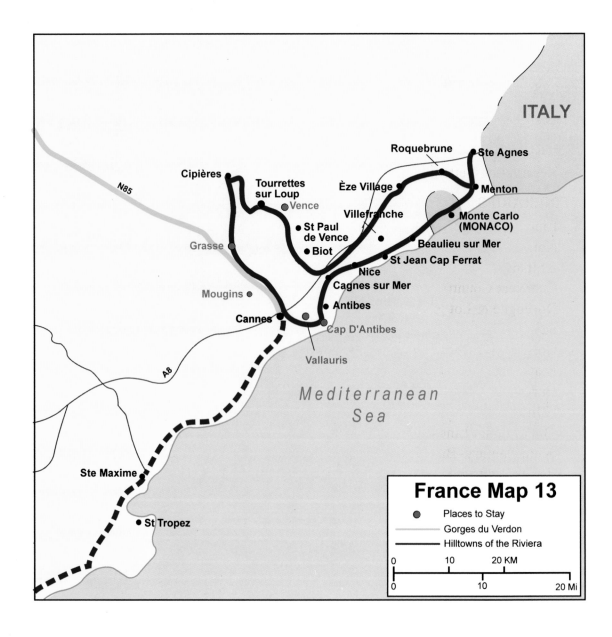

ITALY

Roquebrune

Ste Agnes

Cipières

Tourrettes
sur Loup

Èze Village

Menton

Vence

Villefranche

Monte Carlo
(MONACO)

St Paul
de Vence

Beaulieu sur Mer

Grasse

Biot

St Jean Cap Ferrat

Nice

Mougins

Cagnes sur Mer

Antibes

Cannes

Cap D'Antibes

Vallauris

N85

A8

*Mediterranean
Sea*

Ste Maxime

St Tropez

France Map 13

● Places to Stay
— Gorges du Verdon
— Hilltowns of the Riviera

0   10   20 KM
0   10   20 Mi

Contents

MAPS

Places to Stay & Itineraries   Color Section at Front of Book

INTRODUCTION   1–20

     Reservation Letter in French   20

ITINERARIES   21–174

     Itineraries Overview Map   21

     Normandy   23–34

     Brittany   35–42

     Châteaux Country   43–52

     Dordogne & Lot River Valleys   53–66

     Pays Basque   67–78

     Gorges du Tarn & Beyond   79–88

     Provence   89–100

     Gorges du Verdon   101–106

     Hilltowns of the French Riviera   107–120

     The Maginot Line & Exploring Lorraine   121–134

     Wine Country–Burgundy   135–148

     Wine Country–Alsace   149–158

     Wine Country–Champagne   159–166

     The French Alps   167–174

BED & BREAKFAST DESCRIPTIONS   175–316

INDEX   317–330

Wishing
Marie and Philippe
and her beautiful daughters,
Jessie and Chloé,
A Lifetime of Happiness and Love

2009 Cover Painting: Château de Messey, Ozenay

Authors: Karen Brown and Clare Brown.

Contributing Author: Marie Collins Notot.

Editors: Clare Brown, Karen Brown, June Eveleigh Brown, Debbie Tokumoto, Melissa Jaworski.

Illustrations: Barbara Maclurcan Tapp.

Color photos: Ben Kong.

Cover painting: Jann Pollard.

Maps: Rachael Kircher-Randolph.

Technical support: Andrew Harris.

Distributed by National Book Network, 15200 NBN Way, Blue Ridge Summit, PA 17214, USA. Tel: 717-794-3800 or 1-800-462-6420, Fax: 1-800-338-4500, Email: custserv@nbnbooks.com

A catalog record for this book is available from the British Library.

ISSN 1535-7368

Introduction

Travelers with a sense of adventure can truly experience France and get to know the French people by journeying beyond Paris and exploring the countryside. The way of life outside Paris ("in the provinces" as the French say) is a fascinating reflection of French history and culture—the impact of modern civilization is felt, but a pronounced respect for tradition and quality of life remains. Beyond Paris, the land is like a treasure chest: royal forests with graceful deer, romantic castles casting their images onto serene lakes, picturesque villages with half-timbered houses, vineyards edged with roses, meadows of fragrant lavender, fields of vibrant yellow sunflowers, medieval walled cities perched upon mountain tops, and wild coastlines—all waiting to be discovered.

PURPOSE OF THIS GUIDE

This guide is written with two main objectives: to describe the most charming, beguiling lodgings throughout France and to "tie" them together with itineraries to enable travelers to plan their own holiday. The aim is not simply to inform you of the fact that these places exist, but to encourage you to go and see for yourself: explore towns and villages not emphasized on tours and stay at properties that truly reflect the French lifestyle. This book contains all of the necessary ingredients to assist you with your travel arrangements: easy-to-follow driving itineraries that take you deep into the lovely French countryside, and, most importantly, a selective listing of bed and breakfasts that we have seen and enjoy. It might be an elegant château dominating a bank of the River Loire or a cozy mill tucked into the landscape of the Dordogne Valley, but there is a common denominator—they all have charm, an enticing location, and comfort. Our theory is that where you stay each night matters: the bed and breakfasts should add the touch of perfection that makes your holiday very special. The memories you bring home should be of more than just museums, landmarks, and palace tours. Such sights are important, but with this guide you can add a romantic element to your trip: traveling the enchanting back roads of France and staying in picturesque hideaways.

If you also enjoy staying at small hotels and inns, we suggest you refer to our companion guide, *France Hotels: Exceptional Places to Stay & Itineraries*. Like the bed and breakfasts, the properties we have selected for the "inns" guide have been personally visited and reflect a wide range of accommodation: from very elegant hotels to charming country inns. Offering a different level of service, an itinerary incorporating stays at bed and breakfasts, as well as country inns, can result in a wonderful and memorable trip.

We encourage you to buy new editions of our guide as in each new edition we add new discoveries; update prices, phone and fax numbers; and delete places that no longer meet our standards. This 2009 edition proudly boasts 140 bed and breakfast recommendations and fourteen wonderful driving itineraries that weave a journey through the landscape of the French countryside.

ABOUT BED & BREAKFAST TRAVEL

The bed and breakfast formula is for any traveler who wants to experience the *real* France, its people and culture. There is a social aspect to this style of travel that is not found in the normal tourist experience. You have ample opportunities to meet and exchange ideas with other travelers (usually Europeans) as well as to get to know your hosts and their families, many times making lasting friendships. Single travelers will love the friendliness of bed and breakfast stays because they will not feel alone. Bed and breakfast travel is also tailor-made for families with children—the informality, convenience, and reasonable rates make travel a pleasure. *Note:* Many places also offer family accommodation with several bedrooms and a small kitchen.

ACCOMMODATIONS—WHAT TO EXPECT

Bed and breakfast accommodation, in most cases, means a bedroom rented in the private home of a French family. Oftentimes, the French term *chez* used before a family name translates as "at the home of" and is an accurate phrase when describing the type of accommodation and ambiance that you can expect. However, do not feel that to travel the bed and breakfast route means you will be roughing it. Although some of the least expensive choices in our guide offer very simple rooms, it is possible to choose places to stay that offer sumptuous accommodations—as beautiful as you will find in the most luxurious hotels, at a fraction of the cost. So, this book is definitely not just for the budget-conscious traveler, but for anyone who wants to meet the French people and experience their exceptional hospitality.

The dividing line between a bed and breakfast and a "regular" hotel is sometimes very obscure. In essence, hotels are larger and offer more commercial amenities than a bed and breakfast—hotels usually have a reception desk, a staff member always on the premises, a public restaurant, telephones in the rooms, and a porter for luggage. However, nothing is truly black and white. Some of the bed and breakfasts featured in this guide are very sophisticated and offer every imaginable nicety including exquisite linens, fluffy bathrobes, towel warmers, hairdryers, and an assortment of the finest toiletries. As a rule of thumb, you will find that bed and breakfast accommodations are far less expensive than comparable rooms in a hotel, offer a more personalized warmth of welcome, and provide a better opportunity to meet other guests. *Note:* We have intentionally included a few simple, well-priced, small hotels with charm that are located in areas where the destination warrants a stay where we could not find a suitable bed and breakfast to offer you.

Hosts cover the entire spectrum of French society, from titled counts and countesses to country farmers. All who are listed in this guide are hospitable and have a true desire to meet and interact with their guests. It takes a special kind of person to open his home to strangers, and the French who do so are genuinely warm and friendly.

Bed and breakfasts are called *chambres d'hôtes* (literally, "guest bedrooms") and are most frequently situated in rural settings. This guide offers lodging selections in or near major tourist sites as well as in unspoiled, less-visited regions. Most hosts prefer that their bed and breakfast guests take the time to unwind by staying at least three nights (Americans have a reputation for always being in a hurry). Frequently discounts are offered for stays of a week or longer, but the advantages of longer stays in one place are far greater than just financial: it is great fun to become friends with the owners and other guests, to just *settle in*—no packing and unpacking every night. Frequently a house-party atmosphere prevails as you gather with other guests in the evening to share your travel adventures. We strongly urge you to choose one place to stay and make it your hub, going off in a different direction each day to explore the countryside. Spend time in a medieval stone-walled château evoking dreams of knights and their ladies or experience the sights and sounds of a simple farm surrounded by bucolic pasturelands. Careful reading of the descriptions in this guide will ensure that the homes you select will provide the type of welcome and accommodation you prefer. Each home is, of course, unique, offering its own special charm, yet all share one wonderful common denominator: the welcoming feeling of being treated as a cherished guest in a friend's home. We unequivocally feel there is no finer or more rewarding way to travel in France.

We personally visited hundreds of bed and breakfasts, traveling to remote villages and hamlets throughout France to find the finest places to stay. Even after honing down our list by prior research, we usually included only about one out of every three places seen. We made our personal selection based on individual charm, antique ambiance, romantic feel, and, above all, warmth of welcome. We chose each place to stay on its merit alone. We selected in each region the most outstanding accommodations in various price ranges. Our choices are very subjective: we have handpicked for you those places that we like the most and think you will also enjoy.

AIRFARE

Karen Brown's Guides have long recommended Auto Europe for their excellent car rental services. Their air travel division, Destination Europe, an airline broker working with major American and European carriers, offers deeply discounted coach- and business-class fares to over 200 European gateway cities. It also gives Karen Brown travelers an additional 5% discount off its already highly competitive prices (cannot be combined with any other offers or promotions). We recommend making reservations by phone at (800) 835-1555. When phoning, be sure to use the Karen Brown ID number 99006187 to secure your discount.

CAR RENTAL

Readers frequently ask our advice on car rental companies. We always use Auto Europe, a car rental broker that works with the major car rental companies to find the lowest possible price. They also offer motor homes and chauffeur services. Auto Europe's toll-free phone service from every European country connects you to their U.S.-based, 24-hour reservation center (ask for the European Phone Number Card to be sent to you). Auto Europe offers our readers a discount, and occasionally free upgrades. Be sure to use the Karen Brown ID number 99006187 to receive your discount and any special offers.

Make your own reservations for Auto Europe online via our website, *www.karenbrown.com* (select *Auto Europe* from the home page), or by telephone (800-223-5555).

CELLPHONES

Cellphones are wonderful to have as many bed and breakfasts do not have direct-dial phones in the guestrooms and if you used the hosts' personal phone for phone calls or computer hookup, it would be an inconvenience both to you and to them, as well as hard to determine charges. Also, cellphones are wonderfully convenient when you are on the road and want to call for directions, advise of a changed arrival time, or simply make sure that someone is home—especially since public phones in France are no longer coin-operated but require that you purchase a phone card.

Cellphones can be rented through your car rental company, at the airport or train stations, or you can purchase an international phone once you are overseas. If you are considering taking your cellphone from home, check with your carrier to make sure that your phone even has international capability. Sometimes it is necessary to make arrangements before you depart to activate a special service. We would also recommend getting international phone access numbers and inquiring about international access charges or rates so there are no billing surprises.

CHILDREN

Generally, bed and breakfasts are wonderful places to stay at when traveling with children. For the bed and breakfasts that have advised us that their home is appropriate for children, we have indicated their policy by listing the symbol ♨ with the description information. While legally children cannot be refused accommodation, as parents, we really want to stay where our children are genuinely welcome.

CLOTHING

France stretches some 1,200 kilometers from Calais on the north coast to Nice on the Riviera in the south, so there is a great range of weather conditions, regardless of the season. For winter bring warm coats, sweaters, gloves, snug hats, and boots. The rest of the year a layered approach will equip you for any kind of weather: skirts or trousers combined with blouses or shirts that can be "built upon" with layers of sweaters depending upon the chill of the day. A raincoat is a necessity, along with a folding umbrella. Sturdy, comfortable walking shoes are recommended not only for roaming the countryside and mountain trails, but also for negotiating cobbled streets. Daytime dress is casual, but in the evening it is courteous to dress up for dinner.

CREDIT CARDS

Whether or not an establishment accepts credit cards is indicated in the list of icons at the bottom of each description by the symbol . We have also indicated the specific cards accepted by using the following codes: AX–American Express, MC–MasterCard, VS–Visa, or simply, all major. *Note:* Even if an inn does not accept credit card payment, it will perhaps request your account number as a guarantee of arrival.

CURRENCY

All rates are quoted in euros, using the " € " symbol. The euro is now the official currency of most European Union countries, including France, having completely replaced national currencies as of February 2002. Visit our website (*www.karenbrown.com*) for an easy-to-use online currency converter.

When traveling, an increasingly popular and convenient way to obtain foreign currency is simply to use your bankcard at an ATM machine. You pay a fixed fee for this but, depending on the amount you withdraw, it is usually less than the percentage-based fee charged to exchange currency or travelers' checks. Be sure to check with your bank or credit card company about fees and necessary pin numbers prior to departure.

DRIVING & DIRECTIONS

It is important to understand some basic directions in French when locating bed and breakfasts. Signs directing you to chambres d'hôtes are often accompanied by either *1ère à droite* (first road on the right) or *1ère à gauche* (first road on the left). Chambres d'hôtes signs can vary from region to region, but many have adopted the national green-and-yellow sign of the Gîtes de France organization of which many of them are members.

Maps label the roads with their proper numbers, but you will find when driving that signs usually indicate a city direction instead of a road number. For example, instead of finding a sign for N909 north, you will see a sign for Lyon, so you must figure out by referring to your map whether Lyon is north of where you are and if N909 leads there. The city that is signposted is often a major city quite a distance away. This may seem awkward at first, but is actually an easy system once you understand the logic.

Most bed and breakfast homes and farmhouses are located outside the town or village under which they are listed and are often difficult to find. To make finding your destination easier, specific driving instructions are given in each bed and breakfast description. However, we strongly recommend that you ask for detailed directions and a map when making your reservation, or go to *www.karenbrown.com* and link through to the property's own website, where in many cases detailed directions are available and can be printed out for future reference. An added suggestion: Always plan to arrive at your destination before nightfall—road signs are difficult to see after dark.

BELTS: It is mandatory and strictly enforced in France that every passenger wears a seat belt. Children under ten years of age must sit in the back seat.

DRIVER'S LICENSE: A valid driver's license from your home country is accepted in France if your stay does not exceed one year. The minimum driving age is 18.

GASOLINE: Americans are shocked by the high price of gasoline in Europe, especially when they realize published prices are for liters—only one fourth of a gallon. At some self-service stations you must pay in advance, before using the pumps (credit cards such as MasterCard and Visa are now often accepted). "Fill her up, please" translates as *"Faîtes le plein, s'il vous plaît."*

PARKING: It is illegal to park a car in the same place for more than 24 hours. In larger towns it is often customary that on the first 15 days of a month parking is permitted on the side of the road whose building addresses are odd numbers, and from the 16th to the end of the month on the even-numbered side of the road. Parking is prohibited in front of hospitals, police stations, and post offices. Blue Zones restrict parking to just one hour and require that you place a disc in your car window on Monday to Saturday from 9 am to 12:30 pm and again from 2:30 to 7 pm. Discs can be purchased at police stations and tobacco shops. Gray Zones are metered zones and a fee must be paid between the hours of 9 am and 7 pm.

ROADS: The French highway network consists of *autoroutes* (freeways or motorways), *péages* (autoroutes on which a toll is charged), and secondary roads (also excellent highways). Charges on toll roads are assessed according to the distance traveled. A travel ticket is issued on entry and you pay the toll on leaving the autoroute. The ticket will outline costs for distance traveled for various types of vehicles. It is expensive to travel on toll roads, so weigh carefully the advantage of time versus cost. If you have unlimited time and a limited budget, you may prefer the smaller highways and country roads. A suggestion would be to use the autoroutes to navigate in and out of, or bypass large cities and then return to the country roads. Credit cards are now accepted at tollbooths.

SPEED: Posted speed limits are strictly enforced and fines are hefty. Traffic moves fast on the autoroutes and toll roads with speed limits of 130 kph (81 mph). On the secondary highways the speed limit is 90 kph (56 mph). The speed limit within city and town boundaries is usually 60 kph (38 mph). Keep a lookout for the *gendarmes*!

ELECTRICAL CURRENT

If you are taking any electrical appliances made for use in the United States, you will need a transformer plus a two-pin adapter. A voltage of 220 AC current at 50 cycles per second is almost countrywide, though in remote areas you may encounter 120V. The voltage is often displayed on the socket. Even though we recommend that you purchase appliances with dual-voltage options whenever possible, it will still be necessary to have the appropriate socket adapter. Also, be especially careful with expensive equipment such as computers—verify the adapter/converter capabilities and requirements.

ICONS

Icons allow us to provide additional information about our recommended properties. We have introduced these icons in the guidebooks and there are more on our website, *www.karenbrown.com*. ✳ Air conditioning in rooms, ⏉ Beach nearby, ☙ Breakfast included in room rate, ⅍ Children welcome, ♨ Cooking classes offered, ▣ Credit cards accepted, ☎ Direct-dial telephone in room, ⛰ Dinner served upon request, 🐕 Dogs by special request, ▦ Elevator, ⫙ Exercise room, @ Internet access, ⅄ Mini-refrigerator in guestrooms, ⊗ Some non-smoking rooms, P Parking available, ¶ Restaurant, ✿ Spa, ⍋ Swimming pool, ⫏ Tennis, ▣ Television with English channels, ⌕ Wedding facilities, ♿ Wheelchair friendly, W Wireless available for guests, ⫟ Golf course nearby, ⫚ Hiking trails nearby, ⛷ Horseback riding nearby, ⛷ Skiing nearby, ⚓ Water sports nearby, ♥ Wineries nearby.

ITINERARIES

Fourteen driving itineraries are included in this guide to help you map a route through the various regions of France. Previously, these itineraries were only published in our guide, *France Hotels: Exceptional Places to Stay & Itineraries* because we made the assumption that travelers would purchase both our titles on France and we did not want to duplicate the information. However, it seems many people only purchase one of the guides and we now want to make the suggested countryside routes available to all, regardless of which book you choose. Depending on your time and interests, you might want to patchwork together a trip encompassing a couple of itineraries.

An overview map that shows all 14 itineraries is found on page 21. At the beginning of each itinerary we suggest our recommended pacing to help you decide the amount of time to allocate to each region.

LANGUAGES & LEVEL OF ENGLISH SPOKEN

Possessing even the most rudimentary knowledge of French will make your trip a thousand times more rewarding and enjoyable. Spend a little time reviewing and practicing your French learned in school before you go. You can always get by—usually there is someone around who speaks at least a little English, and the French are accustomed to dealing with non-French-speaking travelers. It is helpful to carry paper and pencil to write down numbers for ease of comprehension, as well as a French phrase book and a French/English dictionary. If pronunciation seems to be a problem, you can then indicate the word or phrase in writing.

The level of English spoken in the bed and breakfasts in this guide runs the gamut from excellent to none at all. Because some of you will have fun practicing your high-school French while others will feel more comfortable communicating freely in English, we have indicated under each bed and breakfast description what you can expect. Levels of the hosts' English are indicated according to the following guidelines:

No or very little English—a few words at best.

Some English—a little more than the most rudimentary, or perhaps their children speak schoolroom English. More is understood than spoken.

Good English—easy conversational English, but no long, involved conversations. More is understood than can be expressed verbally. Speak slowly and clearly.

Fluent English—can understand and communicate with ease—frequently the person has lived in Britain or the United States.

Other languages: We also note if your hosts can communicate in a language other than French or English. Perhaps you might find your "common" language is German!

MAPS

Each itinerary is preceded by a map showing the suggested route and sightseeing town locations. At the front of the book, in the Color-Map section, the maps reference the location of every town where we recommend a bed and breakfast as well as an outline of the various countryside itineraries. All maps included in this guide are intended to provide a general impression of a region and itinerary route, and an approximate location of the towns where recommended places are found. These maps were drawn by an artist and are not intended to replace accurate commercial maps.

Detailed maps are essential for identifying, navigating, and exploring all the wonderful country roads and finding secluded countryside properties, and we recommend purchasing them in advance of your trip, both to aid in the planning of your journey and to avoid spending vacation time searching for the appropriate maps. We find Michelin maps are good and dependable and we refer to them in this book for bed and breakfast locations. Since we ourselves often had difficulty finding all the maps we wanted from one source, for our readers' convenience we stock a full inventory of the Michelin maps referenced in our guides, in addition to other Michelin products. You can easily order maps online through our website, *www.karenbrown.com*, and we will ship them out immediately.

MEALS

BREAKFAST in a bed and breakfast is usually the Continental type, including a choice of coffee (black or with hot milk), tea, hot chocolate, bread (sometimes a croissant or wheat bread for variety), butter, and jam. The evening before, hosts will customarily ask when you want breakfast and what beverage you prefer. Sometimes they will offer a choice of location such as outside in the garden or indoors in the dining area or kitchen.

As the term "bed & breakfast" implies, breakfast is almost always included in the room rate, which is confirmed in the list of icons at the bottom of each description by the symbol ☕. It is mentioned if breakfast is not included and the price is quoted per person.

RESTAURANTS: In the few instances where a property we recommend in this book actually has a restaurant and serves meals to non-guests, we have indicated this with the symbol ⑪ in the list of icons at the bottom of the description.

TABLE D'HÔTE means that the host serves an evening meal. Of all the special features of a bed and breakfast experience, this is one of the most outstanding—if you see "Table d'hôte" (also identified by the icon, ⛰) offered under the bed and breakfast description, be sure to request it! You will not have a choice of menu, but you will have a delicious, home-cooked dinner (usually the ingredients are fresh from the garden) and be able to meet fellow guests. Most frequently meals are served at one large table with the hosts joining you and the other guests, but sometimes they are served at individual or shared tables. Expect at least three courses (an appetizer, a main course, and dessert), often four or five courses (with salad and cheese being served between the entree and dessert).

Prices quoted are *always* per person. The price depends upon how elaborate the meal is, the sophistication of the service, the number of courses, and what beverages are included. However, whether the meal is simple or gourmet, whenever you take advantage of the table d'hôte option, you will enjoy a great value and a memorable experience.

Sometimes even wine is included in the price, making this an even greater value. In a simple bed and breakfast, this is usually a house wine of the region—not fancy, but usually very good. Some of the deluxe places to stay often offer an aperitif before dinner, a selection of wines with the meal, and a nightcap afterwards.

VERY IMPORTANT: When we indicate in the bed and breakfast description that table d'hôte is available, it is *always available only by prior arrangement*—and how often varies tremendously. Some bed and breakfasts offer table d'hôte every day; others serve dinner only when a minimum number of guests want to dine or on certain nights of the week. A few hosts seem to cook only when the whim strikes them. So, in other words—always take advantage of table d'hôte when it is offered, but be sure to check with your hosts to see if the option is available then make a dinner reservation when you book your room. Also, inquire what time the meal will be served. Be sure to call your host from along the way if you are running late.

The French do not have large freezers stocked with frozen supplies nor microwaves to defrost a quick meal. Food is usually fresh and purchased with care the day it is prepared, making it difficult to produce an impromptu meal. If you are a late arrival and have not eaten, sometimes your host will offer a plate of cold cuts, salad, and bread, but do not expect this, as it is not standard procedure. A few French terms to describe food services in conjunction with accommodation are as follows.

DEMI-PENSION means the room rate includes the price of two meals, usually breakfast and dinner (sometimes lunch), and is quoted on a per person basis. Usually a good value, it is often necessary to stay multiple nights before being offered the option of demi-pension.

PENSION COMPLÈTE includes breakfast, lunch, and dinner with prices quoted per person. This formula is rarely an option since most travelers prefer to be on their own for lunch.

FERME AUBERGE is a family-style restaurant, open to the public, on a working farm. These inns are actually controlled by the French government in so far as the products served must come mainly from the farm itself. The fare is usually simple and hearty, utilizing fresh meats and vegetables. The hosts do not generally sit down and share meals with their guests because they are often too busy serving.

MEMBERSHIP AFFILIATIONS

A number of properties recommended in our guides also belong to private membership organizations. These associations impose their own criteria for selection and membership standards and have established a reputation for the particular type of property they include. One affiliation that is very well recognized throughout France is Châteaux & Hôtels de France and a number of properties that we recommend are members. We are familiar with their selection process, criteria, and membership standards and we feel comfortable in recommending this association to our readers. If a property that we recommend is also a member of the Châteaux & Hôtels de France group, we publish the reference at the bottom of the description page.

RATES

In each bed and breakfast listing, 2009 rates are given for two persons in a double room, including tax, service, and Continental breakfast. (In the few instances where breakfast is additional, it is noted.) Often rooms can accommodate up to four persons at additional charge, and cribs and extra beds are usually available for children. Prices frequently go down if a stay is longer than three to five nights. Many places also offer small apartments or separate cottages (often referred to as Gîtes in French) with cooking facilities that are ideal for families. Apartment rates do not include breakfast and are based on a week's stay (reservations are rarely accepted for periods of less than a week). Beautifully furnished country homes and castles can be real bargains although they will cost more if located in one of the prime tourist centers. Rates quoted were given to us at the time of publication and are subject to change. Be sure to verify the current price when making a reservation.

RESERVATIONS—GENERAL INFORMATION

A few bed and breakfasts in this guide offer a degree of sophistication that approaches that of a deluxe hotel. But remember, the very essence of bed and breakfast accommodation is what makes it so special—these are private homes. It is not appropriate to just knock on the door and expect accommodation: *prior reservations are essential*. This also works to your advantage because most bed and breakfasts are tucked away in remote areas and it is frustrating to drive far out of your way, only to find everything is sold out or that they decided to close up and go out for the night as they weren't expecting guests. If you want to be footloose and not confined to a rigid schedule, phone from along the way to see if a room is available.

When making your reservations be sure to identify yourself as a "Karen Brown Traveler." We hear over and over again that the people who use our guides are such wonderful guests. The properties we recommend appreciate your visit, value their inclusion in our guide, and frequently tell us they will take special care of our readers.

RESERVATIONS—DEPOSITS: Deposits are preferred if you are reserving several months ahead of your arrival date. Deposits are usually requested in euros: this is for your own protection against fluctuating exchange rates. Drafts in euros can be purchased at the main branch of many large banks. Credit cards are rarely accepted at bed and breakfasts, although they are sometimes taken as a guarantee of arrival. Be aware that once you have paid your deposit, it is usually non-refundable.

RESERVATIONS BY EMAIL: This is our preferred way of making a reservation. All bed and breakfasts featured on the Karen Brown website that also have email addresses will have those addresses listed on their web pages (this information is constantly kept updated and correct). You can link directly to a property from its page on our website using its email hyperlink. *Note:* In any written correspondence be sure to spell out the month since Europeans reverse the American system for dates. As an example, in France 4/8/09 means August 4, 2009 not April 8, 2009.

RESERVATIONS BY FAX: The majority of bed and breakfasts have fax machines and if so, this is a very efficient way to request a reservation (you can use our reservation letter on page 20). Be sure to spell out the month—see note in previous paragraph. For dialing instructions see "Reservations by Telephone."

RESERVATIONS BY MAIL: Writing a letter is the most popular method for booking accommodations, but allow plenty of time. It is advisable to write well in advance so that you will have time to write to your second choice if your first is unavailable. Allow at least a week each way for airmail to and from France. If you do not speak French, you can make a copy and use the reservation letter supplied on page 20.

RESERVATIONS BY TELEPHONE: If you speak French (or if we have indicated under the bed and breakfast description that fluent English is spoken by the owner), we recommend you call for a reservation. With a telephone call you can discuss what is available and most suited to your needs. It is best to always follow up with a letter and a deposit in euros if requested. Telephone reservations are accepted by most bed and breakfast homes, but if there is a language barrier, it will be frustrating and difficult to communicate your wants. (Remember the time difference when calling: Paris is six hours ahead of New York.) To place a call, dial the international code (011 from the United States), then the country code for France (33) followed by the telephone number (dropping the initial 0). If dialing within France, dial the initial 0.

RESERVATIONS & CANCELLATIONS: If it is necessary for you to cancel your reservation for any reason, please phone (or write far in advance) to alert the proprietor. Bed and breakfasts often have only a few rooms to rent and are thus severely impacted financially if they hold a room for a "no-show."

RESERVATIONS & CHECK-IN: Bed and breakfasts are not hotels—they are private homes. There is not always someone "at the front desk" to check you in, so it is courteous to call the day you are expected to reconfirm your reservation, and to advise what time you anticipate arriving. If you have made arrangements to dine, ask what hour dinner will be served and be sure to be on time.

TELEPHONES

TELEPHONES—HOW TO CALL WITHIN FRANCE: It is very important to know how to make telephone calls within France. There are no longer any coin phones in France. The public telephones accept only special credit cards and although at first this seems complicated, it is actually easy. Stop by a post office (*bureau de poste*), a newsstand (*bureau de tabac*), or a highway gas station and buy a card for a specified amount of credit. You place this card into a slot in the telephone then, when you complete your call, the cost is automatically subtracted from the total available credit.

You might also want to consider renting or bringing a cellphone for convenience and ease of calling. Please see "Cellphones" in this introduction for our recommendations.

TELEPHONES—HOW TO CALL THE USA: Unlike hotels, most bed and breakfasts rarely have direct-dial telephones in the guestrooms. If your hosts do not have a telephone you can use, public telephones are readily available. The best bet is to use an international telephone card from your long-distance company—with one of these you can make a local call within France and be connected with your USA operator (before leaving home, ask your long-distance carrier what access number to use).

TOURIST INFORMATION

Syndicat d'Initiative is the name for the tourist offices found in all towns and resorts in France. When you are on the road, it is very helpful to pop into one of these offices signposted with a large "I". The agents gladly give advice on local events, timetables for local trains, buses, and boats, and often have maps and brochures on the region's points of interest. They can also help with locating bed and breakfast accommodations. Before you depart for France, call their general information number in the USA at (410) 286-8310 or visit their website: *www.franceguide.com*. Additional information can be obtained by writing or faxing to one of the following tourist offices as published below:

FRENCH GOVERNMENT TOURIST OFFICES

USA: 444 Madison Ave., 16th Floor, New York, NY 10022-6903, tel: (212) 838-7800

USA: 9454 Wilshire Blvd., Suite 715, Beverly Hills, CA 90212-2967, tel: (310) 271-6665

USA: 676 N. Michigan Ave., Suite 3214, Chicago, IL 60611, tel: (312) 327-0290

UK: 178 Piccadilly, London W1V 9AL, England, tel: (020) 7399 3500

CA: 1981 Ave., McGill College, Ste 490, Montreal, Quebec H3A 2W9, tel: (514) 288-4264

TRAINS

If you plan to travel by train within France or to other destinations in Europe, you can research schedules and availability online. Also, important to note, many special fares and passes are available only if purchased in the United States. For information on the best possible fares and to book tickets online, visit our website, *www.karenbrown.com*.

TRIP CANCELLATION INSURANCE

Because unexpected medical or personal emergencies—or other situations beyond our control—sometimes result in the need to alter or cancel travel plans, we strongly recommend travel insurance. Prepaid travel expenses such as airline tickets, car rentals, and train fares are not always refundable and most bed and breakfasts will expect payment of some, if not all, of your booking, even in an emergency. Many of the properties in our guides have relatively few rooms, so it is difficult for them to absorb the cost of a cancellation. A link on our website (*www.karenbrown.com*) will connect you to insurance policies that can be purchased online.

WEBSITE

Please visit the Karen Brown website (www.karenbrown.com) in conjunction with this book. Our website provides trip planning assistance, new discoveries, post-press updates, feedback from you, our readers, the opportunity to purchase goods and services that we recommend (rail tickets, car rental, travel insurance, etc.), and one-stop shopping for our guides, associated maps and watercolor prints. Most of our favorite places to stay are featured with color photos and direct website and email links. Also, we invite you to participate in the Karen Brown's Readers' Choice Awards. Be sure to visit our website and vote so your favorite properties will be honored.

WHEELCHAIR ACCESSIBILITY

If an inn has *at least* one guestroom that is accessible by wheelchair, it is noted with the symbol &. This is not the same as saying it meets full disability standards.

Reservation Letter

To: Bed and Breakfast, name and address

Monsieur/Madame:

Nous serons _____ personnes.
We have (number) of persons in our party

Nous voudrions réserver pour _____ nuit(s)
We would like to reserve for (number of nights)

    du _____
    from (date of arrival)

    au _____
    to (date of departure),

    une chambre à deux lits _____
    a room(s) with twin beds

    une chambre au grand lit _____
    a room(s) with double bed(s)

    une chambre avec un lit supplémentaire _____
    room(s) with an extra bed

    avec toilette et baignoire ou douche privée _____
    with private toilet and bathtub or shower

Veuilliez confirmer la réservation en nous communicant le prix de la chambre et la somme d'arrhes que vous souhaitez. Dans l'attente de votre réponse, nous vous prions d'agréer, Messieurs, Mesdames, l'expression de nos sentiments distingués.

Please advise availability, rate of room, and deposit needed. We will be waiting for your confirmation and send our kindest regards.

Your name and address, email address, and fax number (if applicable).

Be sure to spell out the month to avoid any confusion—see previous note in "email" paragraph.

Itinerary Overview

Rouen

Champagne

Luxembourg

Mont St. Michel

Caen

Reims

Épernay

Metz

Strasbourg

Normandy

St. Malo

Rennes

PARIS

Maginot Line

Colmar

Brittany

Quimper

Angers

Tours

Orléans

Vézelay

Alsace

Nantes

Châteaux Country

Burgundy

Dijon

Beaune

Geneva

The French Alps

Annecy

Lyon

Megève

Brantôme

Dordogne & Lot River Valleys

Gorges du Verdon

Les Eyzies

Sarlat

Conques

Moustiers Ste. Marie

Trigance

Cahors

Pays Basque

Cordes

Millau

Ste. Enimie

Avignon

Vence

Nice

Biarritz

Cambo les Bains

Gordes

Grasse

St Jean de Luz

Nîmes

Arles

Aix

Sare

Gorges du Tarn & Beyond

Hilltowns of the Riviera

St Jean Pied de Port

Carcassonne

Provence

Perpignan

Collioure

21

Normandy

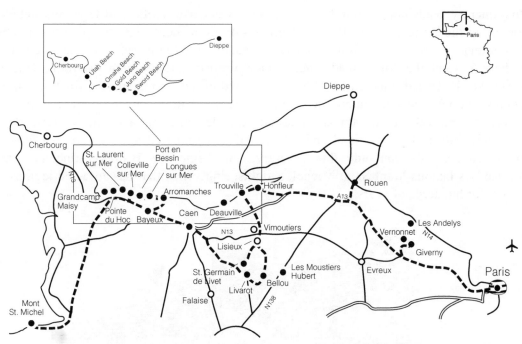

O Orientation
● Sightseeing
- - - Itinerary route

Paris

Dieppe

Cherbourg
Utah Beach
Omaha Beach
Gold Beach
Juno Beach
Sword Beach

Dieppe

Cherbourg

St. Laurent
sur Mer
Colleville
sur Mer

Port en
Bessin
Longues
sur Mer

Arromanches

Trouville

Honfleur

Rouen

N13

Grandcamp
Maisy

Pointe
du Hoc

Bayeux

Caen

Deauville

Vimoutiers

A13

Les Andelys
Vernonnet

Giverny

Lisieux

Evreux

Paris

St. Germain
de Livet

Les Moustiers
Hubert

N13

Livarot

Bellou

Falaise

N138

Mont
St. Michel

N14

Normandy

This itinerary heads north from Paris to Monet's wonderful gardens at Giverny, includes a detour to the historic city of Rouen, continues on to the coast with the picturesque port of Honfleur, and to the world-famous D-Day beaches and the Normandy coastline where on June 6, 1944 the Allies made their major offensive, reinforcing the turnaround in World War II. Decades have passed but abandoned pillboxes remain, the floating harbor endures, and museums document the events of the war. Turning inland, you visit historic Bayeux to marvel at its almost-thousand-year-old tapestry and the hinterland of Normandy with rolling farmland and villages of half-timbered houses—an area famous for its cheese. We conclude this itinerary, and begin the Brittany itinerary, with Normandy's famous Mont Saint Michel, a sightseeing venue that has attracted legions of visitors for hundreds of years.

Recommended Pacing: While you can use the heart of Normandy as a base for this itinerary (except for visiting Mont Saint Michel), our preference is to spend at least one night near Giverny, possibly a night near Rouen, a night near Honfleur, and a minimum of two nights at the heart of Normandy to visit Bayeux, explore the D-Day beaches, and allow a day to follow the scenic roads through the lush countryside.

Follow the Seine north out of Paris (Porte d'Auteuil) on the A13 and exit at Bonnières sur Seine. Travel a scenic route following the N15 north along the Seine to Vernon. As you cross the Seine with the village of **Vernonette** sitting at the crossroads, you see the remains of a picturesque 12th-century bridge and an ancient timbered dungeon (a great picnic spot!). Just a few kilometers upstream lies the village of **Giverny**, a name synonymous worldwide with artist Claude Monet who came to live in the village in 1883.

Monet converted the barn into his studio, where he loved to paint, smoke, and reflect on his work. Now it's a visitors' center and gift shop selling all things Monet from posters of his masterpieces to key-rings. The walls are hung with reproductions of some of his larger canvases and photos of the famous artist at work. Monet's sun-washed peach stucco home with green shutters is decorated much as it was when he lived there—the walls hung with Japanese-style paintings and family pictures. From the striking blue-and-yellow dining room with its matching china, through his bedroom, to the cozy tiled kitchen, you get a feeling for the home life of this famous artist.

The magic of a visit to Giverny is the gardens, a multicolored tapestry of flowers, meandering paths shaded by trellises of roses, and the enchanting oasis of the water garden, whose green waters are covered with lily pads and crossed by Japanese bridges hung with white and mauve wisteria. Monet loved to paint outdoors and it is memorable to search out just the spot where he stood and painted a masterpiece. There is only one problem: you are not alone in your endeavors—Giverny attracts a multitude of pilgrims. However, the influx of tourists also means that this tiny village has a surprising number of facilities, including cafés, restaurants, and gift stores. (*Open Apr to Oct, closed Mon.*)

Another wonderful highlight and attraction, just a couple of hundred yards from Giverny, is the **Musée d'Art Américan**, which is dedicated to the appreciation of American art, focusing on the historical connection between French and American artists throughout the Impressionist and other 19th- and 20th-century periods. During the time of Claude Monet many American artists made pilgrimages to France to partake of the cultural and artistic fever of the time and be inspired by the beauty of the French countryside. If you desire a private tour, it can be scheduled directly through the museum: Musée d'Art Américan, 99, Rue Claude Monet, 27620 Giverny, tel: 02.32.51.94.65, fax: 02.32.51.94.67. (*Open Apr to Oct, closed Mon.*)

From Giverny, we recommend venturing farther on in the direction of Rouen and the coast. You can either go directly to Rouen by first returning to Vernon from Giverny and from there following signposts for that historic city, or consider a short detour to the scenic town of **Les Andelys.** Les Andelys is located on the banks of the Seine. It was once the hub of Franco-English relations during the Middle Ages and one can visit the ruins of the **Château Gaillard** whose hillside location affords a wonderful view of the path of the Seine as it loops north in the direction of Rouen. To reach Les Andelys, from Giverny, return to Vernonette and then follow the D313 (approximately 22 km) as it makes a scenic journey along the banks of the Seine. To continue on to Rouen from Les Andelys, cross the river to the south of town and follow the D135 to intersect with Autoroute and follow direction Rouen.

Rich in history, **Rouen** is termed the "museum city," but it is also famous for its magnificent cathedral and its connection with **Joan of Arc** and the Dauphin. Don't let the size of the city or its industrial outskirts intimidate you—it is easy to navigate to the charming heart of the old city and parking garages are well signed and convenient for exploring the historic pedestrian district.

Captured near Compiègne, Joan of Arc was brought to Rouen for judgment, charged with heresy, and sentenced to be burned at the stake. Before English authorities, church officials, and the masses, on May 30, 1431, she was burned alive at the Old Market Square. You can walk the square; visit the Tour de la Purcelle, the tower of the fortress where she was held prisoner; visit the neighboring Tour Jeanne d'Arc, the tower where she was threatened with torture before officials backed down, fearful of her religious demeanor; visit the Saint Ouén cemetery behind the town hall, where she was taken to renounce her sins; tour the Archevéché, the ecclesiastical court where the verdict was cast; and walk across the Pont Jeanne d'Arc which spans the river where her ashes and unburnt heart were cast into the water.

Rouen is also famous for its 11th-century **cathedral** with its striking Norman tower and 14th-century embellishments which was captured on canvas in every mood and light by Monet. Monet moved here to be with his brother in 1872 and at the peak of the Impressionist period painted the cathedral, the river, the factories—all acclaimed paintings, many of which now hang in the Musée Marmottan in Paris. Many other masters (Caravaggio, Velasquez, Fragonard, Géricault, and Sisley) were also inspired by the city and Rouen's **Musée des Beaux-Arts** has a wealth of their art on display. Rouen's many attractions include two 15th-century churches, a palace of justice, a big clock, and the 16th-century Bourgtheroulde Mansion.

From Rouen, continue the journey on to the coast by following signs to Caen along the A13. Exit the autoroute at Beuzeville and travel north on the D22 and then west on the D180 to Honfleur. **Honfleur** is a gem, its narrow, 17th-century harbor filled with tall-masted boats and lined with tall, slender, pastel-washed houses. Narrow cobbled streets lined with ancient timbered houses lead up from the harbor. Cafés and restaurants set up tables and umbrellas outside so that customers can enjoy the sun and the picturesque location. It is a small wonder that this pretty port has inspired artists, writers, and musicians. Markets are held every Saturday on Saint Catherine's Square with its unusual wooden belfry, a tall bell-tower and bell-ringer's home, standing apart from the nearby church. Just off the square, farther up the hillside, on Rue de l'Homme de Bois, is the interesting **Eugène Boudin Museum** with its impressive collection of pre-Impressionist and contemporary paintings by Norman artists: Boudin, Dubourg, Dufy, Monet, Friesz, and Gernez. There are also displays of Norman costumes and paintings depicting life in 18th- and 19th-century Normandy. (*Closed Tues, tel: 02.31.89.54.00.*)

Just by the harbor, in a former church, the **Musée Marine** traces the history of the port of Honfleur. Nearby, the ancient timbered prison is now the **Musée d'Art Populaire**, consisting of 12 rooms depicting the interiors of Norman houses including a weaver's workshop and a manor-house dining room. (*Closed Mondays, tel: 02.31.89.14.12.*) In addition to having quaint shops and inviting fish restaurants, Honfleur is a haven for artists and there are a number of galleries to visit.

Our advice is that if you visit Honfleur, stay for the night because this will give you the opportunity to enjoy this scenic town without the hordes of daytime visitors.

For a contrast to the quaintness of Honfleur you may choose to visit her two famous neighbors, Trouville and Deauville. **Trouville** has set the pace on the Côte Fleurie since 1852. A stretch of water divides it from its very close neighbor, **Deauville**, a much ritzier resort where row upon row of beach cabanas line the sands and well-heeled folks parade the streets. The casinos are a hub of activity, and if you visit in the late summer, you will

Honfleur

experience the excitement and sophistication of a major summer playground for the rich and famous. For a few weeks each August there is the allure of the racetracks, polo fields, glamorous luncheons, and black-tie dinners. Celebrities and the wealthy international set come here to cheer on their prize thoroughbreds.

From Honfleur dip south into a region of Normandy referred to as the **Pays d'Auge**, a lush region sandwiched between the Risle and Dives rivers. Here quaint villages of timbered and some thatched houses cluster on rolling green hillsides grazed by cows or planted with apple orchards. It is a region to experience by driving along its quiet country roads. The drive we suggest is a leisurely half-day outing beginning at **Lisieux**, the region's commercial center. If you are fortunate enough to arrive on Saturday, enjoy the town's colorful farmers' market where stalls offer everything from live chickens, vegetables, and cheese to underwear and shoes.

Leave Lisieux in the direction of Vimoutiers (D579), travel for just a few kilometers, and take a left turn down a country lane to **Saint Germain de Livet**, a hamlet at the bottom of the valley. Here you see a picture-postcard timbered farm, a couple of cottages, a church, and the adorable 15th-century **Château Saint Germain de Livet**. This whimsical little château with pepper-pot turrets and pretty pink-and-white-checkerboard façade sits in geometric gardens behind a high wall. The interior contains some attractive furniture and some paintings and frescoes. (*Closed Tues, tel: 02.31.31.00.03.*) Leaving the château, follow signposts for Vimoutiers (D268) till you reach the D47, which you follow into Fervaques, a picturesque village in a green valley. Drive past its château, a vast 16th-century stone building, to the village with its timbered cottages set round a quiet square. Here you pick up signposts for **Route de Fromage**, a tourist route that guides you through this lush and scenic cheese-producing region.

Follow the well-signposted Route de Fromage into **Les Moutiers Hubert**, a hamlet of farms along the road, up to **Bellou** with its large brown timbered manor house, and on to Lisores with its little church, ivy-covered houses, and farms in the valley. Regain the main road heading towards Livarot (D579) and travel for a few kilometers before being directed right by the Route de Fromage onto a back road that brings you by a more scenic route into the heart of the attractive old town of **Livarot**, home of the cheese that bears the same name. On the edge of town (driving in the direction of Caen), it is worth a stop to see the **Musée du Fromage** in the basement of one of the town's grand old homes. Here you watch a video on the production of Livarot, Pont l'Évêque, and Camembert cheeses, and tour a replica of an old dairy farm with its traditional cheese-making shop and old-fashioned dairy. (*Open all year, tel: 02.31.48.20.10.*)

As you continue on to Caen (40 kilometers), the countryside is pancake-flat. **Caen**, a large port situated on the banks of the Orne and one of Normandy's largest cities, lost nearly all of its 10,000 buildings in the Allied invasion of 1944. It is also the city that William the Conqueror made his seat of government. Your destination in Caen is the **Memorial** (Memorial to Peace). The museum is well signposted and has its own exit off the autoroute (exit 7 off the Caen ring road). Displays, films, tapes, and photos cover the events that led up to the outbreak of World War II, the invasion of France, total war, D-Day, the Battle of Normandy, and hope for lasting world peace. A good look round takes several hours, an in-depth visit all day. (*Closed Dec 25, Jan 1 to 15, tel: 02.31.06.06.44.*)

A 15-minute drive down the N13 brings you to **Bayeux**, a lovely old town where inviting shops and honey-colored stone houses line narrow streets. **Saint Patrice** square is filled with colorful market stalls on Saturday and Wednesday mornings. There has been a town on this site since Roman times: it was invaded by the Bretons, the Saxons, and the Vikings, but thankfully escaped the Allied bombers. It's a great place for shopping and serves as a convenient base for visiting the landing beaches.

Apart from the town itself, your premier destination in Bayeux is the **Musée de la Tapisserie**, which displays the famous tapestry that Odo, Bishop of Bayeux, had the English embroider following the conquest of England by his half-brother William the Conqueror in 1066. The color and richness of the tapestry make the little stick figures look as if they were stitched just yesterday, not over 900 years ago. With the aid of earphones the intricately embroidered scenes come alive. We found we needed to go past it twice—once quickly to appreciate its enormous proportions and the second time to hear the story it tells. (*Open all year, tel: 02.31.51.25.50.*)

Bayeux Tapestry

Next to the cathedral, the **Musée Baron Gérard** has some lovely examples of porcelain and lace manufactured in Bayeux. (*Open all year, tel: 02.31.92.14.21.*)

With World War II still recent history, for those who witnessed and experienced the Normandy Invasion, a trip to this region is a sentimental and poignant journey. Towns have been restored; but abandoned fortifications on the beaches as well as in the water, numerous museums, memorials, and cemeteries hauntingly remain as testaments and reminders of that heroic and tragic battle. There are eight itineraries that are well signposted and offer the traveler a trail based on the chronological sequence of events of this incredible battle. One could easily spend weeks here following the individual itineraries and the historical trail of each military force and mission. (The eight itineraries are signed on the roadways as follows: Overlord—The Assault or *Overlord—L'Assaut*; D-Day—The Onslaught or *D-Day—LeChoc*; Objective—A Port or *Objectif—Un Port;* The Confrontation or *L'Affrontement;* Cobra—The Breakout or *Cobra—La Percée*; The Counter Attack or *La Contre-Attaque*; The Encirclement or *L'Encerclement*; The Outcome or *Le Denouement*.) However, for the purposes of this itinerary, we propose a route that serves as an introduction to the major events and battles that so greatly influenced the outcome of the Second World War.

Bayeux was the first French town to be liberated and it seems appropriate to begin our D-Day journey here. On the main ring road around the old town is the **1944 Battle of Normandy Museum** with its exhibitions of tanks, guns, and armored vehicles used in the battle. (*Open all year, tel: 02.31.30.47.60.*) On the other side of the ring road, opposite the museum, is the **British Cemetery and Memorial**, honoring the memory of 1,837 missing servicemen.

From Bayeux, in search of the D-Day landmarks and beaches you will travel a scenic route that follows the coast, through the seaside villages that lay exposed to the battle, which took place on five principal landing beaches—Sword (farthest to the east), Juno, Gold, Omaha, and Utah (to the northwest). You will also weave through little gray-stone villages whose tall walled farmhouses and barns form their own little fortifications scattered around the fields. Although different route numbers identify various segments, there is basically one road that hugs the coastline.

To reach the coast, travel approximately 10 kilometers northeast of Bayeux to **Gold Beach** and **Arromanches**. Arromanches is a lively seaside town whose broad crescent of golden sand was one of the D-Day landing beaches dominated by the British troops. In June, 1944 a huge floating harbor was erected in a gigantic U in the bay. Designed by British engineers, the harbor was comprised of massive concrete blocks, floating pier-heads, and 10 kilometers of floating pier "roads." It was towed across the Channel and erected here, enabling the Allies to unload half-a-million tons of materials in a three-month period. After nearly 60 years of Atlantic storms much of the harbor is still in place and you can get an up-close look at several enormous sections marooned on the beach. Beside the beach is the **D-Day Museum** with its displays of models, photographs, and films of the military operations of June, 1944. (*Closed Jan, tel: 02.31.22.34.31.*) On the hillside above town is **Arromanches 360**, where an 18-minute production, *The Price of Freedom*, is dramatically shown on nine screens of this theater in the round. (*Closed Jan, tel: 02.31.22.30.30.*)

If time allows, you might want to continue east to explore the beaches of **Juno** and **Sword**, but for the purposes of this itinerary we direct you west along the coast from Arromanches to the village of **Longues sur Mer**. A country road from Longues sur Mer dead-ends on the bluffs at an open-air museum where you can walk along a path that weaves through the wheat fields to abandoned gun emplacements, overlooking the stretch of coastline that the German artillery so fiercely guarded. Longues sur Mer is the only naval artillery battery on the Normandy coast that still has its guns. *(Open all year, tel: 02.31.06.06.44)*

On the coast just 5 kilometers away, tucked on an inlet, is the small, charming port and fishing village of **Port en Bessin**, not far from our starting point, Bayeux. Port en Bessin has a museum with a collection of remains found on the sunken warships. *(Open Apr to Oct, tel: 02.31.21.17.06.)*

The road travels inland from the water's edge from Port en Bessin to **Colleville sur Mer**, where a road takes you out to the **American Cemetery** and an expansive 170-acre plot overlooking Omaha Beach. A dignified tribute to those who gave their lives in battle, 9,387 white crosses stand in perfect alignment on acreage that looks out to a backdrop of sand and ocean. The memory of this gorgeous setting, the beautiful paths that weave along the bluffs, the chapel, and the dramatic memorial will linger. *(Open all year, tel: 02.31.51.62.00.)*

Continue along the length of Omaha Beach to the town of **Saint Laurent sur Mer**. This town hosts a museum just yards from the sand, **Musée Omaha**, which boasts a collection of vehicles, weapons, uniforms, and insignia found on the sandy battlefield. *(Open Feb 15 to Nov 20, tel: 02.31.21.97.44.)* Both **Omaha Beach** and **Utah Beach** to the northwest are where the American army landed under the direction of General Bradley.

Follow the coast around Pointe et Raz de la Percée to the dramatic vantage point of **Pointe du Hoc**. As you stand on this rugged stretch of coastline, pockmarked by bombs, on the ruins of the German fortifications, it is hard to comprehend the courage of the American soldiers who braved the cliffs and blindly stormed the enemy believing this was a strategic stronghold. From here it is approximately 5 kilometers on to **Grandcamp Maisy**. Here the **Musée des Rangers** focuses on the specially-trained American unit and the capture of Pointe du Hoc.

From here you can easily travel the stretch north along the coast to Utah Beach or leave the coast and travel south via St. Lô to Mont Saint Michel where this itinerary concludes. Straddling the border of Brittany and Normandy, **Mont Saint Michel** is France's most visited tourist attraction. Joined to the mainland by a narrow strip of roadway, Mont Saint Michel, initially a place of pilgrimage, then a fortress, and in the 19th century a prison, clings to a rock island and towers 150 meters above sea level. Depending on the tide, it is either almost surrounded by water or by marshes and quicksand. Wander up the narrow cobblestoned streets to the crowning 12th-century abbey and visit the remarkable Gothic and Romanesque complex, culminating in the glories of the *Merveille* (Marvel)—the group of buildings on the north side of the mount. Saint Michael, the militant archangel, is the saint for the beaches you have just seen.

From Mont Saint Michel you can return to Paris, join the *Châteaux Country* itinerary, or continue on the following itinerary into Brittany.

Breton Women in Traditional Dress

Normandy

Brittany

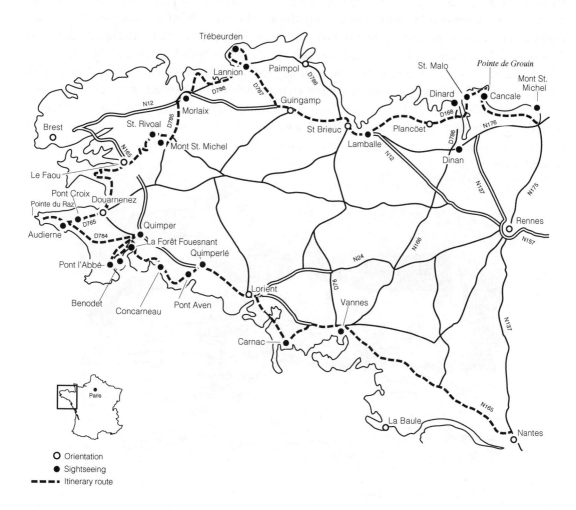

Trébeurden

Lannion
Paimpol

St. Malo
Pointe de Grouin

Mont St. Michel

Dinard
Cancale

Guingamp

N12

Morlaix

St. Rivoal

St Brieuc
Plancöet

Brest

Mont St. Michel
Lamballe

Dinan

Le Faou

Pont Croix
Douarnenez

Pointe du Raz

Audierne

Quimper

La Forêt Fouesnant

Quimperlé

Rennes

Pont l'Abbé

Benodet
Concarneau
Pont Aven

Lorient

Vannes

Carnac

Paris

○ Orientation
● Sightseeing
▬ ▬ ▬ Itinerary route

La Baule

Nantes

35

Brittany

Brittany is a rugged region of beautiful forests bounded by nearly 1,000 kilometers of coastline. This peninsula, jutting out from the northwest side of France, was for many years isolated from the rest of the country and regarded by Bretons as a separate country. The regional language is Breton and you see signposts in both French and Breton. Most of the houses are fresh white stucco with angled blue-gray roofs. *Crêpes* filled with butter, sugar, chocolate, or jam, *galettes* (wheat crêpes) enhanced with cheese, ham, onions, or mushrooms, and cider are Brittany's culinary specialties. This itinerary begins on Brittany's border at Mont Saint Michel and explores the coast before it ventures into the forested interior, culminating on the southern coast at Vannes with its charming old walled town.

Breton Coastal Village

Brittany

Recommended Pacing: Select a location in northern Brittany for the northern portion of the itinerary and one on the southwestern coast for the southern portion. Two nights in each spot should give you ample time to explore the peninsula.

While **Mont Saint Michel** is technically in Normandy, it is geographically in Brittany. Mont Saint Michel is France's premier tourist attraction, and although it is wonderful, we think it best to warn our readers that in high season, the effort of pushing your way uphill through teeming crowds, past souvenir shops, to reach the abbey at the summit is not enjoyable. The appearance of the town is that of a child's sand castle, with narrow, cobblestoned streets winding up to the 12th-century abbey and lovely Romanesque church, dedicated to Archangel Michael. Depending on the tide, the mount is either almost surrounded by water or by marshland and quicksand. Drive across the paved causeway that joins the mount to the mainland, park in the car park, and explore on foot.

Leaving Mont Saint Michel, take the D976 to Dol. Follow signposts for Saint Malo across the flat farmland to **Cancale** whose beachside port is full of lobsters, mussels, oysters, and clams, and whose attractive little town is nestled on the cliffs above. Follow signposts for *Saint Malo par la Côte* to Pointe du Grouin, a windswept headland and promontory. Rounding the point, you are rewarded by vistas of coastline stretching into the far distance.

Saint Malo corsairs, who menaced British seafarers during the 16th century, were pirates with royal permission to take foreign ships. With its tall 13th- and 14th-century ramparts facing the sea and enormous harbor (the terminal of ferries from Portsmouth and the Channel Islands), the town is almost surrounded by water. Within the walls are narrow streets lined with interesting shops and small restaurants. Much was destroyed in battle between Germans and Americans in 1944 but it has all been magnificently restored. Walk round the walls (stairs by Saint Vincent's gate), visit the courtyard of the 14th-century castle (now the town hall), and sample *crêpes* or *galettes*.

Following the D168, cross the *barrière* (low pontoon bridge) over the bay to **Dinard**, a popular beach resort. Once a sleepy fishing village, its confusion of one-way streets and seafront hotels (blocking views) discourage you from leaving the main highway.

Approximately 25 kilometers south of Dinard is the wonderful walled town of **Dinan**. Embraced by medieval ramparts, it is a charming city with cobbled streets, half-timbered houses, a historic convent, and castle ruins. It is a great place to spend an afternoon exploring the maze of streets, from its picturesque port to the encircling ramparts. Known as "the city of art history," Dinan has intriguing stores, a multitude of art galleries, and inviting sidewalk cafés.

A 45-kilometer drive through Plancoët brings you to **Lamballe**. At the heart of Lamballe's industrial sprawl are some fine old houses on the Place du Martrai, including the executioner's house, which is now the tourist office. The traffic is congested.

Join the N12 bypassing Saint Brieuc and Guigamp (the town where gingham was first woven) and take the D767 northwest to Lannion. **Lannion** is an attractive town beside the fast-flowing River Léguer with some fine medieval houses at its center, near the Place Général Leclerc. Follow signposts for Perros Guirec then **Trébeurden**, an attractive seaside resort with a small sheltered harbor separated from a curve of sandy beach by a wooded peninsula. Make your way back to Lannion along the beautiful stretch of coast and take the D786 towards Morlaix. At Saint Michel the road traces a vast sandy curve of beach and exposes vistas of succeeding headlands. Just as the road leaves the bay, turn right following signposts for *Morlaix par la Côte,* which gives you the opportunity to sample another small stretch of very attractive coastline. At Locquirec turn inland through Guimaéc and Lanmeur to regain the D786 to Morlaix.

Morlaix is a central market town whose quays shelter boats that travel the passage inland from the sea. You do not have to deal with city traffic as you follow the N12 (signposted Brest) around the town for a short distance to the D785 (signposted Pleyben Christ), which leads you into the **Regional Parc d'Amorique**. After the very gray little towns of Pleyben Christ and Plounéour Ménez the scenery becomes more interesting as the road leads you up onto moorlands where rock escarpments jut out from the highest hill. A narrow road winds up to the little chapel high atop **Mont Saint Michel** (an isolated windswept spot very different from its famous namesake). Return to the D785 for a short distance taking the first right turn to **Saint Rivoal**, which has a **Maison Cornic**, a small park with an interesting collection of old Breton houses.

Following signposts for Le Faou, you travel up the escarpment to be rewarded by sky-wide views of the distant coast. Travel through Forêt du Cranou with its majestic oak trees to Le Faou where you continue straight (signposted Crozon). The route hugs the Aulne estuary and offers lovely vistas of houses dotting the far shore, then gives way to wooded fjords before crossing a high bridge and turning away from the coast. At Tar-ar-Groas make an almost 180-degree turn in the center of the village and continue the very pleasant drive following signposts for Douarnenez, a large fishing port that you skirt on the D765 following signposts for Audierne. **Pont Croix** is built on terraces up from the River Goyen. Leading to the bridge, its photogenic narrow streets are lined with old houses. **Audierne** is a pretty fishing port on the estuary of the Goyen where fishing boats bring in their harvest of lobsters, crayfish, and tunny.

Your destination is **Pointe du Raz**, the Land's End of France. Thankfully it is less commercial than England's, but it is certainly not isolated. Uniformly sized white holiday cottages dot the landscape and a large café and enormous museum lie at road's end. If you can ignore the commercialism, you will find the views across the windswept headlands spectacular. This journey is not recommended in the height of summer when roads are congested.

An hour's drive (60 kilometers on the D784) brings you to the large town of **Quimper**, set where the Odet and Steir rivers meet. Park by the river, wander the town's pleasant streets and visit the **Musée de la Faïence** with its displays of attractive regional pottery. *(Open mid-Apr to end-Oct, closed Sundays, tel: 02.98.90.12.72.)* If the name of Quimper pottery is not familiar, it is, however, likely that you will immediately recognize the endearing figures painted in warm washes of predominantly blues and yellows that are now appreciated and recognized worldwide. The paintings on the pottery depict country folk in the old traditional dress and costume of Brittany.

This itinerary now explores Brittany's southern coast. The individual towns are very attractive but we were disappointed not to find more scenic countryside between them. Your first stop is **Pont l'Abbé**, set deep in a sheltered estuary. The squat castle contains a museum, **Musée Bigoudin**, of costume and furniture, with some fine examples of the tall white lace coifs that Breton women wear on their heads for festivals. (*Open Mar to end-*

Concarneau, Ville Close

Sep) A pleasant park borders the river and the town square has a large covered market. Cross the high bridge that spans the River Odet and catch a panoramic view of **Benodet**. If you go into its crowded streets, follow signs for the port, which bring you to its yacht harbor—from here the coast road weaves past sandy bays and holiday hotels to the casino. In summer do not tackle the crowded streets; we recommend that you just admire the town from the bridge.

40 *Brittany*

Ten kilometers away lies **Fouesnant**, a traditional center for cider production. Its pretty port, **La Forêt Fouesnant**, with its harbor full of yachts and small arc of golden sand, lies just a few kilometers away. Leaving the village, follow signs for *Concarneau par la Côte*, which quickly takes you on a scenic back road into town.

Ignore **Concarneau's** bustling town and park by the harbor as close as possible to **Ville Close**, the 14th-century walled town sitting amidst a vast harbor of colorful boats varying from sleek yachts to commercial fishing trawlers. The old town, with its narrow streets and old houses full of crêperies and gift shops, is fun to explore. Visit the interesting **Musée de la Pêche**, which covers all things nautical inside and has three old fishing boats tied up outside of what was once the town's arsenal. (*Open all year, tel: 02.98.97.10.20.*) Climbing the walls gives you good views of the inner harbor where fishing boats unload their catch.

From Concarneau the D783 brings you to **Pont Aven**, a pretty resort by the River Aven made famous by Gauguin and his school of artists who moved here in the 1890s. Gauguin with his bohemian ways was not popular with the locals and he soon moved on. There are a great many galleries and in summer it's a colorful and crowded spot.

Turning inland, the D783 brings you to **Quimperlé** (20 kilometers) where the rivers Ellé and Isole converge to form the Lafta. One of the town's central streets is cobbled and lined with old houses. From here head through the large town of Hennebont for the 27-kilometer (D9 and D781) drive to the rather dull seaside town of **Carnac**. In the windswept fields on the edge of town are over 2,700 standing stones (*menhirs*) arranged in lines (*alignements*). The stones, believed to have been erected between 4,000 and 2,000 B.C., consist of three groups each arranged in patterns of 10 to 13 rows. The area is somewhat divided by country roads but the site is large enough that you can meander around and enjoy the groupings unhindered by the milling crowds and ticket barriers that impede your enjoyment of the British counterpart, Stonehenge. The **Musée de la Préhistoire** will help you interpret the stones. (*Open all year, tel: 02.97.52.22.04.*)

Leaving Carnac, follow signposts to **Vannes**, the region's largest city, complete with all the traffic and navigation headaches that plague so many downtown areas. The old walled town surrounding **Saint Peter's Cathedral** is delightful. The cathedral was built between the 13th and 19th centuries and has a great mixture of styles. The nearby parliament building has been converted to a covered market for artists, leather workers, metalworkers, and crêperies. There is a maze of old streets with beautiful timbered and gabled houses. Market days are Wednesdays and Saturdays on the Place des Lices.

This section of Brittany with its rocky promontories serves as a dramatic and wonderful base from which to explore Brittany's rugged south coast before leaving the region.

From Vannes the N165 whisks you around Nantes and onto the A11, which brings you to Angers, a convenient point to join our *Châteaux Country* itinerary.

Carnac

Brittany

Châteaux Country

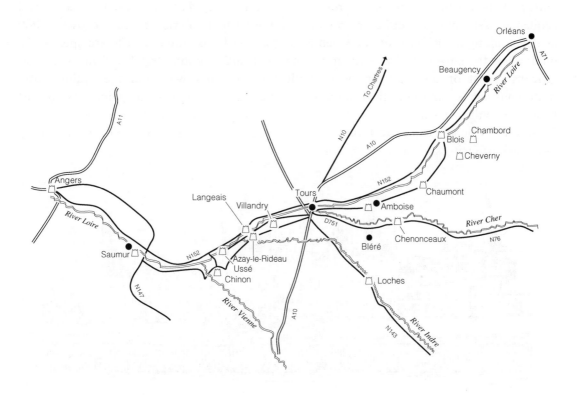

Paris

O Orientation
● Sightseeing
⌂ Châteaux

Châteaux Country

A highlight of any holiday in France is a visit to the elegant châteaux of the Loire river valley. This itinerary suggests a route for visiting the châteaux based on a logical sequence assuming you either begin or end your trip in Paris. There are over 1,000 châteaux along the River Loire between Nantes and Orléans, and over 100 are open to the public. For the purposes of this itinerary, the Châteaux Country stretches from Angers to Orléans. Most of the châteaux were built for love, not war, and they range from traditional castles and grandiose homes to romantic ruins: we try to paint a picture of what you will see when you tour each château. In our opinion the best are Azay-le-Rideau and Chenonceaux. Be forewarned that in July and August you will be caught up in a crush of visitors.

Chambord

Recommended Pacing: Any property from Map 3 makes an ideal base for exploring the châteaux country. If you are going to spend just a few days and visit the most famous châteaux, select a place to stay at the heart of the region. If you plan an extensive visit to the valley and numerous châteaux, you might want to consider first stopping en route from Paris along the river to the northeast, then settle at its heart and, finally, continue on to its western outskirts. This region has a wealth of marvelous places to stay and they vary from small country farmhouses or inns to elegant, regal châteaux. In terms of how to pace your sightseeing—please do not try to visit all the châteaux we describe—it would be just too many for one trip. Rather, read our descriptions and choose those that appeal most to you. As we do not tell you how to get from château to château, we recommend Michelin maps 517 and 518 for outlining your route. Three nights in the region should give you all the time you need—one can visit only so many castles. Allow more if you are an avid fan of French furniture, French gardens, or the like, and want to explore properties in depth.

Many visitors spend time in Paris before coming to the Loire Valley and an excellent sightseeing venue on the way is **Chartres**, about an hour and a half southwest of Paris (97 kilometers). **Chartres Cathedral** towers high above the town and stands proud on the horizon. Light from three 13th-century stained-glass windows dapple the inside of the church with color. It's a magnificent edifice and the old city surrounding the cathedral has been lovingly restored. It's delightful to explore its old winding streets.

From Chartres the N10 takes you to Tours (130 kilometers, about a 2-hour drive). Located at the junction of the Cher and Loire rivers, Tours is a convenient starting point for our itinerary.

Begin your adventures in the Loire Valley by a visit to **Langeais**, one of the region's smaller châteaux. Remarkably, it has not been altered since it was built between 1465 and 1471 for Louis XI as a defense against Bretons. It is beautifully furnished and wax figurines commemorate the royal wedding of Charles VIII and Anne of Brittany, which took place on a cold December morning in 1491. On a nearby ridge are the ruins of a

10th-century stone *donjon* or keep, one of Europe's first. This was a stronghold of the notorious Fulk Nerra the Black, Count of Anjou. (*Open all year, tel: 02.47.96.72.60.*)

Angers was the former capital of the Dukes of Anjou and is now a city full of factories with an old town and its 13th-century fortress at its heart. During the 16th century many of the 17 massive towers were dismantled, on royal command, to the level of the wall-walk. The castle has some spectacular displays of tapestries, including the Apocalypse Tapestry, the longest ever woven in France, displayed in a special gallery. It was originally 164 meters long but during the Revolution it was thrown over the walls into the street and citizens snipped bits off. In 1843 the bishop managed to repiece two-thirds of it and about 100 meters are on display. (*Open all year, tel: 02.41.87.43.47.*)

Saumur lies on the edge of the River Loire. Rising from the town are the walls of Saumur castle, a 14th-century fortification built atop a sheer cliff. (*Tel: 02.41.40.24.40.*)

For horse enthusiasts, on the outskirts of the city of Saumur is an internationally acclaimed equestrian center, ***L'École Nationale d'Équitation***, and school for the famous riders and horses of the *Cadre Noir*. It is possible to take guided tours of the facility and observe the training. Riding events and staged performances are seasonal. (*Open Apr 1 to Sep 30, Tues through Sat, tel: 02.41.53.50.60.*)

Chinon is a huge crumbling fortress set high above the River Vienne, with a medieval town and tree-lined boulevard at its feet. Henry II of England died here, his son Richard the Lionheart owned it, King John lost it to the French, and Joan of Arc came here to plead with Charles VII for an army. It is an interesting walk around the skeleton of this fortification, but be prepared to fill in large chunks of the interior with your imagination. There is an interesting museum celebrating Joan of Arc. (*Open all year, tel: 02.47.93.13.45.*)

Ussé overlooks the River Indre and is everything you expect a château to be, with turrets, towers, chimneys, dormers, and enchantment. The house is completely furnished in period style, illustrating the way things were in the 16th and 17th centuries, complete with wax figurines dressed in period costume.

Châteaux Country

Magnificent Flemish tapestries grace the Great Gallery of the Château d'Ussé and while you are waiting for your guided tour (narrated in French with English description sheets), you can climb the tower whose turret rooms are furnished with scenes from *Sleeping Beauty*. Conjecture has it that Ussé was the château that inspired Perault to write the famous fairy tale. (*Closed Nov to mid-Feb, tel: 02.47.95.54.05.*)

Azay-le-Rideau and its elegant Renaissance château are not far from Ussé. Azay-le-Rideau's graceful façade is framed by wispy trees and is reflected in its lake and the River Indre, from whose banks it rises on one side. It was built by Gilles Berthelot, the treasurer to Francis I between 1518 and 1527. Francis accused Gilles of fiddling the nation's books and confiscated this ornate château. It was not until the 19th century that it was completed. You can accompany a knowledgeable guide on a detailed tour or explore on your own, walking from one showpiece room to the next, admiring the fine furniture and tapestries. This is one of our favorite châteaux. (*Open all year, tel: 02.47.45.42.04.*)

Villandry is known for its formal, geometric French gardens—even the paths are raked into designs. While you can tour the house, the real reason for visiting Villandry is to spend time in the gardens wandering along the little paths between the neatly clipped box hedges. Even the vegetable garden has been planted to produce geometric patterns. Be sure to capture the bird's-eye view of this colorful quilt of a garden from the upper terrace. (*Gardens open all year, house open mid-Feb to mid-Nov, tel: 02.47.50.02.09.*)

Southeast of Montbazon is the town of **Loches**, found in the hills along the banks of the Indre, and referred to as the "City of Kings." The ancient castle is the "Acropolis of the Loire;" the buildings around it form what is called *Haute Ville*. It was a favorite retreat of King Charles VII and here you will find a copy of the proceedings of Joan of Arc's trial. The king's mistress, Agnes Sorel, is buried in the tower and her portrait is in one of the rooms. (*Open all year, tel: 02.47.59.07.86.*)

Chenonceaux almost spans the River Cher and is without a doubt one of the loveliest of the Loire's châteaux. This château owes a great deal to each of its six female occupants. Catherine Briconnet built Chenonceaux as a home, not a fortification, and sexy Diane de

Chenonceaux

Poitiers, the mistress of Henry II, added a garden and the bridge between the house and the banks of the River Cher. When Henry died, his jealous wife, Catherine de Medici, took Chenonceaux back and consigned Diane to Château de Chaumont. Catherine had the gallery built on the bridge, laid out the park, and held decadent parties. She bequeathed her home to Louise de Lorraine, her daughter-in-law who, after her husband's death, retired here and went into mourning for the rest of her life. In 1733 it passed to Monsieur Dupin whose intellectual wife was so beloved by the locals that it escaped the Revolution unscathed. In 1864 it was bought by Madame Peolouze who made it her life's work to restore her home. The château is now the home of the Menier family. Chenonceaux merits a leisurely visit: you want to allocate at least two hours for wandering through the park, gardens, and its elegant interior. The grounds also contain a wax museum with scenes from the château's history. (*Open all year, tel: 02.47.23.90.07.*)

Just a few kilometers north of Chenonceaux is the striking castle of **Amboise**. A tour of this large property will fill you with tales of grandeur, intrigue, and gruesome history. Francis I loved to party, reveling in grand balls, masquerades, festivals, and tournaments. He invited Leonardo da Vinci here and the artist spent his last years at the neighboring manor **Clos Lucé**. You can see his bedroom, models of machines he invented, and copies of his drawings. Catherine de Medici brought her young son Francis II and his young bride Mary, later Queen of Scots, to Amboise when the Protestants rose up after the Saint Bartholomew massacre. The Amboise Conspiracy of 1560 involved a group of Protestant reformers who followed the royal court from Blois to Amboise under the pretense of asking the king for permission to practice their religion. However, their plot was betrayed to the powerful Duke of Guise (Scarface) and upon arrival they were tortured, hung from the battlements, and left twisting in pain for days—the court and the royal family would come out to watch them. (*Open all year, fax: 02.47.57.62.88.*)

From Amboise follow the Loire to **Chaumont**, a château that has more appeal viewed from across the river than up close. Catherine de Medici was reputedly living here when her husband Henry II was killed and she became regent. She supposedly bought the château so that she could swap it with Diane de Poitiers (her husband's mistress) for Chenonceaux. Diane found it did not match up to Chenonceaux and left—you can understand why. Later Benjamin Franklin paid a visit to sit for an Italian sculptor who had set up his headquarters in the stables. Approached across a drawbridge, the château has three wings—the fourth side was pulled down in 1739—opening up to a fine view of the Loire Valley. You can tour the apartments and the stables. (*Open all year, tel: 02.54.51.26.26.*)

Blois sits on the north bank of the River Loire. The Chamber of the States General and part of a tower are all that remain of the 13th-century fortification that occupied this site. Much of the magnificent edifice you see today is due to Francis I's trying to keep his brother Gaston d'Orléans (who was always conspiring against him) out of trouble. In 1662 he banished him to Blois and gave him the project of restoring the château. Gaston hired the famous architect Mansart. The château has its stories of love, intrigue, and politicking, but its most famous is the murder of the Duke of Guise. In 1688 the powerful Henri de Guise called the States General here with the intention of deposing Henry III and making himself king. Henry found out about the plot and murdered the Duke. Who did what and where is explained in great detail on the tour. The most interesting room on the tour is Catherine de Medici's bedchamber with its many secret wall panels, used in the true Medici tradition to hide jewels, documents, and poisons. (*Open all year, tel: 02.54.90.33.33.*)

Cheverny

Châteaux Country

Ten kilometers from Blois lies **Cheverny**, a château built in 1634 for the Hurault family. It is smaller than Blois and Chambord and more interesting to tour because it still has its 17th-century decorations and furnishings. The Hurault family has carefully preserved their inheritance with its exquisite painted woodwork, tapestries, and furniture—in fact Cheverny is one of the most magnificently furnished châteaux in the Loire. One can also tour the acres of park by electric cart or by boat traveling the canals. Cheverny is also famous for its kennels. The grounds are home to 70 hounds and watching them patiently line up for dinner is a popular event. (*Feedings: Apr to mid-Sep except Sat and Sun 5 pm, otherwise 3 pm except Tues and weekends.*) In another outbuilding is a collection of 2,000 deer antlers, the family's hunting trophies. (*Open all year, tel: 02.54.79.96.29.*)

Standing on a grassy expanse amidst vast acres of forest, **Chambord** is enormous. Francis I built Chambord as a hunting lodge, but he believed that bigger was better so the vast edifice has 440 rooms and 80 staircases. Francis spent only 40 days at his huge home, which now has far less furniture than many other properties and is owned by the state. Apart from its impressive size and isolated location, Chambord's most interesting feature is the double-spiral staircase in the center of the building. (*Open all year, tel: 08.25.82.60.88.*)

The last stretch along the Loire takes you to the lovely old town of **Beaugency** with its historic church, **Nôtre Dame**. A magnificent bridge with 22 arches spans the river. The French blew it apart in 1940 to delay the Germans, but it has been completely restored (the central arches are original) and provides an ideal viewpoint for looking at the river and this delightful little town with its narrow medieval streets.

Orléans is a modern town rebuilt after the destruction of World War II. This was the scene of Joan of Arc's greatest triumph, when she successfully drove the English from France in 1429. There is little left for Joan of Arc fans to visit except her statue in Place Martoi.

From Orléans it is a 120-kilometer drive on the autoroute A10 back to Paris.

Azay le Rideau

Châteaux Country

Dordogne & Lot River Valleys

Dordogne & Lot River Valleys

The lazy Dordogne and Lot rivers wind gracefully through some of France's most picturesque countryside past villages dressed with grand castles, through peaceful meadows dotted with farms, beneath towering cliffs, and into pretty woodlands. However, this itinerary is more than just traveling along river valleys, for the region is France's prehistoric capital: the Cro-Magnon skull was discovered at Les Eyzies; colorful 15,000-year-old paintings decorate the Lascaux, Font de Gaume, and Les Combarelles caves; and man occupied the terraces on the cliffside of La Roque Saint Christophe as long ago as 70,000 B.C. Visit Rocamadour, an ancient village that tumbles down a rocky canyon, and Conques, a medieval village on a dramatic hillside site.

View of the Dordogne River from Domme

Recommended Pacing: You could happily spend a couple of weeks in the Dordogne, venturing along the river valley then adding unscheduled meanderings up little side roads to country villages. For the purposes of this itinerary, an efficient pacing would be to base yourself a night or two in the northern region, two to three nights close to the river itself (more if you make reservations at several of the caves), a night or two near Rocamadour, (using Rocamadour as a base for the journey to Turenne for a daytrip loop), and then continue south to the River Lot where you will need two nights to explore this lovely river valley and include a visit to the hillside village of Conques at its eastern boundary.

In the northern region of the Dordogne, **Brantôme** is a delightful little town on the banks of the River Dronne with narrow winding streets and a riverside park that leads you across the famous 16th-century elbow bridge to the old abbey, nestled at the foot of a rocky cliff. Founded by Charlemagne in 769, the abbey was reconstructed in the 11th century after it was ransacked by the Normans. The church and adjoining buildings were constructed and modified between the 14th and 18th centuries.

Follow the River Dronne for 10 kilometers on the D78 into the very pretty village of **Bourdeilles**. A little bridge takes you across the river to its 12th-century castle which the English and French squabbled about for years. From Bourdeilles country roads direct you to the D939 and on to Périgueux.

Périgueux changed allies twice in the 100 Years' War, eventually opting for France. It's a pleasant, large market town with an interesting domed cathedral resplendent with little turrets. From Périgueux follow signposts towards Brive (D47) and at Thenon take the D67 to Montignac (40 kilometers).

Montignac is a popular tourist town because on its outskirts are the wondrous **Lascaux Caves** with their magnificent 15,000-year-old paintings. In 1963 these caves were closed to the public because the paintings were being damaged by the rise and fall in temperature as hordes of visitors came and went. It took ten years to construct an exact replica—**Lascaux II**. Except for the even, non-slip floor you will not know that you are not in the real Lascaux. The bulls, bison, and stags appear to be moving around the cave—so skillfully did the artists utilize every feature of the rocks that bumps appear as humps, cheekbones, and haunches. In July and August the quota of 2,000 tickets a day go on sale at 9 am at the *Syndicat d'Initiative* (Tourist Office) in Montignac. Tickets are not available in advance. For the rest of the year tickets are sold at the site on a first come, first served basis, so you may arrive at 11 am and find that you are offered a 4 pm tour. Tours are given in English and French.

Leaving Lascaux II, watch for signs that will direct you to Le Thot along the D65. The admission ticket for Lascaux includes admission to **Le Thot** where you can see a film of the building of Lascaux II and displays of large photos of the many prehistoric paintings found in caves in the valley. The grounds also have a park and a re-creation of a prehistoric village.

Leaving Le Thot, follow signposts for **La Roque Saint Christophe**. As the road winds by the river, a sheer cliff rises to a deep natural terrace before continuing upwards. As long ago as 70,000 B.C. man took advantage of this natural terrace for shelter and by medieval times it was home to over 1,000 people. The thousands of niches that you see today were used to hold up supporting beams for the houses and the rings you see carved into the rock were used to hang lamps and to tether animals. (*Open all year, tel: 05.53.50.70.45.*)

Following the winding River Vézère, the D706 brings you into **Les Eyzies de Tayac**. The caves in the cliff that towers above the town were home to prehistoric man who took shelter here during the second Ice Age. People lived here for tens of thousands of years. Archaeologists have uncovered flints, pottery, jewelry, and skeletons that have been identified as those of Cro-Magnon man found in the cave behind the hotel of the same name. Visit the **Musée National de la Préhistoire** in the 11th-century castle set high on the cliff beneath the overhanging rock, guarded by the gigantic sculpture of Cro-Magnon man. (*Open all year, tel: 05.53.06.45.45.*)

Nearby, the **Font de Gaume** cave has prehistoric wall paintings of horses, bison, mammoths, and reindeer with colors still so rich that it is hard to comprehend the actual passage of time. The caves are a bit damp and dark and entail a steep 400-meter climb to reach the entrance. The grotto is deep, winding, and narrow in parts. There are some 230 drawings, of which about 30 are presented and discussed. Displayed in three tiers, some drawings are marred by graffiti, others are not clearly visible as the walls tower above the floor of the cave. Entrance is limited to 200 people per day but you can make reservations in advance by calling the tourist office in Les Eyzies (*tel: 05.53.06.97.05, fax: 05.53.06.90.79*). There is a small additional charge for advance booking. With the closure of more caves each year, it is uncertain how much longer the opportunity to visit Font de Gaume will continue. (*Open all year.*)

A short distance from Font de Guam is **Les Combarelles**, a cave discovered in 1901. The entrance is about a 100-meter (level) walk from the car park. The cave is a winding passage with engravings of mammoth, ibex, bears, reindeer, bison, and horses—and man in the last 70 meters. Entrance is limited to 140 visitors per day and the cave is closed every Wednesday. Advance booking and hours of opening are identical to Font de Gaume.

From Les Eyzies follow the scenic D706 to **Campagne** with its abandoned château sitting behind padlocked gates. From Campagne take the pretty D35 to **Saint Cyprien**, an attractive town just a short distance from the Dordogne. It has more shops and cafés than most small towns in the valley, making it an appealing and interesting place to break your journey.

Through pretty countryside follow the Dordogne river valley, just out of sight of the river. As you approach **Beynac**, you are presented with a lovely picture of a small village huddled beneath a cliff crowned by a 12th-century fortress before a broad sweep of the Dordogne. The castle, while its furnishings are sparse, is well worth visiting for the spectacular views. (*Open all year.*) On the water's edge is **Hôtel Bonnet**, recommended not for its accommodation, but as a scenic and excellent choice for lunch under vine-covered trellises.

Have your cameras ready as you approach **La Roque Gageac**. The town, clinging to the hillside above the River Dordogne and framed by lacy trees, is a photographer's dream. There's a grassy area on the riverbank with a few picnic tables and an inviting path, following the curves of the river, tempts you farther.

Just upstream, cross the bridge and climb the hill to **Domme**, a medieval walled village that has for centuries stood guard high above the river and commanded a magnificent panorama. The town itself is enchanting, with ramparts that date from the 13th century and narrow streets that wind through its old quarter and past a lovely 14th-century **Hôtel de Ville**. At the town center under the old market place, you find access to some interesting stalactite and stalagmite grottos. However, most visitors come to Domme for its spectacular views—the best vantage point is from the **Terrasse de la Barre**.

Because it is more scenic on the north side of the river, retrace your steps across the bridge and continue downriver on the D703 to **Château de Montfort**, a majestic castle shadowing a wide loop in the river. Built by one of the region's most powerful barons,

Château de Montfort

this intimate, restored castle, furnished like a private residence, rises out of a rocky ledge. The **Cingle de Montfort** offers some delightful views of the river. When the D703 intersects with the D704, take a short detour north to the city of **Sarlat**. Sarlat has a delightful old quarter with narrow cobbled streets that wind through a maze of magnificent gourmet shops. The church and the Episcopal palace create a roomy space along the narrow bustling streets. Sarlat bustles with activity and color on market day.

After visiting Sarlat, return to the banks of the Dordogne and continue east once again along its shore, this time in the direction of **Souillac**. When the D703 reaches this lovely riverside town, travel south following the N20 in the direction of Cahors. As you leave houses behind you, turn left on the D43 (rather than crossing the river) and begin a very picturesque stretch of the valley. As you cross a single-lane wooden bridge spanning the Dordogne, take note of the picture-postcard **Château de la Treyne**, one of our favorite hotels in the region, (recommended in our France hotel guide), perched above the riverbank. **Lacave** is also known for some spectacular geological formations in its caves, which you can tour on a diminutive train. As you climb out of Lacave towards Rocamadour, the fields are filled with bustling geese being fattened for *foie gras* and you get a picturesque view of a castle sitting high above the distant Dordogne. A scenic country road winds to where the ground disappears into an abyss and the village of **Rocamadour** tumbles down the narrow canyon.

Our preference is to park in the large car park adjacent to the castle, but if it is full, head for the valley floor and park in one of the grassy car parks. A stairway leads down, from beside the castle to the chapels, houses, and narrow streets that cling precipitously to the rock face, to the little chapels and the large basilica that incorporates the cliff face as one wall of the building. From the 12th century onwards Rocamadour was a popular pilgrimage site. There are lots of tourist shops and, thankfully, cafés providing a spot to sit and rest after climbing up and down the staircases. If steep climbs are not for you, buy a ticket on the elevator that goes up and down the hillside. From Rocamadour you can either travel directly on to the Lot river valley to the south or take a scenic detour of approximately 100 kilometers north to some enchanting and picturesque villages.

For a scenic loop north from Rocamadour travel east on D673 for just 4 kilometers, cross the N140, continue on D673 as it winds through the village of Alvignac, and then travel on to Padirac.

Château de la Treyne

At Padirac, detour off on the D90 to **Gouffre de Padirac**. A gouffre is a great opening in the ground, and this wide circular chimney of Padirac was formed by the roof of a cave falling in. This impressive grotto leads over 100 meters underground to a mysterious river where the visitor can negotiate a stretch of some 500 meters by boat to discover the sparkling Lac de la Pluie (Lake of Rain) and its huge stalactite in the immense Great Dome room with its vault rising up 90 meters. The roof lies quite near the surface and it is almost inevitable that it too will one day collapse to form another chasm. (*Open Apr to Oct. Allow approximately 1½ hours for a guided tour, tel: 05.65.33.64.56.*)

Retrace your trail back to Padirac and then wind along the D38 traveling east and then north in the direction of Autoire. This scenic drive winds down a hill to reveal the beautiful village of **Autoire** set in a rich green valley shadowed by majestic, towering limestone cliffs. Autoire is lovely with its old stone houses topped with slate roofs clustering together along the narrow alleyways. Windowboxes overflow with flowers to provide a profusion of color against the mellowed stone of the buildings.

From Autoire, travel the few short kilometers to the picturesque village of **Loubressac**. Crowning the mountaintop, Loubressac appears dramatically on the horizon—another charming village, with a picturesque main square.

From Loubressac you enjoy gorgeous views across the river valley to the medieval fortress of **Castelnau** on the opposite bank in the town of **Bretenoux**. Impressive from a distance, the long façade of the fortress dominates the village skyline. Colored in the rusty red of the regional rock, the castle is remarkably preserved and impressive from the massive wooden portal to splendid interior furnishings. (*Open all year, closed Tues Oct to Mar, tel: 05.65.10.98.00.*) Crossing back to Loubressac, wind down to the river and then detour east to the Renaissance Château de Montal. The château is beautifully furnished and definitely worth a visit. (*Open Easter to Nov, closed Sat, tel: 05.65.38.13.72.*)

From the Château de Montal, it is a short distance farther on to the pretty market town of **Saint Céré** whose square comes alive and is particularly colorful when the commodity for sale is livestock. Worthy of a visit on the outskirts of Saint Céré in **Le Tours de Saint Laurent** is a tapestry museum, the **Atelier Musée Jean Lurçat**. (*Open mid-Jul to Oct, telephone number for the tourist office in Saint Céré: 05.65.38.11.85.*)

From Saint Céré journey back along the D30, once again following the path of the Dordogne to the pretty village of **Carennac**, set just above the river. This idyllic little village is even more picturesque because of the river that weaves through it, in the shadow of the lovely old timbered homes and a handsome church sheltered behind an arched entry.

From Carennac, cross the river and travel north to **Turenne**. This charming, picturesque village is surrounded by a patchwork of farmland. Narrow, cobbled streets wind steeply up to a crowning church and castle. (*Open Apr to Oct.*) Views from the top of the castle are very peaceful and pretty.

Saint Cirq Lapopie

From Turenne, according to the map, there is a road that appears to cross almost directly over to **Collonges la Rouge** (the D150 to connect with the D38, just 5 kilometers west of Collonges) but it is extremely difficult to find—I never discovered how to access it from Turenne. It might prove easier, as I found, to detour north on the D8 to just north of Monplaisir and then turn east on the D38 and on to Collonges la Rouge, a lovely village favored by local artisans, with cobbled streets winding through a maze of stone buildings all rich in a hue of burnt red. Probably the regional town most geared for tourists, it has a number of interesting craft shops to tempt you indoors. Collonges la Rouge is most beautiful on a clear day when the sun washes the stone in a rich, warm red against a backdrop of blue.

From Collonges la Rouge, return west on the D38 in the direction of Brive; and then just past Maranzat, jog south on the D8 and then almost immediately west on the D158 to Noailles and the junction of N20. Traveling south on the N20 at the town of Payrac, you will pass the junction of D673 which travels the rocky valley east to Rocamadour where you begin this scenic northern loop. From Payrac it is another 50 kilometers on to Cahors and the magical Lot River Valley.

Although it appears to be a large city, **Cahors**, in reality, is an enchanting, medieval city set on the bend of the River Lot. I would definitely recommend that you take time to venture into the city. Embraced by the banks of the river the city is famous for its architectural richness: the dramatic **Pont Valentré** bridge built in the 14th century, the Arc de Diane, a remnant of a vast Gallo-Roman thermal establishment, the Saint Etienne Cathedral from the 11th and 12th centuries, the tower of Pope John XXII, and the Saint Barthelemy Church. Not to be missed at the heart of the city is the old core with its houses, mansions, gates, lanes and squares. There are lots of restaurants, sidewalk cafes and interesting shops. With lots of character and a quiet pace, this is a city to explore on foot, or take advantage of the bike paths that follow the banks of the river Lot. Cahors serves as an excellent focal point for exploring the region and sampling its wonderful wines.

A destination in its own right, and dramatic in terms of a landmark, just a few kilometers west from Cahors, towering over the river is a magnificent château-hotel, the **Château de Mercuès**. (Recommended in our France hotel guide.)

From the outskirts of Cahors travel east, following signposts for Figeac along the north bank of the river. This portion of the **Lot River Valley** can be driven in half a day on roads that wind along a riverbank that is narrower and quieter than that of the Dordogne. The River Lot winds along the curves of the wide canyon, cutting into its chalky walls. At some stretches the route follows the level of the river and at others it straddles the clifftops. Vistas are dramatic at every turn although the restricting narrow roads will frustrate the eye of any photographer because there is rarely a place to stop.

Cross the river at **Bouzies** and take a moment to look back across the bridge and see the medieval buildings constructed into the walls of the canyon above the small tunnel. This is also the departure point for many boat trips as evidenced by the many tethered rental boats. Just outside Bouzies, the road (D40) climbs and winds precipitously to the top of the cliff and rounding a bend, you find **Saint Cirq Lapopie** clinging precipitously to the sheer canyon walls and cascading back down towards the river. Drive around the village to one of the car parks and walk back up the hill to explore. Many of the buildings have been restored and only a few of the houses are lived in. It's most enjoyable to wander the quiet streets without being overwhelmed by tourist shops.

Travel down to the Lot and cross to its northernmost bank. As the river guides you farther, it presents a number of lovely towns and with each turn reveals another angle and view of the valley. **La Toulzanie** is a small, pretty village nestled into a bend of the river, interesting because of its houses built into the limestone cliffs. Calvignac is an ancient village clinging to the top of the cliff on the opposite bank. At Cajarc be careful to keep to the river road (D662). A short drive brings you to the village of **Montbrun**, a village that rises in tiers on jutting rock by steep cliffs. It looks down on the Lot, up at its ruined castle, and across the river to *Saut de la Mounine* (Jump of the Monkey). Legend recalls that to punish his daughter for falling in love with the son of a rival baron, a father ordered daughter to be thrown from the cliffs. A monkey was dressed in her clothes and thrown to its death instead. Father, regretting his harsh judgment, was overcome with joy when he discovered the substitution. Set on a plateau, the **Château de Larroque Toirac** is open to visitors and makes an impressive silhouette against the chalky cliffs and the village of **Saint Pierre Toirac**.

Less than 10 kilometers to the north of the Lot on the River Célé is the larger market town of **Figeac**. A wonderful example of 12th-century architecture, Figeac is an attractive river town and it is fun to explore the shops along its cobbled streets and alleyways.

Continue on to Conques, a bonus to this itinerary that requires that you journey farther along the winding Lot (on the N140 signposted Decazeville and then D963 and D42 signposted Entraygues). The route weaves through some beautiful farmland and attractive little villages. At La Vinzelle leave the Lot river valley and climb up the D901 to **Conques**, a tiny medieval town on a dramatic hillside site. Tucked a considerable distance off the beaten track, it is a delightful, unspoiled village that was once an important pilgrimage stop on the way to Santiago de Compostela in Spain.

Conques's pride is its 11th-century **Abbaye Sainte Foy** whose simple rounded arches give it the look of a Gothic cathedral. The carving of the Last Judgment in a semi-circle over the central door shows 124 characters—the grimacing devils and tortured souls are far more amusing than the somber few who are selected to go to heaven. The abbey's treasure is the 10th-century Sainte Foy reliquary, a statue sheathed in gold leaf and decorated with precious stones.

If time allows, linger in the town into early evening, when evening light plays on the wonderful old stone and cobbled streets. It is magical to hear the melodious bells as their sound echoes through the town.

Conques

Dordogne & Lot River Valleys

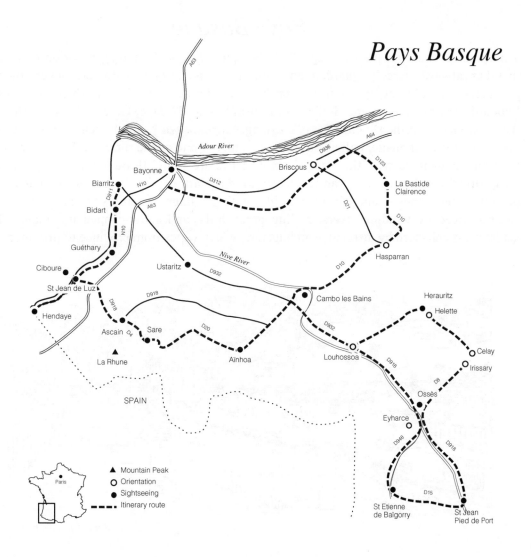

Pays Basque

Adour River

Bayonne

Biarritz
D911
Bidart
N10
A63
N10

Guéthary

Ciboure

St Jean de Luz
D918
D918

Hendaye

Ascain D4 Sare

▲
La Rhune

SPAIN

Ainhoa

D20

Ustaritz
D932
Nive River

D312
N10

Briscous
D936
A64
D123

La Bastide
Clairence

D21

D10

Hasparran

Cambo les Bains
D932

D10

Herauritz
Helette

Louhossoa

D918

Celay

Irissary

D8

Ossès

Eyharce

D948

St Etienne
de Baïgorry
D15

St Jean
Pied de Port

D918

Paris

▲ Mountain Peak
○ Orientation
● Sightseeing
- - - Itinerary route

67

Pays Basque

This itinerary traces a path through Pays Basque (Basque Country), a region of France that has always fiercely guarded and preserved its unique character. Seven Basque provinces straddle the western border between France and Spain; three in France: Labourd, Basse-Navarre, and Soule, and four in Spain: Biscaye, Guipuzcoa, Navarre, and Alava. Concerning the seven there is a saying, *"zazpiak bat,"* which means "seven equals one." The local language, called Euskara, considered one of the oldest in Europe, and the traditions associated with the Basque style of life are found throughout the region. The area, stretching from the Atlantic Ocean to the start of the Pyrenees, abounds with beautiful landscapes—sandy beaches, old whaling villages, picturesque ports, beautiful valleys sliced by winding rivers, rolling green hills, and snow-capped mountains. The landscape is enhanced by distinctive architecture, which varies from province to province.

Saint Jean Pied de Port

The Basque people, with their strong sense of tradition, add their own color to this fascinating region with their local festivals and in their dress—they often wear traditional costume and are never without a beret or espadrilles.

This itinerary takes you to two of the French Basque provinces, exploring the coast and hilltowns of Labourd and then weaving deeper into the countryside to the heart of Basse-Navarre. Labourd, with its beaches, port towns, and green foothills, is the province with the most diverse landscape. Basse-Navarre is rich with lush countryside, rolling green pastures, a scenic valley cut by the path of the River Nive, and small farming communities that have become famous for their ewes' cheese.

Diverse in their landscape, the provinces are just as distinctive in architecture, influenced by both setting and tradition. Especially charming are the colorful, red-roofed, timbered houses of Labourd, which are intentionally built with their backs to the sea, with one side more richly decorated, and also strategically positioned east to face the rising sun and a new day. These houses are painted in the national red and green colors of Basque and it is fascinating to learn that ox blood was actually once used to stain the timbers red! Traditionally, Labourd homes are passed down to the oldest child and many have been in the same family for hundreds of years. To weather the more rugged climate, the homes of Basse-Navarre are built from the locally quarried stone and have distinctive circular balconies. The ground floor and entryway of Basque homes used to house the animals, with the family living above and drying hay serving to insulate the roof. You will notice in Labourd homes that one side of the roof extends further than the other—this gave the family the opportunity to expand the living quarters under the existing roof when financially able.

As well as being rich in tradition, landscape, and architecture, the region also offers a wealth of food specialties. To fully appreciate their culture, be sure to sample the rich ewes' cheeses, delicious macaroons, a complex fish soup often referred to as *ttoro*, a butter tart filled with delicious black cherry filling (*gâteau basque*), the salty, dried ham (*jamon de Bayonne*), and a side dish called *piperade*, which is a compote of cooked tomatoes, onions, eggplant, garlic, and pimentos (the origin of its name). The vineyards of Irouleguy produce a red and a rosé and there is said to be a secret recipe with ingredients cultivated from over 20 regional plants to produce the two varieties of *Izarra*, a green or yellow liquor.

Recommended Pacing: Biarritz and Bayonne, on the coast, are both logical and convenient cities from which to begin and conclude a circle trip of these gorgeous and diverse districts of Pays Basque. Plan to spend at least two nights on the coast in order to explore the beaches, charming towns, and fishing villages with either Biarritz or Saint Jean de Luz as a base, a night in the hilltown village of Sare, and continue on into the heart of Basse-Navarre, overnighting in Saint Etienne de Baïgorry. Continue back to the coast and the capital city of Bayonne, including a stop in the picturesque village of La Bastide-Clairence.

Biarritz is a wonderful introduction to the style and life of Pays Basque. Once a whaling station, it is now recognized as a seaside resort of international renown. Don't let its size intimidate you—as the residents will tell you, this is still a small town in heart and soul—locals claim not even to lock their cars! Biarritz is captivating and charming and the center of the old town is very easy to explore on foot. Its central stretch of beach is flanked by a promenade and a few casinos, the most spectacular of which, the **Hôtel du Palais**, is also a hotel and an historic landmark, dating back to the days of the Spanish Countess, Eugenie of Montijo who married the Emperor Napoleon III. Being fond of Biarritz, she had the Hôtel du Palais (originally referred to as Villa Eugenie) built as a holiday home, hosted European aristocracy, and introduced them to the charms and festivities of the town. The Countess is fondly referred to as the "godmother" of the town. The nightlife is perhaps a bit more tame than in her time, but people are still attracted to Biarritz for the casinos, racecourses, nightclubs, and special events including the surf festival, pelota tournament, and numerous golf tournaments. While exploring Biarritz, be sure to visit the **Marine Museum** located in front of the Rocher de la Vierge (Virgin Rock) for its display of marine fauna and aquariums; the **Historical Museum**, which features fishing and agricultural influences through costumes, paintings, artifacts, and documents; and, for gourmands, the **Chocolate Museum**, whose sculptures are a delicious and interesting testament to the fact that chocolate originated in the Basque Country during the reign of Louis XIV.

With its absolutely gorgeous setting, Biarritz also inspires you to spend some time outdoors. Include a visit to the **Biarritz Lighthouse**, dating back to 1831, which towers 73 meters above the sea and (after a climb of 248 steps) offers an exceptional view of the town and Basque coastline. From the lighthouse follow the headland to the **Côte des Basque** beach with its dramatic offshore rocks of the Basta, the Madonna, and the Atalaye Plateau and most definitely include a walk along the Port des Pêcheurs, the old fishing village now referred to as the **Port Vieux** or Old Port. This is an enchanting path to walk at sunset: taking you from the beach around the old harbor, along its breakwater, which protects its active fishing fleet and intimate seafood restaurants, to a picturesque point and then wrapping around the other side of Biarritz below an exclusive residential district. It was from the old harbor where whaling ships used to sail out to the Bay of Biscaye.

Traditional Labourd Home

There are several charming villages that hug the coast south from Biarritz in a span of just 108 kilometers to the Spanish border. A few roads run parallel down the coast: we left Biarritz on the D911 and then opted for the smallest road, the N10, which wasn't the most direct but ribboned through the center of each of the villages. **Bidart**—with its quaint main square banded by timbered houses and its nearby church, which is characteristic of the fortress-style churches of the 16th century—is a typical Basque village in the Labourd style and was also once a bustling whaling and fishing port. For another wonderful view of the Basque coast, turn right off the square on the narrow street that leads to the cliffs, to the site of the Sainte-Madeline Chapel, dedicated to Basque mariners.

From Bidart's lovely beach, the road winds up through the coastal hills to **Guéthary**, the coast's smallest village, nestled in the hills above the beautiful expanse of blue ocean. Guéthary derives its name from the Latin word "to observe" as its setting provided a wonderful vantage point from which to spot whales. Its numerous villas, many of them lovely red-and-green timbered and shuttered houses, are a testament to its days as a very popular and wealthy seaside community. Don't leave without visiting its picturesque port and driving by the charming cliff-top railway station. Like Bidart, Guéthary boasts some lovely neighboring beaches (quite popular with surfers) and interesting shops.

Farther south is the larger town of **Saint Jean de Luz**, separated by a bridge and the mouth of the River Nivelle from the equally picturesque town of Ciboure. With its lovely expanse of beach, sheltered harbor, grassy beach promenade, distinctive regional architecture, quaint town square, outdoor cafés, and local artists, it is easy to understand the enduring popularity of this enchanting town. To complement its beauty it also has a rich and colorful history—the lavish homes are evidence of the wealth acquired by whalers-turned-pirates (the French—*corsaires*—sounds more dignified!) who sailed under the blessing of the French King. The town reached its peak of dignity and glory in 1660 with the arranged political union of Louis XIV of France and Marie-Thérèse of Spain. Still standing on either side of the town's main square are the two houses where they each awaited their marriage. (The Louis XIV House can be visited in summer months.) Also interesting to visit is the Church of St. John the Baptist, whose doorway was walled up immediately after the couple's departure so that no one else could cross the royal threshold. The interior is worth a visit for its simple architecture, high altar, and classic wooden Basque balconies. Although a popular tourist town, Saint Jean de Luz still has an active fishing industry, with anchovies, tuna, and sardines playing a vital role in its commercial success.

With a beautiful setting banded by ocean and hillside, **Ciboure** has always been considered an extension of Saint Jean de Luz; but because it is across the river, it became a comfortable refuge for the Bohemian set and remains a community of fishermen, artists, and musicians.

From Ciboure it is just a short distance traveling along the Corniche Basque following the D912 to the lovely town of **Hendaye** with its gorgeous 3-kilometer stretch of sandy beach (considered the region's safest beach for swimming). Right on the Spanish border, Hendaye has played an important historical role as a frontier town.

From Hendaye, cut east over to the N10, travel north back to the outskirts of Saint Jean de Luz, and then leave the coast and head inland on the D918. The scenery changes almost immediately as you leave the ocean behind and the road follows a picturesque sweep of the River Nivelle with a gorgeous backdrop of verdant mountain. The D918 travels across the river and passes right through the center of **Ascain**, a charming town nestled amongst fields of sheep and cattle. After Ascain take the D4, a road that winds a scenic route up from the town, and on its outskirts at the Col de St. Ignace, a number of parked cars will draw your attention to a little rack railway that climbs 905 meters up to the highest peak in Pays Basque, **La Rhune**, on the Spanish border. From La Rhune you enjoy spectacular vistas looking over the Pyrenees and to the distant coastline. The train trip takes approximately 30 minutes and at the top there are a few souvenir shops and places to eat. You can return to the bottom on foot, if you prefer. (*Mid-Mar to Nov 02, first departure 9:30 am, tel: 05.59.54.20.26, fax: 05.59.47.50.76, www.rhune.com.*)

Soon after you leave La Rhune a tree-lined drive winds down to the valley and the quiet, endearing village of **Sare**. I will always have fond memories of Sare that date to my early research years (now a quarter of a century ago!); memories of a typical timbered Labourd village whose central square at the time of my first visit was a stage for a colorful local festival with traditionally costumed dancers and musicians.

Historically, Sare, so close to the Spanish border, has played a dominant role in smuggling goods across the frontier—termed "night work" by the locals!

Although not on sightseeing maps, close to Sare there is a completely non-commercial, storybook-perfect hamlet of timbered homes that is worth a quick drive-by. To step back into this world of yesterday and visit a single-street village that was once a 16th-century farm, leave the center of Sare in the direction of Cambo les Bains and just on Sare's outskirts, at the roundabout, make a detour left, up the tree-lined road.

Return to the roundabout, take the D4 in the direction of Saint Pée, cross over a small bridge and travel through farmland, first on the D4 then the D305, a narrow road and lush, scenic route. The road jogs onto the D20 and brings you to Aïnhoa. Located halfway between Sare and Cambo les Bains, **Aïnhoa** is one of France's most beautiful villages, traditional and typically Basque. Dating back to the Middle Ages, Aïnhoa, just 2 kilometers from the Spanish border, served as a convenient stopover for pilgrims making their journey to Santiago de Compostella. Although almost totally destroyed by the Spanish in 1629, it was rebuilt in the 17th and 18th centuries and its one main street lined by timbered and shuttered homes represents the essence of Pays Basque. All the typical, essential, and fundamental elements in a traditional Basque village are present in Aïnhoa: the town hall, the church, and the *fronton* (the rounded wall used for playing the classic Basque game of pelota).

From Aïnhoa return to the main road, following the D20 in the direction of Espelette and then the D918 in the direction of Bayonne, to the larger town of Cambo les Bains.

Proudly distinguished as a *ville fleurie* ("flowering village" is an award recognizing towns with dramatic flower displays), **Cambo les Bains**, with its pretty setting and mild climate, became a popular tourist spot because of the two thermal springs found in the village. The oldest homes are located in Bas Cambo down from the town on the other side of the river. You can also visit **Arnaga**, Edmond Rostand's magnificent château-home and gardens. Now a national monument, it is also a museum dedicated to this much-celebrated author of *Cyrano de Bergerac*. (*Open Apr to Nov, tel: 05.59.29.70.25.*)

Following the path of the River Nive from Cambo les Bains, it is a pretty drive on the D918 through lush countryside to the heart of Basse-Navarre and two wonderful towns, Saint Etienne de Baïgorry and Saint Jean Pied du Port. You will want to overnight in the area in order to explore the region and towns. I would select Saint Etienne de Baïgorry if you want a quieter setting, and Saint Jean Pied du Port if you want stay in one of France's most beautiful walled villages. The D918 goes directly to Saint Jean Pied de Port, but to reach Saint Etienne de Baïgorry, you leave the D918 on the D948 at Saint Martin d'Arrossa. From Saint Etienne de Baïgorry you can then drive 11 kilometers on the D15 to Saint Jean Pied de Port.

With the mountains as a dramatic backdrop, **Saint Etienne de Baïgorry** enjoys a beautiful, serene setting in the valley of the Aldudes, nestled among the vineyards of the Irouléguy. Now a sportsman's paradise (hiking, rafting, rock climbing), this rugged terrain was, for those who tended the land, hard to work and many of the summer festivals and the famous "Force Basque Games" are based on the old farming chores and challenges of mountain life.

The capital of Basse-Navarre and a border crossing into Spain, the fortified town of **Saint Jean Pied de Port** enjoys a strategic location at the base of the mountains and straddling the Nive River. The name Pied de Port translates to "foot of the pass" and refers to the famous Roncevaux Pass where Charlemagne was defeated by the Basques. This pass was also used by the Romans and by the pilgrims en route to the tomb of St. James at Santiago de Compostella—the scallop shell used as an emblem by the pilgrims of St. James appears as a carved decoration on many of the town's homes.

You can drive to the summit (1032 meters) of Roncevaux Pass and of interest, just after the summit, is a 13th-century Gothic church, cloister, and small chapel housing the tomb of the Basque King Sancho VII, the Strong of Navarre.

Saint Jean Pied de Port is pretty and distinctive, with many of its houses constructed in rose-colored granite. A picturesque medieval bridge spanning the Nive connects the two sections of town and cobbled, narrow streets wind up to the crowning citadel. It is a fun town with lots of outdoor cafés and shops selling regional goods, and is the principal market town for the region (*market day Mon*).

From Saint Jean Pied de Port you can drive directly back to the coast following the D918 or, if time allows for a scenic detour, leave the D918 at Eyharce and take the D8, crossing the river at Ossès, a cute town whose church has a distinctively striped steeple, on to Irissary. Here you pick up the D22 at Celay traveling north to the neighboring villages of Helette and Herauritz. This is definitely farm country and the drive is picturesque as it cuts a path right through the rich pastures and dairy farms, a route often appropriately signed *Route du Fromage* (Cheese Road). If you want to stop and sample the regional ewes' cheese, the tasting room of Fromage de Brebis, just past Herauritz, is well signed along this charming country road.

From Herauritz, take the D119 and travel back to Louhossoa and the junction of D918. The D918 will take you back to the outskirts of Cambo les Bains. Here you can continue on the D918, which becomes the D932 past Cambo les Bains, to Bayonne.

But for another rewarding detour, travel the D10 through Cambo les Bains to Hasparren and then the lovely Basque village of **La Bastide Clairence**. This is a sweet village made up entirely of timbered homes and, with the honor of being designated one of France's most beautiful villages, it serves as a wonderful last countryside stop before you continue back to the coast and the larger port city of Bayonne.

The regional capital, **Bayonne**, has played an important role in history as a strategic commercial port city located at the junction of two rivers, the Nive and the Adour, on the constantly challenged border between France and Spain. It is a relatively easy city to navigate in and out of and is most definitely well worth the effort. Travel to the heart of this captivating port city, which was once a Roman garrison and was ruled at different times by both the French and English crowns. Shaded by old, leaning timbered buildings, cobbled streets wind up from the river that cuts a path through its center. Bayonne flourished during the 300-year English reign of Eleanor of Aquitaine and Henry Plantagenet. Their son Richard the Lionheart found his bride here—a Basque princess from Navarre. The town was penetrated by canals until the 17th century and you can still see the unusual arcades that once housed merchants serving the seamen.

To walk the streets of this river town, still protected behind its old stone walls, is to discover a lovely city of pedestrian passages, quaysides, and wonderful stone and half-timbered houses. Visit **St. Mary's Cathedral**, built in the 13th and 14th centuries, and the **medieval cellars**—in fact, medieval shops—that are found under the upper and older part of the town surrounding the cathedral. Bayonne is home to the **Bonnat Museum**, which houses a fine collection of art, considered one of the most prestigious collections outside Paris, including works by Goya, Raphael, Delacroix, Michelangelo, and Constable. For an in-depth study and presentation of the history of Bayonne as well as Basque culture, you might also want to visit the **Basque Museum**.

Before leaving Basque allow yourself to be tempted into one of the many tea rooms that specialize in a regional decadence. Basque is intensely proud of its claim of introducing hot chocolate to the world.

In South America, Christopher Columbus came upon this strange concoction that was used by the Indians not for barter but as the necessary ingredient for a rich, strong drink. The explorers returned home with the distinctive bean and shared the secret technique for turning cacao into chocolate. The Jews became experts in its production and brought it to the southwest of France when fleeing the Inquisitions. It is said that Bayonne became the first town to taste this delicious new beverage. The church at first disapproved of it, claiming it to be an aphrodisiac! However, the threatened wrath of the church was quickly ignored for something so delicious and chocolate became one of Bayonne's most famous exports. Don't leave Basque without sampling some of this "devil's brew"!

Gorges du Tarn
& Beyond

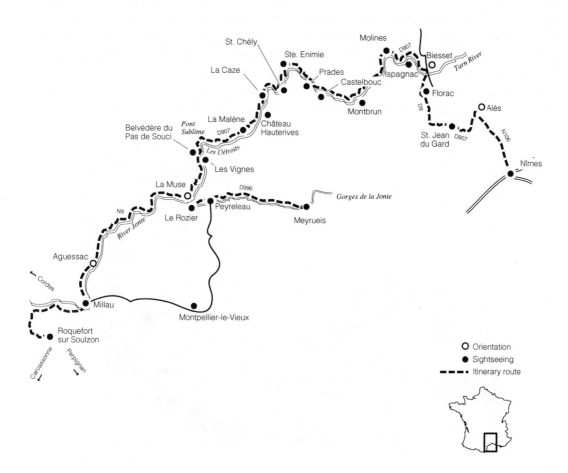

St. Chély

Molines

Biesset

Tarn River

Ste. Enimie

D907

La Caze

Prades

Ispagnac

Castelbouc

Florac

Montbrun

Alès

La Malène

D9

St. Jean
du Gard

D907

N106

Belvédère du
Pas de Souci

Pont
Sublime

D907

Château
Hauterives

Les Détroits

Nîmes

Les Vignes

La Muse

D996

N9

Le Rozier

Peyreleau

Gorges de la Jonte

River Jonte

Meyrueis

Aguessac

Cordes

Millau

Montpellier-le-Vieux

Roquefort
sur Soulzon

Carcassonne

Perpignan

O Orientation
● Sightseeing
▬ ▬ ▬ Itinerary route

Gorges du Tarn & Beyond

This itinerary follows the truly spectacular River Tarn as it winds back and forth along the Tarn Canyon or *Gorges du Tarn*. With each turn the drive becomes more beautiful, never monotonous. The road cuts through the canyon, hugging its walls, always in sight of the peaceful waters of the Tarn and its picturesque villages, clusters of warm stone buildings that nestle above its shore. Encased in deep limestone cliffs, the river canyon is at its most glorious in early autumn—a perfect time to visit. In the fall the traffic has subsided and nature's colors contrast beautifully with the canyon walls: grass carpets the mountains, making hillsides lush in all shades of green, and the trees blaze gold, red, and orange in the sunlight. But whatever time of year, the Gorges du Tarn is lovely.

Gorges du Tarn & Beyond

Recommended Pacing: This itinerary covers approximately 220 kilometers and can be driven in about 4 hours. The stretch along the canyon from Florac to Millau, about 75 kilometers, is sometimes crowded, often narrows to two lanes, and there are no short cuts once you're following the river. If you plan to cover the distance in a day's journey, get an early start. We suggest that you overnight near the river and give yourself two full days to drive, walk, picnic, and even float your way through the Tarn Canyon. At its conclusion, since this is relatively a short itinerary and based on the assumption that you will want to extend your trip into other regions of France, there are two suggestions for continuing your journey. Both suggestions incorporate a trip to the walled town of Carcassonne, one heads further west to visit the lovely cities of Albi and Toulouse, and the medieval, hill-town of Cordes; while the other recommends that once you leave Carcassonne, you efficiently span the distance, traveling the autoroutes, to the geographic, southwest corner where France neighbors Spain and overlooks the beautiful Mediterranean Sea.

With either **Avignon** or **Nîmes** on the western edge of Provence as a point of reference, travel northwest in the direction of Alès. Using a good map to plan the best route depending on your origin, travel southwest of Alès to the D907, going north in the direction of Saint Jean du Gard. **Saint Jean du Gard** is a very scenic village, located just before the **Corniche des Cevennes**. Just outside Saint Jean du Gard you are faced with the option of traveling the corniche along the canyon's south or north rim. This itinerary travels the D9, which follows the north rim and is the more scenic and better of the two roads. The drive is lovely, traveling through and above the forests of the region. At the northern tip of the corniche the road number changes from D9 to D983 and travels 6 kilometers to the junction of D907. Follow the D907 north just over 5 kilometers to **Florac** and then join the N106, continuing north in the direction of Mende, but at the tiny village of Biesset veer off and head west on the D907 bis. It is here that your true journey of the Tarn Canyon begins.

To appreciate the region you need to simply travel it: each turn affords a lovely vista or breathtakingly beautiful portrait of a hillside village. Opportunities to stop along the roadside are limited and will frustrate most photographers, but drive it leisurely and stop when possible to explore the little hamlets. The following is an overview of the river and its path, and some of its most picturesque highlights. With a good map in hand, enjoy its scenic journey.

The **Ispagnac Basin**, located at the entrance to the canyon, is filled with fruit trees, vineyards, and strawberries. Here towns are scattered artistically about; châteaux and ruins appear often enough to add enchantment. A lovely wide bridge spans the river at **Ispagnac** and farther along at **Molines**, set in the bend of the river, the canyon boasts a picturesque mill and castle. As the road hugs the hillside, the pretty town of **Montbrun** blends into the hillside on the opposite side of the river. The road then narrows and winds along the base of the canyon, looking up to rugged canyon walls and down to stretches of green along the river's edge. **Castelbouc**, on the other side of the river, is idyllically nestled on the hillside and is spectacular when illuminated on summer evenings. Just a short distance beyond Castelbouc the road carves a path to the north, providing a scenic overlook of the neighboring castle of **Prades**. One of the larger settlements in the region, **Sainte Énimie** is a charming village caught in the bend of the canyon where an old attractive bridge arches across the river and a church wedged into the mountainside piques the curiosity. From Sainte Énimie the road tunnels into the canyon walls colored in orange, gold, and green. **Saint Chély du Tarn** is nestled on the sides of the canyon wall and is illuminated in a spectacle of sound and light. A short distance south of Saint Chély, majestically positioned above the Tarn, is a fairy-tale castle offering accommodation, the **Château de la Caze**. (Recommended in our France hotel guide.)

From the spectacular setting of La Caze, the road follows the river as it bends past the **Château Hauterives** and then passes through the lovely and probably most active village on the riverbank, **La Malène**. Many companies offer raft, kayak, and canoe trips departing from La Malène. From the river you have a better view of some of the old medieval towns and a section of the Tarn referred to as **Les Détroits**, the Straits, not visible from the road. Here the river is only a few meters wide, towered by canyon cliffs rising more than 300 meters straight above. From La Malène the road winds through the canyon rock and a cluster of buildings appears huddled on the other bank, just at the entrance to Les Détroits. Farther on, numerous buses stop at **Belvédère du Pas de Souci** and you can join the crowds to climb the steep metal stairway to views of the pools below (for an admission fee). From Pas de Souci, the river widens and the canyon walls turn to gentle slopes at the little village of **Les Vignes**. From Les Vignes it is worth a short detour following signs to **Point Sublime**. It is a steep climb up to one of the most impressive viewpoints of the canyon, 400 meters above the river.

Cross the river at La Muse to the village of **Le Rozier**, which enjoys a pretty setting at the junction of the Tarn and Jonte rivers. From Le Rozier you have a couple of options to extend your visit in this lovely region and explore another river canyon before continuing along the D907 the last 20 kilometers along the Tarn to Millau.

To extend your visit, venture east from Le Rozier, crossing the bridge, to the neighboring, picturesque village of **Peyreleau**. Straddling both sides of the river, buildings huddle on the narrow river ledges as mountain and canyon walls rise from this narrow stretch of the valley. As common as postcards in most towns, walking sticks are for sale at every shop and suggest that you should park your car and take time to explore the region on foot. If nothing else, cross the narrow bridge that spans the river and make the climb up the narrow streets to Peyreleau's dramatic castle.

From Peyreleau you can continue traveling the D996, a narrow, often roughly paved road following the dramatic and rugged **Gorges de la Jonte**. Overpowered by the towering Jonte canyon walls, this is a gorgeous drive and establishing an endpoint of the scenic journey is the picturesque village of **Meyrueis**. A charming village, located approximately 21 kilometers east of Le Rozier, the handsome buildings of Meyrueis huddle together along the banks of the Jonte. There are numerous outdoor restaurants that take advantage of the views and setting.

Another option from Peyreleau, rather than continuing east, exploring the Gorges de la Jonte, there is a narrow, winding road that travels 10 kilometers south to **Montpellier le Vieux**—a landscape of intriguing rock formations. There is an admission charge for driving through this complex of rock and then from here one continues another twisting stretch of almost 20 kilometers on to Millau. **Millau** is a lovely, large city located at the junction of two rivers, the Tarn and the Dourbie, known for its leather goods, particularly gloves. Millau marks the end of the canyon.

Because a visit of the Gorges du Tarn can be achieved in a few days time, we assume you will want to extend your trip and continue your journey into other regions of France. It would be easy to circle back to Provence; make the journey west to the Dordogne and Lot River Valleys, or travel west and then south to region Basque. However, the following are a couple of suggestions for some sightseeing that would necessitate just a few days in terms of an appendage to your itinerary.

SUGGESTION ONE: From Millau it is feasible to follow an itinerary loop that journeys southwest in the direction of Carcassonne, with the suggestion that you incorporate stops in Roquefort sur Soulzon, Albi, and the hilltown of Cordes-sur-Ciel (a short detour) and then circle back to the walled fortress of Carcassonne. **Roquefort sur Soulzon** is home to the distinctive Roquefort cheese: if this regional specialty appeals, you might enjoy a tour of one of the cheese cellars. **Albi**, a large city, is about a two-hour drive through farmland from Roquefort. With its cathedral dominating the entire city, Albi, mostly built of brick, is also referred to as "Albi the red." The **Musée Toulouse Lautrec** is one of its more interesting attractions. From Albi it is another half-hour drive to the medieval town of **Cordes-sur-Ciel**, also known as "Cordes in the Heavens," above the Cerou Valley. This is an enchanting hilltop village, a treasure that will prove a highlight of any itinerary. Known for its leather goods and hand-woven fabrics, Cordes-sur-Ciel offers many *ateliers* (craft shops) along its cobblestoned streets.

Retracing your path back to Albi, it is an undemanding drive south along the N112 and the D118 to Carcassonne. Europe's largest medieval fortress, **Carcassonne** is a highlight of any visit to France and a wonderful grand finale to this itinerary; Vieux Carcassonne rises above the vineyards at the foot of the Cevennes and Pyrenees.

Gorges du Tarn & Beyond

The massive protecting walls of Carcassonne were first raised by the Romans in the 1st century B.C. Though never conquered in battle, the mighty city was lost to nature's weathering elements and has since been restored so that it looks as it did when constructed centuries ago. Stroll through the powerful gates along its winding cobbled streets and wander back into history. The walled city boasts numerous touristy shops and delightful restaurants and places to stay.

MAP OF SUGGESTION ONE:

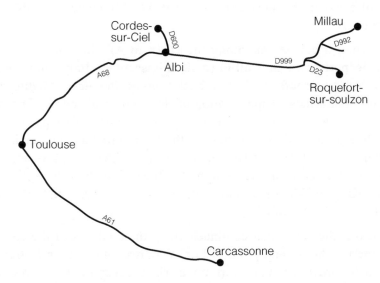

SUGGESTION TWO: This suggestion would be to head directly southwest to Carcassonne, visit the walled city and from there, make use of the Autoroutes to efficiently cover the distance to the southwest corner of France on the Spanish border.

Travel first on Autoroute 61 west to Narbonne and then connect with Autoroute 9 south, following the Mediterranean coast in the direction of Perpignan and the Spanish border.

Your goal is a very distinctive and enchanting region of France—one I have only just begun to discover and intend to explore in greater depth in the near future. Referred to as **Terre Catalane**, it is a region strongly influenced by its neighbor in its ambiance, flavor and the easy-going and relaxed style and warmth of the people who live here.

To begin your journey, exit the Autoroute at Le Boulou and travel approximately 10 km southwest to **Céret,** a charming hillside town of stucco buildings and tiled roofs. Home to many artists, Céret's seemingly greatest renown is for its *cerises* (cherries) as evidenced in the late spring and early summer by the many stands, banners and festivals. Céret is also the address of a wonderful museum, **Musée d'Art Moderne**. (*tel: 04.68.87.27.76, www.musee-ceret.com*)

From Céret, now chart a course east along the D618 to Argelès and then south on the D114 to the idyllic port town of **Collioure**. Reminiscent of Italy with pastel-colored stucco buildings and tile roofs against a backdrop of the deep Mediterranean sea, Collioure has long lured artists in appreciation of its beauty and setting. The heart of the port boasts narrow passageways that weave through a multitude of shops and restaurants, as well as access to a pretty little beach right in the town, protected and embraced by the breakwater. Center stage is **Château Royal,** which in its time served as both a strategic meeting point of the Mediterranean Sea and the Pyrenees mountains as well as a fortress. It was home to the Kings of Mallorca in the 13th and 14th centuries and was converted to a citadel in the 16th and 17th centuries.

From Collioure, travel the N114 that continues along the contours of the coast, possibly detouring out to the lighthouse and point of Port Vendres, and then on to **Banyuls**. Just north of the Spanish border, Banyuls warrants a trip because of its marvelous museum honoring one of France's most acclaimed sculpturers, the **Musée Maillol** (*Open all year, tel: 04.68.88.57.11*). It is also the impressive site of the cellars of **Cellier des Templiers** where you can enjoy a free, guided tour, sample wines from a region that has been producing wines for over seven centuries, and enjoy panoramic views of the surrounding, terraced vineyards. (*Open all year, tel: 04.68.98.36.92*)

Unless you want to continue south to Spain, from Banyuls I would recommend retracing your path back north to **Perpignan,** where you will find both train and planes convenient options for continuing your travels.

MAP OF SUGGESTION TWO:

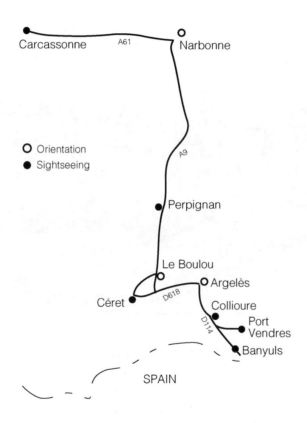

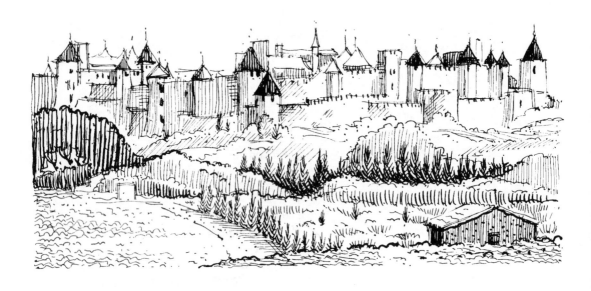

Walled City of Carcassonne

Gorges du Tarn & Beyond

Provence

Orientation
Sightseeing
Itinerary route

Paris

Crillon le Brave

Vénasque

Le Thor

Saumane de Vaucluse

Villeneuve les Avignon

L'Isle sur la Sorgue

Fontaine de Vaucluse

Senanque

Joucas

Pont du Gard

Avignon

Gordes

Roussillon

Remoulins

Cavaillon

Nîmes

Ménerbes

Apt

St. Rémy de Provence

Bonnieux

Eygalières

Les Antiques

Glanum

Loumarin

Les Baux de Provence

Silvacane

Fontvieille

Maussane les Alpilles

Abbaye de Montmajour

Moulin de Daudet

Lignane

Meyrargues

Arles

Aqueduct

Aix en Provence

Marseille

A9
D981
N86
A9
A54
N570
D571
D5
D17
N113
A7
D2
D149
D4
N100
D36
D943
D543
A51
N7
A7
A51
N8
A55
A52
D28
D177
D4
D938

89

Provence

Provence, settled by the Romans around 120 B.C., is a region of contrasts and colors. This delightful region of the French *Midi* (the South) is associated with warm breezes, a mild climate, and rolling hillsides covered in the gray washes of olive trees and lavender. Its rich soil in the bath of the warm southern sun produces a bounty of produce that is incorporated into its regional cuisine. Some of the world's most popular wines are produced here and complement the delicious local dishes. The romance and beauty of Provence has inspired artists and writers for generations.

Pont du Gard

Recommended Pacing: This itinerary assumes the large port city of Marseille as a starting point, winds north to the beautiful university city of Aix en Provence, into the hilltowns of Haute Provence, and then circles back to the heart of the region and the lovely towns set in its valley. It is possible to see Provence in just a few days, but the countryside calls for you to linger, to settle and absorb the climate, the beauty, and the landscape. Our ideal would be a night to explore Aix en Provence, one to two nights in one of the hilltowns of Haute Provence, and at least three nights at the heart of Provence.

Marseille is the second-largest city in France. Settled as a Phoenician colony, this major Mediterranean port is where our Provence itinerary begins. Apart from the Roman docks and fortified church of Saint Victor, there are few monuments to its past within the city. However, you must see **La Canebière**, a major boulevard that captures the activity, gaiety, and pace of Marseille. The old port has a number of museums to draw your interest; the **Musée Grobet-Labadie** has a beautiful collection of tapestries, furniture, paintings, musical instruments, pottery, and sculpture. (*Open daily 10 am to 5 pm, Sun noon to 7 pm.*)

From Marseille drive north following either the N8 or the Autoroute 51 to the southern periphery of **Aix en Provence**, an elegant city that deserves an overnight stay. (Recommendations for places to stay can also be found in our France hotel guide.) Aix achieved fame when "Good King René," count of Provence, and his wife chose it as their preferred residence in the 1450s. Upon his death Aix fell under the rule of the French crown and was made the seat of parliament. The city flourished in the 17th and 18th centuries and became one of the most prosperous metropolises of the region. Much of Aix's elegant architecture is attributed to this period of affluence. Today it is predominantly a university town, home to some 40,000 students who represent almost a third of the city's population. Numerous fountains adorn the elegant tree-lined Cours Mirabeau, edged by aristocratic residences and numerous cafés. The Cours Mirabeau separates the Quartier Mazarin to the south from the Quartier Ancien on the north. The Quartier Mazarin attracted dignitaries and many lovely parliamentary homes still stand in this neighborhood. By contrast, the Quartier Ancien is the heart of the city, with a bustle of activity along its charming little back streets lined with numerous cafés and restaurants.

Aix is an enchanting, beautiful and aristocratic city to explore. The beckoning cobblestoned streets of its **Old Quarter** are intriguing to wander along at night and the illuminated tree-lined Cours Mirabeau is enchanting—a bit reminiscent of Paris with its many sidewalk cafés. Nineteen 17th-century tapestries from Beauvois are on display in the **Museum of Tapestries**. Another fifteen Flemish tapestries can be found in the **Cathedral Saint Sauveur**. (*Closed noon to 2:00 pm and all day Tues.*) Aix is also the birthplace of Paul Cézanne who was born here in 1839 but left to join his colleagues and the impressionistic fever that prevailed in Paris. He returned to his hometown in 1870 and settled here until his death in 1906. You can visit the studio he built, **Atelier Paul Cézanne**, set behind a little wooden gate just north of the old quarter. Paul Cézanne studied in Aix with Émile Zola and the distant Mont Saint Victoire, which inspired much of his work, can be seen from various vantage points in the city. (*Closed noon to 2 pm except in summer–noon to 2:30 pm, and all day Tues.*)

From Aix en Provence you travel north on country roads through groves of olive trees and acres of vineyards to the hilltowns of Haute Provence. Less traveled, the medieval hillside perched villages of this region are intriguing to explore.

From Aix follow the N7 northwest in the direction of Saint Cannat. Turn north 6 kilometers out of Aix at Lignane, following the D543 north across the Chaîne de la Tréversse, to Silvacane on the waters of the River Durance and the Canal de Marseille. Cross the river and the D543 becomes the D943, traveling first to Cadenet and then on to **Loumarin**, the capital of this region of Luberon. Loumarin is a small city surrounded by the bounty of the region: fruit trees, flowers, and produce. The château on the outskirts of town is a school for artists.

From Loumarin, the D943 enjoys the beautiful path of the Aigue Brun for 6 kilometers and then you take the D36 just a few kilometers farther west to the hillside village of **Bonnieux**. From Bonnieux you can wind a course northeast to the thriving city of **Apt**, known for its crystallized fruits and preserves, truffles, lavender perfume, and old Sainte Anne Cathedral, which is still the site of an annual pilgrimage. From Apt follow the N100 west for 4½ kilometers to the D4 north to the turnoff west to Roussillon. Another

Gordes

option is to navigate a course directly north to Roussillon, an exploration along countryside roads.

Whichever the route, **Roussillon** is worth the effort to find. This lovely village is a maze of narrow streets, small shops, and restaurants that climb to the town's summit. In various shades of ochres, Roussillon is an enchanting village, especially on a clear day when the sun warms and intensifies the colors.

From Roussillon travel first north on the D105 and then west on the D2 to the neighboring village of **Gordes**, perched at one end of the Vaucluse Plateau and dominating the Imergue Valley. Bathed in tones of gray, this is a wonderful place. Off its main square are some inviting cafés, restaurants, and shops selling Provence's wonderful bounties: lavender, olive oils, wines, regional dolls *(santons)*, and garments in the charming local fabrics. Gordes is also known for the ancient village of 20 restored *bories,* or dry-stone huts, that lie in its shadow. Unusual in their round or rectangular shapes, these intriguing buildings (many of which accommodate 20th-century comforts) are thought to date from the 17th century.

Across from Gordes, **Joucas** is a perfectly preserved jewel of a village perched above the Luberon Valley.

Just four kilometers to the north of Gordes is **Senanque**, a 12th-century Cistercian abbey standing dramatically isolated at the edge of the mountainside surrounded by lavender and oak trees. Vacated by the monks in 1869 and accessible on foot by a 2-kilometer path up from the car park, the abbey is now a religious cultural center and hosts concerts in the summer months.

A Restaurant Housed in a Borie

From Senanque follow the small country road (D177) north to connect with the D4 and then travel west through the dense Forest of Vénasque to the beautiful and striking hilltop village of **Vénasque**. Charmingly untouched by civilization, this village is tucked in a dense forest cupped between two steep hills and is notable for its 6th-century **Église de Notre Dame** and the 17th-century **Chapelle Notre Dame de Vie**. The town comes to life during the early summer when it is the market center for the region's cherry crop. Near Vénasque is another lovely hilltop village, **Crillon le Brave**.

From Vénasque weave a course south in the direction of the market town of **Cavaillon**. Known for its melon fields, Cavaillon is another village to include on your itinerary if your schedule permits. On the outskirts of Cavaillon, detour east to the amazing **Fontaine de Vaucluse,** fed by rainwater that seeps through the Vaucluse Plateau. In the late afternoon as the sun begins its descent, walk around this celebrated natural fountain: at certain times of the year the shooting water is so powerful that it becomes dangerous and the fountain is closed to observers. The most dramatic seasons to visit the spewing fountain are winter and spring. Over a million tourists travel to Vaucluse each year to see the fountain, but few venture the 4 kilometers farther to the idyllic perched village of **Saumane de Vaucluse** whose hillside location affords an idyllic spot from which to watch the sun bathe the countryside in the soft hues so characteristic of Provence.

Retrace a path back in the direction of Cavaillon from Fontaine de Vaucluse and take the N100 southwest in the direction of Avignon. A wonderful place to stop en route, especially if you like antiques, is the country town of **L'Isle sur la Sorgue**, known for its many shops.

Considered a gateway to Provence, **Avignon** is one of France's most interesting and beautiful cities. Easy to navigate, its medieval encasement is encircled by one main boulevard and various gates allow entry into the walled city. The Porte de l'Oulle on the northwestern perimeter has parking just outside the wall and a small tourist booth with maps and information, and provides convenient access into the heart of the old city. The Porte de la Republique on the south side is opposite the train station and opens onto the Cour Jean Jaures, the location of the main tourist office. The Cour Jean Jaures becomes the Rue de la République and leads straight to the Place du Palais on the city's northern border. You might want to inquire at the tourist office about the miniature train that travels the city, highlighting the key points of interest, and the excellent guide service that conducts either full- or half-day walking tours of the city. Avignon is fun to explore—a wonderful selection of shops line its streets, a festive air prevails with numerous street performers, and the historical attractions are monumental.

Avignon was the papal residency from 1309 to 1377 and the **Palais des Papes** is a highlight of a visit to this lovely city—if only to stand on the main square and look up at the long, soft-yellow stone structure that dominates the city skyline, stretching the length of the square and towering against the blue skies of Provence. If time permits, enter the papal city through the Porte des Chapeaux into the Grande Cour. A little shop just off the entrance provides maps, information, and admission into the palace. Just off the entry, the impressive inner courtyard and beginning point for a palace tour is often a stage for the open-air theater performances of the popular summer festival.

Allow approximately an hour to explore the palace effectively, noting the distinction between the old palace, built by Pope Benedict XII from 1334 to 1342, and the new palace commissioned by his successor, Pope Clement VI, and finished in 1348. The tour will take you down the Hall of the Consistory (*Aile du Consistoire*), hung with portraits of popes who resided in Avignon, to the upstairs banqueting hall (*Grand Tinel*), to the impressive Deer Room (*Chambre du Cerf*), whose walls display a beautifully painted fresco by Giovanetti depicting the decadent life of leisure led by the papal court in the 14th century, on to the Audience Hall (*Aile de Grande Audience*), elaborate with its star-studded ceiling, and the magnificent Saint Martial Chapel *(open only on Sun for church service, tel: 04.90.27.50.00)*

Devote the majority of your time to visiting this feudal structure, but don't miss the two lovely churches, **Cathédral de Notre Dame des Doms** and **L'Église Saint Didier**. Just off the Rue Joseph Vernet is the **Musée Calvet**, named for the doctor who bequeathed his personal collection of art and funds to launch it. The museum displays a rich collection of work from artists of the French and Avignon schools of painting and sculpture: Delacroix, Corot, and Manet are some of the impressive masters represented. (*Closed 1 to 2 pm and all day Tues.*)

Although only four of its original twenty-two arches still stand, the **Pont Saint Bénezet** is an impressive sight. A small chapel still sits on one of its piers and shadows the waters of the encircling River Rhône. This is the bridge referred to in the song familiar to all French children, "*Sur le pont d'Avignon, on y dance, on y dance.*" Even if all the arches still stood, passage would be difficult by modern-day transportation as the bridge was constructed at the end of the 12th century with pedestrians and horses in mind.

Villeneuve les Avignon is separated from Avignon by the Rhône. (Cross the river by following the N100 west of the city and then turn immediately on D900 in the direction of Villeneuve.) Villeneuve flourished when the pope held residence in Avignon and a number of cardinals chose it for their magnificent estates. Today it presents a lovely setting on the river, enjoys magnificent views of its neighbor, and yet benefits from a quieter setting and pace. A stronghold that once guarded the frontier of France when Avignon was allied to the Holy Roman Empire, it has towering on its skyline **Fort Saint André** whose vantage point commands a magnificent view across the Rhône to Avignon and the Popes' Palace. Another military structure still standing is the **Philippe le Bel Tower** and the curator is often on hand to provide all the historical facts. The Saturday morning antique and flea market is a popular attraction.

From Avignon it is a very pleasant drive south along a lazy, tree-lined road, the D571, to **Saint Rémy de Provence**, a pretty, sleepy town, nestled in the shade of its plane trees. Of interest in the town are a Romanesque church, Renaissance houses, and a busy public square.

On the outskirts of Saint Rémy, following the D5 south in the direction of Les Baux de Provence, you can visit the **Clinique de Saint Paul** where Van Gogh was nursed back to health after slicing off his earlobe; **Les Antiques**, an impressive arch and mausoleum commissioned by Augustus; and **Glanum**, a thriving point of commerce during the Gallo-Greek years that was virtually destroyed in the 3rd century.

From Saint Rémy it is a beautiful drive along the D5 as it winds through the chalky gray hills referred to as *Les Alpilles* and then turns off to cover the short distance across the valley to the charming Provençal village of **Les Baux de Provence**. (The mineral bauxite was discovered here and derives its name from the town.)

The village appears to be a continuation of the rocky spur from which it rises. This site has been occupied for the past 5,000 years, and is now visited by more than a million visitors every year. A number of craft shops, inviting crêperies, and ice cream vendors are tucked away along the village streets. From Les Baux you have splendid views of the area.

En route to the lovely Roman city of Arles from Les Baux, the D17 travels first to the small roadside town of **Fontvieille**. Fontvieille is home to a wonderful hotel and restaurant, **La Régalido**, (recommended in our France hotel guide), and is also worth a stop to visit the **Moulin de Daudet**, an abandoned mill set on the hillside above town, reputedly where Daudet wrote *Letters from My Windmill*.

Continuing on the back road from Fontvieille, the D33, as it travels beyond the mill, passes the ruins of an old **Roman Aqueduct** that stands unceremoniously in a field just off the road at the intersection of the D82. Head west from the aqueduct along the D82 to connect with the D17 and travel once again in the direction of Arles. On the approach to

Les Baux de Provence

Provence

the city, surrounded by fields, stand the ruins of **Abbaye de Montmajour**, which was built in the 10th century by Benedictine monks.

The skyline of **Arles** can be seen as you approach the city. Abounding in character, this is a truly lovely city whose growth is governed by the banks and curves of the Rhône. It has fierce ties to its Roman past when it thrived as a strong port city and gateway. Arles is glorified because of its magnificent Gallo-Roman arenas and theaters in the heart of the old city. This is a city to explore on foot: it is fun to wander through the narrow maze of winding streets that weave through the old section. Bullfights and festivals are still staged in the magnificent **Amphithéâtre**, or arena, able to accommodate in its prime more than 20,000 spectators. (*Open Jun to Sep all day, Oct to May seasonal hours.*)

The **Théâtre Antique**, although apparently a ruin by day, becomes a lovely stage on summer nights under the soft lights of the Festival d'Arles. (*Same hours as the Amphithéâtre.*) The Place du Forum is bordered by cafés and is a social spot to settle in the afternoons and into the balmy evenings of Provence. Just a block from the Place du Forum, the **Muséon Arlaten** was conceived and funded by the town's poet, Frédéric Mistral, from the money he received for winning the Nobel Prize in literature, to honor all that is Provençal. The museum is rich in its portrayal of the culture and fierce traditions of Provence. (*Closed noon to 2 pm and all day Mon in winter.*) Another fascinating museum in Arles is the **Musée de l'Arles Antique**, just south of the Nouveau Pont, which you can reach by walking along the ramparts on the edge of the Rhône. Large and open, the museum houses a dramatic display of sarcophagi, mosaics, statuary, models, and replicas depicting the dramatic arenas and theaters, as well as jewelry, tools, and pottery that lend a glimpse of life in ancient Arles. It is built on a site overlooking the ruins of the Roman hippodrome and from the rooftop of the museum you can see the outline of the track, which in time they hope to restore to its original dimensions. (*Open Apr to Oct, 9 am to 7 pm daily; rest of year 10 am to 6 pm, closed Tues.*)

At the gateway to the Camargue and nestled at the heart of Provence, Arles is a wonderful base from which to experience the region.

Nîmes lies approximately 35 kilometers west of Arles. A Gaelic capital, it was also popular with the Romans who built its monuments. Without fail see the **Amphithéâtre** that once held 21,000 spectators, the **Arénas**, **Maison Carrée**, the best-preserved Roman temple in the world, and the magnificent **fountain gardens**.

As a final destination, journey just another 20 kilometers or so north of Nîmes (N86 Remoulins, D981) to the spectacular **Pont du Gard**, an aqueduct that impressively bridges the River Gard. Still intact, three tiers of stone arches tower more than 36 meters across the valley. Built by Roman engineers about 20 B.C. as part of a 50-kilometer-long system bringing water from Uzès to Nîmes, the aqueduct remains one of the world's marvels. Park in the car park amid the tourist stalls and food stands and walk a pedestrian road to the span of river that thankfully lies uncluttered, dominated only by the impact and shadow of the towering structure.

From Pont du Gard, you can easily return to Nîmes or complete the circle back to Avignon.

Palais des Papes, Avignon

Gorges du Verdon

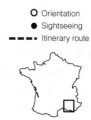

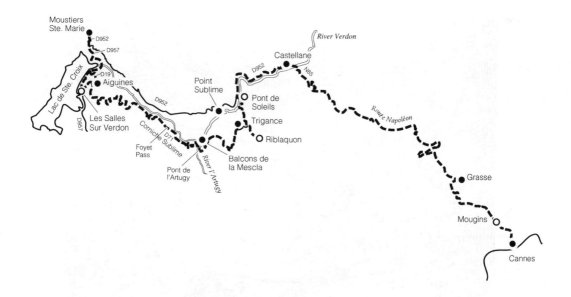

Gorges du Verdon

The Gorges du Verdon is the French equivalent of the Grand Canyon. The striking blue-green water of the Verdon is dramatic in its intensity as it carves through and contrasts with the magnificent limestone plateau. The river then plunges into the spectacular trench-like Gorges du Verdon and is enclosed within its steep jagged walls. When you are traveling between the Riviera and central Provence, the Gorges du Verdon makes for a wonderful detour, and a few days spent in this region will prove memorable.

Gorges du Verdon

Recommended Pacing: This itinerary extends from Castellane to the delightful village of Moustiers Sainte Marie just to the north of Lac de Sainte Croix. The total distance covered is only about 40 kilometers, including the dramatic 20-kilometer span of the canyon from the Pont de Soleils to the town of Aiguines. The most logical access from the Riviera is to follow the N85, a lovely forested road that winds from Grasse northwest along the Route Napoléon to Castellane, a town set on the banks of the Verdon. You can include a visit to the canyon and cover the distance between the Riviera and Provence in one day, but it would require a very early start and make for an exceptionally long day. We recommend an overnight on the edge of the canyon at the Château de Trigance (recommended in our France hotel guide), in the small hillside village of Trigance. Breaking the journey here gives you time to enjoy an unhurried drive along the dramatic canyon rim and then a leisurely next day to explore Moustiers Sainte Marie. We would also recommend including an overnight in Moustiers Sainte Marie—as we are certain the town and its setting will captivate you—before continuing your journey on to Provence.

Castellane is a natural starting point for an exploration of the canyon. It enjoys a lovely setting on the banks of the River Verdon and is famous for its crowning rock that towers above the town, crested by the **Nôtre Dame du Roc Chapel**. Traveling the D952 west following the path of the Verdon, at Pont de Soleils you can either choose to follow the south bank or the north bank of the canyon. (If time and enthusiasm allow, it is also possible to make one grand circle journey traveling both sides of the canyon.) For the purposes of this itinerary, the suggested routing follows the south bank, the *Corniche Sublime*, as it affords spectacular vistas of the canyon and also conveniently passes the enchanting medieval village of Trigance whose thick stone walls guard a wonderful hotel and restaurant, the Château de Trigance. To reach Trigance from Pont de Soleils, travel first south 16 kilometers on the D955 and just before the village of Riblaquon, cross over the Jabron river to the medieval town of **Trigance** on the opposite hillside.

Following the road round the back of Trigance, the D90 travels a short distance (6 kilometers) before it ends at the D71. Turn north on the D71 and you will soon be rewarded with a spectacular vista of the dramatic Verdon at the **Balcons de la Mescla**.

You can pull off here, and there are terraced points from which you can look down at the dramatic loop in the path of the river some 760 meters below. (There is also a small café where you can purchase snacks and postcards.) From Mescla the road winds through sparse vegetation of boxwood and then crosses over a dramatic span, the **Pont de l'Artugy**, a concrete, one-arch bridge that rises precariously high above the waters below. From the bridge, the drive is constantly spectacular in its drama and scenery. It rises and falls above the canyon walls, winding in and out of tunnels impressively cut into its rock face. From Artuby the road climbs on the fringe of the ravine to the **Fayet**

Pass. Here a tunnel carves through the rock and square openings through the thick tunnel walls create windows that afford glimpses of the river's dramatic passage. Every second of the drive following the jagged mouth of the Verdon Canyon is spectacular. The canyon is almost overpowering: the river forges a path through narrow stretches where the canyon sides plunge down to depths far below, and then slows and calms in wider sections, pausing to create glistening, dark-green pools.

The road periodically veers away from the edge of the canyon and rolls past beautiful green meadows dotted by a few mountain cabins and hamlets. In spring, wildflowers bloom everywhere. As the ruggedness and fierceness of the canyon wanes, the road gradually returns to the valley, opening up to vistas of the brilliant blue waters of **Lac de Sainte Croix** where you see **Aiguines**, a rosy-hued village silhouetted against the backdrop of the lake. The numerous docks hint at what a paradise the lake is for sportsmen in summer months. At the water's edge, the road (now numbered D957), travels in the direction of Moustiers Sainte Marie, crossing over the Verdon as it flows into the lake. Be sure to take a moment and park just before the bridge, as it is a beautiful sight looking back up the narrow canyon and if you are fortunate, you might see kayakers at the conclusion of their journey.

Moustiers Sainte Marie is a grand finale to this itinerary. Famous for its pottery, it is a wonderful village whose cluster of buildings with their patchwork of red-tiled roofs hugs the hillside and crawls back into the protection of a sheltered mountain alcove. Monks came here in 433, took shelter in caves dug into the mountainside, and founded the monastery **Nôtre Dame de Beauvoir**, which towers over the village. The church was rebuilt during the 12th century and enlarged in the 16th. You can reach the sanctuary by a winding footpath paved with round stones leading up from the heart of the village.

This is a beautiful Provençal hilltown whose narrow, winding streets offer a wealth of stores displaying the famous Moustiers pottery. As early as 1678, the first master potter created a pattern that originated the style associated with the village. Today, some 15 master potters offer high-quality handmade and hand-decorated products, and pottery is the principal industry in the area. You can actually come to Moustiers and commission a personalized pattern in one of the workshops. Considering the size of the village and its seemingly remote location, it is hard to believe that the workshops of Moustiers Sainte Marie fulfill requests from all over the world for their hand-painted *faïence*.

From Moustiers Sainte Marie, it is a 1½-hour drive to Aix en Provence where you can join our *Provence* itinerary.

Moustiers Sainte Marie

Gorges du Verdon

Hilltowns of the French Riviera

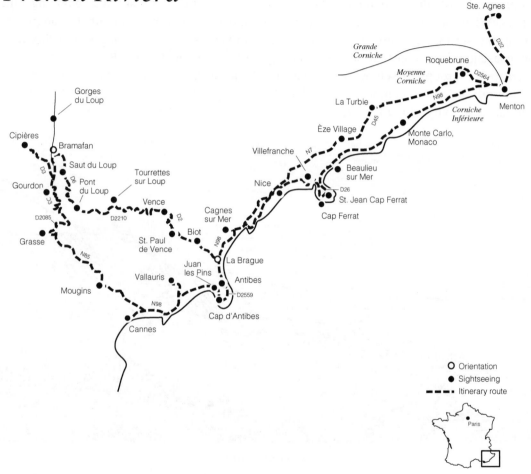

Ste. Agnes

Grande
Corniche

Roquebrune

Moyenne
Corniche

D2564

D22

Menton

Gorges
du Loup

La Turbie

N98

Corniche
Inférieure

Cipières

Bramafan

Saut du Loup

Tourrettes
sur Loup

Èze Village

D45

Monte Carlo,
Monaco

Villefranche

N7

Gourdon

Pont
du Loup

D3

D6

Vence

Nice

Beaulieu
sur Mer

St. Jean Cap Ferrat

D2085

D3

D2210

D2

Cagnes
sur Mer

D26

Grasse

Biot

Cap Ferrat

St. Paul
de Vence

N98

N85

Juan
les Pins

La Brague

Vallauris

Antibes

Mougins

N98

D2559

Cannes

Cap d'Antibes

O Orientation
● Sightseeing
- - - Itinerary route

Paris

107

Hilltowns of the French Riviera

People in the hundreds of thousands flock to the Riviera for its sun and dazzling blue waters. When planning your trip, be aware that most of these sun-worshipers congregate during the spring and summer with the coastal towns as their base and during this time the coastside is a constant hub of activity and excitement. The Riviera attracts an international group, jet-setters here to see and be seen. In the mountains overlooking the Mediterranean are a number of smaller, "hillside-perched" towns, removed from the continuous activity of the Riviera and offering a beautiful setting and escape.

View from Èze Village

Recommended Pacing: We suggest at least three full days to explore the coastal and hilltowns of the French Riviera. Assuming your time is going to be devoted to the Riviera, this itinerary traces a routing that both begins and ends in Nice. Keep in perspective that distances between destinations are short (Nice and Menton are just 23 kilometers apart), and although you can make a circle trip staying at one or two places, it would also be feasible to select one property as a base from which to explore the entire region. Remember that during peak summer months the Riviera is crowded with tourists—it is difficult to find places to stay and dine, negotiate the roads, find parking, and visit museums, so you must incorporate more time into your itinerary to do so. Our suggestion would be to avoid summer on the Riviera and, alternatively, escape up into the hills above the coastal towns.

The French Riviera, or the Côte d'Azur, is the area between Menton and Nice. Its inhabitants are a breed apart: even the French themselves say the *Niçoise* are not typically French—warmed and subdued by the climate, they are more gentle and agreeable. We recommend that you begin your explorations in the region's capital, Nice, "Queen of the Riviera." France's wonderful express trains service the Nice train station and convenient connections can be made from many cities within Europe into the Nice airport (the second busiest in France). Equally appealing, both the train station and airport are small and easy to get around, and car rental agencies are represented at both.

Nice is a large city whose population of 400,000 has carpeted the land with apartments and condominiums bounded only by the ocean and the surrounding hills. Along the waterfront, the **Promenade des Anglais** takes a grand sweep from the city's western edge along the Baie des Anges and the new city to the edge of the picturesque old quarter. The new district of Nice is a mecca for tourists with the promenade along the seashore lined with elegant hotels and casinos. Lighted at night, the promenade is a romantic place for strolling. Just off this majestic promenade is the **Musée International d'Art Naïf** (Avenue Val Marie), which boasts an inventory of over 6,000 paintings from all over the world. (*Open all year, tel: 04.93.71.78.33.*) The **Musée des Beaux-Arts Jules Cheret** (33, Avenue des Baumettes) focuses on a wealth of paintings from the 19th century.

(*Open all year, tel: 04.92.15.28.28.*) A landmark of the promenade is the stately **Hôtel Negresco** whose terrace is a wonderful place to settle and enjoy a café or ice cream, a tradition to be equated with tea at Harrods. Just a little farther on, the Jardin Albert 1 is dressed with fountains and a bandstand that hosts numerous rock concerts. From the Jardin a mini-train departs every 20 minutes to tour the old town, the flower market, and castle gardens. The lovely **Place Masséna** stands proud on the promenade with its dramatic fountains and fronts the area's principal shopping district along the Avenue Jean Médecin. Also leading off the Place Masséna, the Rue Masséna and the Rue de France are charmingly restricted to pedestrian traffic, and banked by cafés, boutiques, and restaurants.

On the other side of the River Paillon is the old quarter of Nice, **La Vieille Ville**, full of character and ambiance. Narrow alleys wind through this district of cobbled streets shaded by towering buildings. The district is colored with flowerboxes and upward glimpses of sky are crisscrossed by banners of laundry. The flower market is very picturesque—a display of color all day and every day on the Cours Saleya, except on Mondays when a flea market of antiques and collectibles invades its space. A bountiful fish market is set out every morning (except Mondays) on the Place Saint François. From the Cours Saleya it is possible to climb the hill, known as the Château (by stairs, a lift, or by strolling up the Rue Ségurane), to some spectacular views of the Baie des Anges. "Château" refers to the château that last stood between the harbor and the old town some 300 years ago. The harbor with its colorful mix of fishing boats and neighboring yachts is fun to explore.

The territory mapped out and referred to as **Cimiez** is where the Romans constructed Cemenelum, a town to rival the then existing Greek town of Nikaia (Nice) in the 1st century B.C. The renovated Roman amphitheater hosts a famous jazz festival that takes place every July. Cimiez also flourishes in March during the *Festival des Cougourdons*, and in May, Sundays are an offering of dances, picnics, and folklore presentations during the *Fêtes des Mais*. Cimiez is also worth the journey to visit the **Musée d'Archéologie**, 160 Avenue des Arènes (*Closed Tuesdays, tel: 04.93.81.59.57*), the **Musée Chagall** at the corner of Boulevard de Cimiez and Avenue Dr Ménard (*Closed Tuesdays, tel: 04.93.53.87.20*), and the **Musée Matisse** in the Villa des Arènes (*Closed Tuesdays, tel: 04.93.81.08.08*). The Musée Chagall houses the largest single collection of the master's work, while the Musée Matisse honors its namesake, who made Nice his home for 20 years, through presentation of the artist's paintings, drawings, and figurines.

Leaving Nice in the direction of Menton, you have a choice of three roads that all run somewhat parallel to each other following the contours of the coast. The **Grande Corniche** or "high" road was built by Napoleon and passes through picturesque *villages perchés*. The **Moyenne Corniche** or "middle" road is a lovely, wide, modern road. The **Corniche Inférieure** or "low" road was built in the 18th century by the Prince of Monaco and enables you to visit the wealthy coastal communities and the principality of Monaco. Each road offers a uniquely appealing route. A suggestion would be to loop in one direction on the Corniche Inférieure to enjoy the water and the coastal towns (this is the busiest road during the summer months), and return via a combination of both the Grande and Moyenne Corniches.

From Nice the Corniche Inférieure, the N98, hugs the contours of the coast and the lovely inlet of **Villefranche sur Mer** whose gentle waters are home to numerous yachts and fishing boats. Round the bay from Villefranche and follow the D26 through the exclusive residential district and peninsula of **Cap Ferrat**.

Sometimes only glimpses are possible of the million-dollar mansions, home to many celebrities, which stand proud behind towering hedges and security gates along this 10-kilometer drive. It is possible to visit the former residence of the Baroness Ephrussi de Rothschild, who commissioned the Italian-style palace to house her personal art collection. It is now owned by the state and open to the public as a museum—the gardens and setting alone merit a visit. Traveling along the peninsula, climb the steps of the lighthouse for a wonderful view. Farther out on the tip is a tower that housed prisoners in the 18th century.

Saint Jean Cap Ferrat is nestled on the other side of the peninsula from Villefranche, enjoying a picturesque setting and a quiet ambiance, with just a few homes, restaurants, and hotels tucked into the hillside. It has lovely views across the towering masts of yachts that grace its waters. From Saint Jean Cap Ferrat, the road winds back to the N98 through another wealthy enclave of homes and luxurious hotels enjoying the protected climate, the town of **Beaulieu sur Mer**.

Saint Jean Cap Ferrat

As the N98 leaves Beaulieu sur Mer, the road hugs the mountain and tunnels through the cliff face just above the Mediterranean, through Cap d'Ail, and into the principality of **Monaco**. First-class hotels and excellent restaurants are numerous in **Monte Carlo**, catering to the millions of annual visitors who come to play in its casino and hope to catch a glimpse of the royal family or resident international celebrities. Monaco is independent of French rule, and an exclusive tax haven for a privileged few. Step inside

Hilltowns of the French Riviera

the **Palais du Casino**, fronted by beautifully manicured gardens. To experience gambling fever, step inside the private salons where high stakes are an everyday agenda.

Beyond Monaco the N98 merges with the N7 and continues on to the graceful city of **Menton**, on the Italian border. Menton boasts streets shaded by fruit trees and stretches of sandy beach in addition to a colorful harbor, casino, and an endless array of shops. At the heart of the old town, Rue Saint Michel is a charming shopping street restricted to foot traffic. The nearby Place aux Herbes and Place du Marché are picturesque with their covered stalls and flower displays. Menton is also known for its gardens, the most famous being the **Jardin des Colombières** (Rue Ferdinand Bac), located on the hill above the town and enjoying lovely views through pines and cypress trees to the waters of the Mediterranean.

From Menton, a 10-kilometer detour into the hills brings you to the picturesque walled town of **Sainte Agnes**. The D22, often just a single lane, winds precariously up into the hills to this attractive mountain village of cobbled streets, a few restaurants, shops, and unsurpassed views of the coastline. (Although the hillside town of **Gorbio** is often recommended in connection with Sainte Agnes, the drive is even more demanding. Sainte Agnes is a little larger and very similar, with better views.)

Returning in the direction of Nice with Menton and the Italian border at your back, follow signs to Roquebrune Cap Martin and you find yourself traveling on the D2564 and the Grande Corniche. **Roquebrune** is divided into two districts: the new town on the water and a medieval village on the hillside dating from the dynasty of Charlemagne. Very picturesque on the approach, the medieval Roquebrune is well worth a detour and some time for exploration. Park on the main square and follow its maze of narrow, cobbled streets to the 13th-century keep, protected at the core of the medieval village.

From Roquebrune, the Grande Corniche continues along a very scenic stretch affording beautiful views of the principality of Monaco stretched out below. Just past the charming hillside town of **La Turbie**, watch for the D45, a short connector to the Moyenne Corniche and the idyllic village of Èze.

Like Roquebrune, there are two divisions of Èze, **Èze Village**, the medieval village perched on the hillside above the Riviera, and **Èze Bord de la Mer**, a modern town on the water's edge. Of all the perched villages along the Riviera, Èze Village, a quaint medieval enclave with cobblestoned streets overlooking the sea, remains a favorite: park your car below the village and explore it on foot. This is a village whose residences have for more than a thousand years soaked up the sun and looked down upon the beautiful blue water associated with the magnificent Côte d'Azur.

Èze Village

From Èze, the Moyenne Corniche follows a beautiful route, the N7, which winds back into Nice. Once in Nice you can either follow the Promenade des Anglais along its waterfront, the N98 in the direction of Cannes, or circumvent the city and traffic by taking the Autoroute A8, exiting at Cagnes Est and following signs to Haut de Cagnes. (If you opt for the N98, take the D18 at Cros de Cagnes and follow signs away from the coast in the direction of Haut de Cagnes.)

Hilltowns of the French Riviera

Cagnes sur Mer is on the waterfront, a port town struggling to resemble the other coastal centers. **Haut de Cagnes**, however, is an old section located on the hill, with an abundance of charm and character. Follow narrow, steep, cobbled streets to the heart of the old village. Opt for the underground parking just on the approach to the village crest—you might find space on the street, but it takes a brave soul to negotiate a spot, and unless you find a generous section, the streets are so narrow, it's never certain that there is enough room left for passing vehicles.

The most visited site in Haut de Cagnes, the **Château Grimaldi** was originally built as a fortress in 1309, commissioned by Raynier Grimaldi, Lord of Monaco and Admiral of France. A citadel was built a year later and then, in the 17th century, Henri Grimaldi had the citadel refurbished into very spacious accommodations. His descendent, Gaspard Grimaldi, was forced to abandon the castle at the time of the French Revolution. During the reign of the Grimaldis, the residents within the walls of this medieval enclave prospered by cultivating wheat, wine, and olives. Mules were used to haul the bounty of produce from the neighboring hillsides and a wealth of seafood from the coast.

On the other side of Cagnes sur Mer from Haut de Cagnes, and definitely worth the hassle of its congested streets, is the absolutely wonderful **Musée Renoir**. (*Closed Oct 20 to Nov 9, and Tues.*) Advised to move to a warmer climate because of ill health, Renoir relocated to the coast and lived his last years in this sun-washed villa above the town. Surrounded by a sprawling, peaceful garden graced with olive trees, rhododendrons, iris, geraniums, and stretches of lawn, you can almost sense the peace and quiet that he must have experienced and the environment that inspired him to paint—artists today frequent the gardens seeking their own inspiration. The town of Cagnes purchased the home, which displays many of Renoir's works, photos, and personal and family memoirs. Especially moving is the sentimental staging in his studio: Renoir's wheelchair is parked in front of the easel, dried flowers rest on the easel's side, and a day bed which enabled Renoir to rest between his efforts is set up nearby. When you study the photo of Renoir during his later years, he appears so old and yet determined to give the world his last ounce of creativity.

Return to the water from Haut de Cagnes and follow the N7 or the N98 along the Baie des Anges in the direction of Antibes. At La Brague detour just a few kilometers off the coastal road following the D4 to the hillside village of **Biot**. Biot, where glassware has been made for just under three decades, has won high acclaim. A visit to a glass factory to see the assortment of styles and types of glassware available is very interesting. Bottles vary from the usual types to the Provençal *calères* or *ponons-bouteilles* that have two long necks and are used for drinking. This medieval village of small narrow streets, lovely little squares, and a maze of galleries and shops is a gem.

After retracing your path back to the coastside, continue to **Antibes**—allow at least half a day for exploring this waterfront fortress. **Fort Carré**, not to be confused with the Château de Grimaldi, is closed to the public and located on the south entrance of town. The fort guards the waters of Antibes, which is home to thousands of yachts berthed in the modern Port Vauban Yacht Harbor. The rectangular towers and battlements of the **Château de Grimaldi** can be seen beyond the fort, within the ramparts of the medieval village. At the heart of the village, the château commands some of the town's best views and now houses some of Picasso's work in the **Musée Picasso**. Picasso resided at the château just after the war in 1946 and, in appreciation of his stay, left much of his work to the town. Spacious and uncluttered, open, bright rooms in the château admirably display his work and photographs of the master when he resided here in addition to contemporary works by Léger, Magnelli, and Max Ernst. Entry to the museum also gives you some of Antibes' most beautiful views of the Mediterranean framed through the thick medieval walls. (*Closed Mon.*) The town with its cobbled streets is charming.

From Antibes a scenic drive follows the D2559 around the peninsula to its point, **Cap d'Antibes**, another exclusive residential community with gorgeous homes, exclusive hotels, and lovely sandy beaches. On the other side of the peninsula from Antibes is the pretty resort town of **Juan les Pins**, which is popular for its lovely stretch of white-sand beach and whose sparkling harbor shelters many attractive boats.

As the N98 hugs the bay of Golfe Juan and before it stretches to **Pointe de la Croisette** in Cannes, you can detour into the hills just up from the town of Golfe Juan to **Vallauris**. Picasso settled in Vallauris after his time in Antibes and tested his skill at the potter's wheel, producing thousands of pieces of pottery using the Madoura pottery shop as his *atelier*. He restored the craft and brought fame to the village and in gratitude the town made him an honorary citizen. He, in turn, showed his appreciation by crafting a life-size bronze statue, which stands on Place Paul Isnard outside the church. A museum, **Musée de Vallauris**, displaying Picasso's work is housed in the château, originally a 13th-century priory rebuilt in the 16th century. There are numerous workshops in Vallauris, now considered the ceramic capital of France—the **Galerie Madoura** remains one of the best, and stores sell a vast assortment of styles and qualities. (*Closed Nov, Sat and Sun, tel: 04.93.64.66.39.*) Over 200 craftsmen reside in Vallauris, creating original designs and copying patterns made famous by Picasso.

From Vallauris, return to the coast and continue on to the cosmopolitan city of Cannes. Located on the Golfe de Napoule, **Cannes** is the center for many festivals, the most famous being the Cannes Film Festival held annually in May. The **Boulevard de la Croisette** is a wide street bordered by palm trees separating the beach from the elaborate grand hotels and apartment buildings. La Croissette is congested with stop-and-go traffic in the summer, and the lovely beaches that it borders are dotted with parasols and covered with tanning bodies. The **old port** (*Vieux Port*) is a melange of fishing boats and sleek luxury craft. You find the flower market, Fortville, along the Allées de la Liberté and the bounty displayed at the covered market is set up every morning except Mondays. The picturesque pedestrian street of Rue Meynadier is worth seeking out for delicious picnic supplies such as cheeses, bread, and paté. Rising above the port at the western end of the popular Boulevard de la Croisette is **Le Suquet**, the old quarter of Cannes, which has a superior view of the colorful port.

It is easy to escape the bustle of the cosmopolitan fever of Cannes by traveling just a few short miles directly north out of the city along the N85 to the hilltown village of **Mougins**. This charming village achieved gastronomic fame when Roger Vergé converted a 16th-century olive mill into an internationally famous restaurant. Other notable chefs have been attracted to the village and Michelin has awarded the village and its restaurants in total four gourmet stars. The fortified town of Mougins is characteristic of many of the medieval towns that are accessible only to pedestrian traffic, which luckily preserves the atmosphere that horns and traffic congestion all too often obliterate. Located in the center of Mougins is a small courtyard decorated with a fountain and flowers and shaded by trees. Here you will discover a few small cafés where locals meet to gossip about society, life, and politics.

Continuing into the coastal hills, you come to a region of lavender, roses, carnations, violets, jasmine, olives, and oranges. Approximately 12 kilometers north of Mougins in the heart of this region is **Grasse**. Grasse's initial industry was the tanning of imported sheepskins from Provence and Italy. It was Catherine de Medicis who introduced the concept of perfume when she commissioned scented gloves from the town in a trade agreement with Tuscany. When gloves fell out of fashion and their sales dwindled, the town refocused on the perfume industry. The town is constantly growing, but the old section is fun to wander through. Interesting tours of perfume factories are given in English by **Fragonard** (at 20 Boulevard Fragonard and at Les 4 Chemins), **Molinard** (60 Boulevard Victor-Hugo), and **Gallimard** (73 Route de Cannes).

Leave Grasse to the northeast on the D2085 and travel for 6 kilometers to the D3, which travels north and winds back and forth along a steep ascent to the beautiful village of Gourdon. Endeared as one of France's most beautiful villages, **Gourdon** is an unspoiled gem that commands an absolutely spectacular setting as it hugs and clings to the walls of the steep hillside. Vistas from the village look north down the Loup Canyon or southeast over the countryside dotted with villages of sun-washed stucco and tiled roofs to the glistening water of the distant Riviera. On clear days you can see from Nice to the Italian border. The village's cobbled streets are lined with delightful, untouristy shops and a handful of restaurants. **Le Nid d'Aigle** on the Place Victoria is a restaurant whose terraces step daringly down the hillside.

From Gourdon, the D3 hugs the hillside and affords glimpses of the twisting River Loup far below. As the road winds down to a lower altitude, you can either drive north on the D603 to the medieval village of **Cipières** and cross the river at a more northerly point or continue on the D3 and cross the Loup on the Pont de Bramafan. After crossing the river, just before Bramafan, follow the D8 south in the direction of Pont du Loup. This 6-kilometer stretch of road winds through the **Gorges du Loup**. The canyon's beauty and its high granite walls beckon you into the ever-narrowing gorge. The River Loup flows far below, only visible to the passenger who might chance a peek over the edge. The road passes through some jaggedly carved tunnels—pathways blasted through sheer rock, which open to glorious vistas of the canyon, trees, and rock. Pull off the road at **Saut du Loup**. The stop requires no more than 15 minutes and, for a fee, you can walk down a short, steep flight of steps to a terrace overlooking magnificent waterfalls and pools. The small riverside village of **Pont du Loup** is situated at the mouth of the canyon, on a bend in the river shadowed by the ruins of a towering bridge. It is a pretty town and a lovely end to the Loup Canyon.

Beyond Pont du Loup, traveling east along the D2210 in the direction of Vence, you pass through a few more towns, each consisting of a cluster of medieval buildings and winding, narrow streets that, without exception, encircle a towering church and its steeple. **Tourrettes sur Loup** is an especially lovely town whose medieval core of clustered rosy-golden-stone houses enjoys a backdrop of the three small towers that give the town its name. Every March the hillsides of Tourettes sur Loup are a mass of violets and the village is dressed with fragrant bouquets for the *Fête des Violettes*. After World War II the town revived its long-abandoned textile production and is one of the world's top *tissage à main* (hand-weaving) centers. The workshops are open to the public.

The D2210 continues from Tourrettes sur Loup and approaches the wonderful old town of **Vence** from the west. Located just 10 kilometers above the coast and Riviera, the hillsides surrounding Vence afford a lovely coastal panorama and are dotted with palatial homes and villas. Entering through the gates into the old village, you find dozens of tiny streets with interesting shops and little cafés where you can enjoy scrumptious pastries.

The Place du Peyra was once the Roman forum and it's now the colorful town marketplace. In 1941 Matisse moved here and, in gratitude for being nursed back to health by the Dominican Sisters, he constructed and decorated the simple **Chapelle du Rosaire**. (Follow the Avenue des Poilus to the Route de Saint Jeannet La Gaude.) (*Closed Sundays, tel: 04.93.58.03.26.*) Vence makes a wonderful base from which to explore the coast and the hilltowns, and its location affords spectacular views across the hills to the blue waters.

A few kilometers beyond Vence (D2 in the direction of Cagnes sur Mer) is the picturesque mountain stronghold of **Saint Paul de Vence**, which once guarded the ancient Var Frontier. Cars are forbidden inside the walls of the old town whose cobbled streets are lined with galleries and tourist shops. From the encircling ramparts you get panoramic views of the hilltowns of the Riviera. Located outside the walled town in the woods along the Cagnes road, the **Foundation Maeght**, a private museum that sponsors and hosts numerous collections of works of some of the world's finest contemporary artists, is one of the principal attractions of Saint Paul de Vence. (*Open Oct to Jun.*) Saint Paul de Vence is also a convenient base from which to explore the Riviera and we recommend a number of places both within its fortified walls on its outskirts. From Saint Paul de Vence it is a short drive back to Nice.

From Nice you can join our *Provence* itinerary by taking the scenic autoroute through the mountains, bridging the distance with our *Gorges du Verdon* itinerary. Or you can follow the coastline, referred to as the Corniche d'Or, between La Napoule (just outside Cannes) and Saint Raphaël, which offers spectacular views: fire-red mountains contrasting dramatically with the dark-blue sea. Saint Raphaël is a small commercial port with a pleasant, tourist-thronged beach. Continuing on, Saint Tropez is easily the most enchanting of the dozens of small ports and beaches that you'll pass. If you choose to continue along the coastal road, take the Corniche des Maures, which hugs the waterfront at the base of the Massif des Maures. At Hyères the scenery wanes, and we suggest you take the A50 to the A8-E80, which travels west to Aix en Provence.

Maginot Line &
Exploring Lorraine

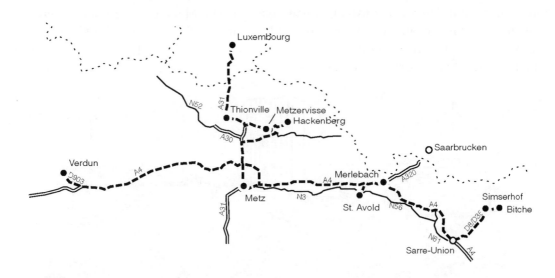

Luxembourg

N52

A31

Thionville   Metzervisse
● Hackenberg

A30

○ Saarbrucken

Verdun
●
D903

A4

Merlebach
●
A4

A320

Simserhof
● ● Bitche

Metz

A31

N3

St. Avold
●

N56

A4

D8/D35

N61

Sarre-Union

Paris

○ Orientation
● Sightseeing
━ ━ ━ Itinerary route

The Maginot Line & Exploring Lorraine

The region of Lorraine, tucked in the northeast corner of France, is bordered to the north by Belgium, Luxemburg and Germany. Stretching along its border to the east is Alsace. However, whereas Alsace is well known for its picturesque villages and lovely wines, Lorraine is well known for its rich military history. If you are intrigued by stories of World War II, you will not want to miss a visit to the Maginot Line, built as a brilliant, but unsuccessful defense against a German invasion. The Maginot Line stands today as a monument to French engineering genius and lost hopes. Also tying in with the history of the World War II, is the beautiful American cemetery in Saint Avold where thousands of simple white crosses mark the graves of American soldiers. A visit here is unforgettable.

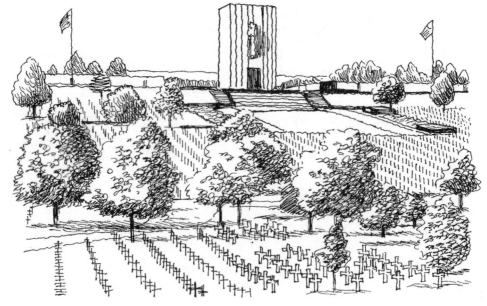

Cemetery of American Soldiers, Saint Avold

As you travel through Lorraine, you cannot help but wonder why this region is not nearly as well-known as Normandy to travelers who are interested in the history of World War II. Here too crucial battles were fought against the Germans under the commands of General George Patton. Here too a heartbreaking number of soldiers sacrificed their lives to restore freedom to France.

Whereas Normandy has hosted many reunions and memorial ceremonies over the years, Lorraine was somewhat forgotten. It wasn't until 2004 (60 years after the allied forces came to the rescue of Lorraine) that the heroism of the men who fought here was truly recognized. What prompted this surge of interest is due to one of General Patton's platoon sergeants, Joseph Stobbe, who was seriously wounded by a by a sniper who was shooting from a window as he entered Metzervisse (a village about 15 kilometers east of Thionville). This was the third time Sergeant Stobbe was wounded while fighting in France (his first two injuries were in the battle of Normandy).

After the war, Sergeant Stobbe returned home, went to school, and opened a medical practice in Salt Lake City. It wasn't until many years later that he returned to Lorraine with his family to share with them memories of his past. As coincidence would have it, an automobile accident hospitalized him once again. The local chief of Police, Pascal Morretti, while investigating the accident was stunned to hear that Dr. Stobbe was one of the young soldiers who had been wounded many years before while liberating his village. Friendships were formed and many of the local people came to the hospital bearing bottles of wine, flowers, flags, and souvenirs. But, patriotic Pascal Morretti thought that more should be done, and a grand reunion was planned to commemorate the 60th anniversary of the liberation of Lorraine. The elaborate plan called for inviting as guests all the veterans of the 90th and 95th Infantry Divisions, as well as the 3rd Cavalry. Amazingly many of the soldiers were still alive and came to France with their families for a week's celebration. The local people turned out en mass and welcomed them royally with banquets, speeches, parades, religious services, and bus tours to the battle fields where new monuments and statues were commemorated. At every stop both the *Star spangled Banner* and the *The Marseille* were played by local bands.

Planning Your Trip: If the Maginot Line is the focus of your trip to the Lorraine, it is essential that you plan in advance and carefully check dates before finalizing your travel arrangements. The reason for this is that the fortresses along the Maginot Line are not always open. Most are only open from spring through fall, and then only on certain days of the week. If you have a group that wants to visit, special arrangements can usually be made. Two of the largest of the fortifications that are open to visitors are the **Hackenberg Fortress** and the **Simserhof Fortress**. If you want to visit the Hackenberg Fortress (which is frequently closed) our suggestion is to stay nearby at the Romantik Hotel L'Horizon in Thionville (recommended in our guide to France Hotels, *www.karenbrown.com/lhorizon.html*) and to mention to the owner, Mr. Speck (who has an astonishing depth of knowledge of the history of World War II) that the purpose of your trip is to see the Hackenberg Fortress. Before making reservations, ask him to advise you if it will be possible to visit it during your intended dates. If you also want to include the Simserhof Fortress, scheduling is much easier since it is open every day from mid-March to mid-November. If the focus of your trip is to visit the American cemetery at **Saint Avold**, planning is easy since the cemetery is open every day all year except Christmas and New Year's.

Recommended Pacing: This itinerary covers a small geographical area so we suggest choosing just one place as your hub of operation. Thionville and Metz (both large industrial cities) are centrally located for sightseeing. To have time to include one or more fortresses along the Maginot Line and also visit the American cemetery at Saint Avold, you need three nights in order to have two full days for sightseeing. One day can be allocated to the Hackenberg fortress and the surrounding area. Another day can be used to visit the Simserhof Fortress and Citadel of Bitche with a stop en route to see the Saint Avold Cemetery (located approximately mid-way between Thionville and Simserhof). If you want to squeeze in some more sightseeing, additional suggestions are given at the end of this itinerary.

The Maginot Line–A bit of history: The Maginot Line, a name and place once so well known, has faded into the background through the years and now is best remembered by those who were alive during World War II and those with a keen interest in history. But, its story is fascinating. Following the Great War (World War I) the French were devastated by the horrors of battle and determined to never again experience such losses at the hands of their mortal enemy, Germany. It is no wonder they were so motivated to find a way to block another German invasion. The loss of life in World War I is almost unimaginable. A staggering number of France's finest young men were lost; few families were spared heartache. The worst casualties of the war took place in **Verdun**, also located in Lorraine. Here the Germans, led by Crown Prince Wilhelm, attempted to conquer France with an onslaught that began in February 1916 and lasted for 10 months. Finally, in spite of great odds against them, the French prevailed, but at an almost inconceivable loss of life. It is estimated that over a million died here, including Germans and French—the greatest fatalities per square meter of any battle of the war.

Knowing the French suffered such heartbreaking losses in the World War I, it is understandable that they were passionate about avoiding another invasion by Germany. And, their fears of just such a scenario happening again grew daily as Hitler blatantly built up his army. The French politicians and military experts debated about the best way to stymie an invasion. After much debate, the plan of the Minister of War, André Maginot, to build string of fortifications along the border was accepted and construction began in 1929 for what became know as The Maginot Line. The concept was grandiose; the engineering top notch. Only the Great Wall of China could compete with the flamboyant plan—to build a series of fortifications stretching for 640 kilometers across the north of France along the borders of Germany, Luxembourg, and Belgium. The strategy called for 108 large fortresses positioned 15 kilometers apart, supplemented by smaller forts, pillboxes, concrete bunkers, and watch posts. The undertaking was awesome: Secreted below the ground would be over 100 kilometers of tunnels accessed by a network of trains, accommodations for thousands of men, hospitals, kitchens, dental offices, lighting systems, cinemas, rail yards, sophisticated plumbing works, maintenance shops, dining rooms, a vast network of phone, and concealed turrets with mechanisms that could raise them as smoothly as a well-run clock to the surface of the earth.

Hackenberg Fortress

Unfortunately, the Maginot Line did not work. On paper, the plan seemed brilliant, but it did not take into consideration changes in warfare. Yes, the German and Luxembourg borders were well protected; however, the section of the fortification along the border with Belgium was weak because the French thought the Germans would never attack through Belgium, which was their ally. They also thought there was little chance the Germans would attack through Belgium since they would have to go through the dense forests of the Ardennes. How wrong they were. Belgium declared neutrality thus Germany had access to France. And, with better equipment, Hitler's panzers plowed right through the forests of the Ardennes which the French had thought were impregnable. In

The Maginot Line & Exploring Lorraine

May 10, 1940, the German army crossed into France over the border with Belgium with 140,000 troops and 1,500 tanks. The only obstacle to their unimpeded conquest of France was the battle at Dunkirk where the Germans surrounded and trapped over 300,000 allied troops. In a drama that will always be remembered as testament to British daring and courage, the soldiers were rescued by the heroic efforts of incredibly brave Englishmen who crossed the English Channel in hundreds of small boats of all shapes and sizes to rescue the stranded soldiers and ferry them back to England. (It was said there were so many boats in the channel that one could almost walk between England and France.) After Dunkirk, the Germans encountered no more resistance. They swept across the country unimpeded, totally avoiding the Maginot Line. By June 15, 1940, Paris had fallen.

The Maginot Line–Hackenberg: If you have time for just one fortification, we suggest Hackenberg Fortress near Veckring. Not only is it near Thionville and Metz, but it is also one of the largest and most important of the fortifications along the Maginot Line. Even Winston Churchill came to take a look at this underground city. To reach the fortification, take exit 37 off the A31 (the exit is between Thionville and Metz). Then take D8 east for about 14 kilometers and turn north on D918 for just a few kilometers, and then go east on D60. Five kilometers before you reach Veckring, there is a M10 tank marking a turnoff to the left to the Hackenberg Fortress, which is tucked into a wooded ridge.

Park your car and walk up to the entrance. Be sure to wear comfortable walking shoes and a warm coat, gloves, and a cap since you will be doing lots of walking and the underground tunnels are damp and cold. You will be greeted by a guide—some of the older ones have known the fortress first hand. Be forewarned that there might not be an English-speaking guide available. If not, join the tour anyway—most of what you see along the way will be self explanatory. The tour usually takes from 2 to 3 hours.

As you start out on foot with your guide and descend ever deeper into the ground through a myriad of tunnels and elevators, it quickly becomes obvious why a guide is absolutely essential. In fact, you will probably hover near to him, like a school child clinging to his teacher, for fear of getting lost in the 10-kilometer maze of dark passages. Just about when you get tired of walking, a train will pull up through one of the long tunnels and you will hop aboard to continue your journey along the narrow gauge railway that was used to transport soldiers, ammunition, and supplies. Along the way you will make many stops where your guide will take you through a labyrinth of small tunnels and with his special key opens the heavy doors leading into locked rooms, flipping on lights so you can see.

The tour is fascinating. Not a sophisticated, sleek Hollywood-style presentation, but rather a simple, well-presented one that shows you everything in homespun, heartfelt way that makes the adventure that much more real. One of the most interesting aspects of the tour is that along the way you will experience what it must have been like to have been one of the more than 1,000 enlisted men and officers who lived here. There are many dioramas which make the scene come alive. You will pass the kitchen where dressed manikins show the chef preparing dinner helped by the solders assigned to mess duty. The daily menu shows that the soldiers were well fed, no doubt an attempt to boost moral in this forsaken assignment. Another vignette is the dentist's chambers where again full size models dressed in uniforms. A hospital, dormitories, officers' quarters, laundry facilities, ammunition depots, huge maintenance rooms, a movie theater, recreation halls, power plants, and reservoirs of water are passed along the way.

Housed in one of the barracks is a museum displaying memorabilia of the war with very interesting photographs of some of the soldiers and a display of weapons and uniforms At another point, a stop is made to see a demonstration of how the hidden gun turrets worked. As you watch, the guide operates the still perfectly-functioning mechanism whose gears slowly raise a camouflaged turret. You climb some steps leading outside where you watch as the gun turret magically rises from its hiding place below and pokes its head above the ground. (*The fortress is open for tours on Saturday and Sunday at 2 pm from April through October. From mid-June to mid-September, weekday tours are added at 3pm.*)

The Maginot Line–Simserhof: If you wish to see more fortifications, visit the Simserhof Fortress, located near the town of Bitche. It is the fourth largest of the fortresses along the Maginot Line. To reach the site, go south on A31 from Thionville, then east on the A4 (bypassing Metz). From the A4, take exit 43 near Rimsdorf, then north for 5 km, then east on the D8 (which becomes D35). When you come to Rohrbach, continue east on D62. Simserhof is located five kilometers before you reach the town of Bitche.

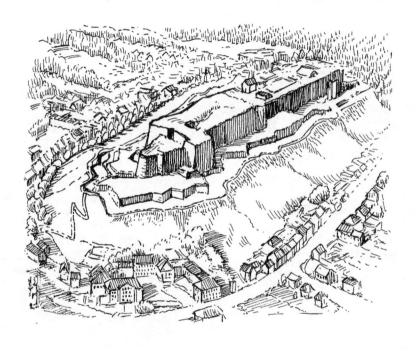

Simserhof Fortress

Simserhof is different from the other fortresses in that it has received outside funding for renovations—whereas most depend almost totally on financial support from their local communities. As a result, the tour is a bit more "polished" than the others along the Maginot Line. The tour begins at the visitors' center where an 18-minute film is shown giving the background of the Maginot Line, including why it was built. Afterwards an open-air electric train takes you 30 meters underground for a short tour. The tour is well done with dioramas demonstrating what it must have been like to have been one of the

Citadel of Bitche

soldiers stationed here. (*The fortress is open daily from mid-March to mid-November, 10am to 5pm.*)

Bitche–The Citadel of Bitche: After visiting the Simserhof Fortress, continue on for another 5 kilometers to the town of Bitche where the strategic military importance of this region of France is once again demonstrated. The town wraps around a flat-topped hill, crowned by the remains of a superb, 18th century fortification, the Citadel of Bitche. A tour of the site relives the battle fought in 1870 during the Franco-Prussian War. There is also a museum here that commemorates the men who fought in the Franco-Prussian War.

Saint Avold American Cemetery: A visit to the Saint Avold American Cemetery adds greater compassion and understanding to the sacrifices made during World War II. It seems that everyone is familiar with the battlefields and cemeteries of Normandy, where thousands of visitors walk the hallowed ground each year. However, it was surprising to us to learn that the largest American cemetery in Europe is the one in Saint Avold.

Saint Avold Cemetery is beautifully set in gently rolling, wooded countryside just north of the town of Saint Avold. Upon arrival, you can leave your car in a parking area just outside of the dramatic gated entrance, which is adorned with a bronze eagle. A short walk leads to undulating lush green lawns that are enclosed by a distant forest. The well-manicured landscaping is elegant with flowering shrubs, walkways bordered by roses, and a lush lawn dotted with oak, beach, maple, and hawthorn trees. There is nothing to mar the beauty. Everything is serene and tasteful. Tears cannot help but come to your eyes as you view row upon row, of simple, pure white, marble crosses that seem to stretch forever. The graves of soldiers of Jewish faith are marked with the Star of David. Four Medal of Honor recipients are buried here: their headstones inscribed in gold leaf. In Saint Avold there are 10,489 graves, including soldiers and airmen from every state in America, as well as fallen soldiers from Puerto Rico, Panama, Canada, Mexico, and England.

Stop to visit the Wall of the Missing, a handsome, impressive monument inscribed with the names of 444 unidentified soldiers. The names of those who were later identified are now marked by a star. While we were at the cemetery we spoke with a family from Virginia who told us the story of their Missing Soldier. For many years the family only knew that their son was missing and had obviously died on the battlefield. It was not until more than 60 years later that they received in the mail a bracelet engraved with his name. A note was attached from a farmer in Lorraine who found the bracelet while working in his field. After vast research, he was finally able to discover where the boy's family lived and sent the token to them. A small group of his family, glad to finally have closure, had come to Saint Avold to commemorate their long-lost loved one.

Before leaving the cemetery, be sure to visit its Memorial, a simple, dignified, beautifully designed, rectangular stone building that stands on a rise overlooking the field of crosses. An inscription reads "In proud remembrance of the achievements of her sons and in humble tribute to their sacrifices, this memorial has been erected by the United States of America." Within, the monument tastefully blends historical information along with a quiet, spiritual mood. At the end of the room, bathed in a stream of light that flood through tall floor to ceiling windows, there are five sculptured figures of white limestone that represent the eternal struggle for freedom. The middle carving is a young man. He is flanked by historic religious and militarily heroes, including King David, Emperor Constantine, King Arthur, and George Washington. Below the sculptures is an alter of green marble, a place where many come to quietly remember about their loved ones and say a silent prayer On the wall is a large glazed, colored ceramic map portraying, and describing, the military operations in Europe beginning with the Normandy landing until the war ended. A special smaller map details the fighting near Avold. A row of flags flutter high on each side wall, representing each part of the United States military service. (*Saint Avold is open daily except Christmas and New Year's, 9am to 5pm*).

Additional sightseeing suggestion–American Cemetery in Hamm, Luxembourg. If your heart was profoundly touched by the American cemetery at Saint Avold, it is well worth the short drive across the border into Luxembourg to visit the American Cemetery where over 5,000 American soldiers are buried near the village of Hamm (about 4 kilometers east of Luxembourg City). It is here that General George Patton, the strong-willed, brilliant military genius who liberated Lorraine is buried. Patton fought in both World War I and World War II and had been wounded three times. However, it was not a battle, but rather a staff car accident that led to the death of this tough general, affectionately called by his men "Old Blood and Guts." Instead of returning home to lie at rest in Arlington Cemetery along with other famous military heroes, he is buried, just as he requested, amongst his soldiers. Thousands of visitors come each year to visit the cemetery and pay their tribute by decorating the graves with wreathes and flowers. The beautiful, 43-acre, wooded site was donated by the people of Luxembourg.

Additional sightseeing suggestion–Metz: If time allows, visit Metz, a city dating back to Roman times. Today it is a large metropolis; however at its heart you find an interesting, pedestrian-only, historic center. Of greatest interest here is the magnificent St. Étienne Cathedral, one of the finest Gothic cathedrals in France. Its beautiful stained glass windows were done by famous artists, including Marc Chagall. The cathedral and many of the nearby historic monuments are romantically illuminated at night.

Additional sightseeing suggestion–Verdun: To expand your understanding of military history, visit Verdun, located about an hour's drive east of either Thionville or Metz. It was in Verdun in World War I that France's most horrendous 10-month battle took place. Its battlefields and memorials can easily be visited in a day. For more information on Verdun, see the previous section: "The Maginot Line: a bit of history."

When finished with your explorations in Lorraine, it is an easy drive southeast along the A4 to the exceptionally lovely city of Strasbourg. From here, you can continue along our Alsace Itinerary, tasting delicious wines and visiting charming small villages.

St. Étienne Cathedral

The Maginot Line & Exploring Lorraine

Wine Country – Burgundy

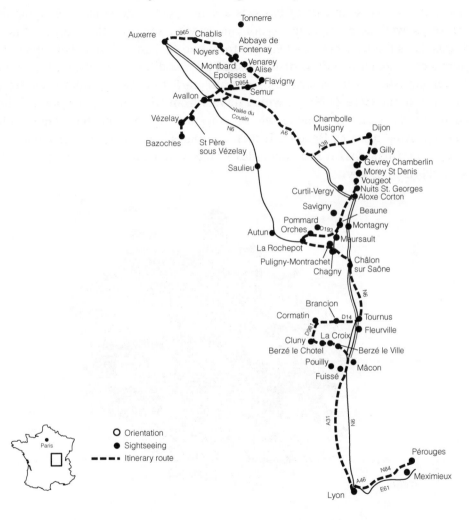

Tonnerre

Auxerre D965 Chablis

Abbaye de
Fontenay

Noyers

Montbard Venarey
Alise

Epoisses D954 Flavigny

Semur

Avallon

Vézelay

Valée du
Cousin

Bazoches N6

St Père
sous Vézelay A6

Chambolle
Musigny Dijon

Gilly

Gevrey Chamberlin

Saulieu Morey St Denis

Vougeot

Curtil-Vergy Nuits St. Georges

Savigny Aloxe Corton

Beaune

Pommard Montagny

Orches D193

Autun Meursault

La Rochepot

Puligny-Montrachet Châlon
sur Saône

Chagny

Brancion

Cormatin D14 Tournus

D981 Fleurville

Cluny La Croix

Berzé le Chotel Berzé le Ville

Pouilly Mâcon

Fuissé

A31 N6

A6

O Orientation

Paris ● Sightseeing

- - - Itinerary route

Pérouges

N84 Meximieux

A46 E61

Lyon

135

Wine Country–Burgundy

Burgundy, which lies to the southeast of Paris, is a name used to designate a geographic region of France as well as a reference synonymous with some of the world's finest wines. Vineyards dress the landscape and stretch from one enchanting, steepled village to the next. In terms of wine, Burgundy is distinguished by five different areas, each with its own special characteristics. The backbone of this itinerary follows the Côte d'Or from Chablis in the north to the Côte de Nuits, which travels from Dijon to beyond Nuits Saint Georges, and on to the Côte de Beaune whose vineyards spider web the countryside around the magical wine town of Beaune. It then continues south from Chagny into the region of the Côte de Chalonnaise and concludes in the wine district of Mâconnais with Mâcon as its southern boundary.

Vézelay

In addition to a focus on wine, this itinerary weaves a path through some enchanting and historic towns and monuments. In the vicinity of Chablis is the memorable Abbaye de Fontenay that was declared a World Heritage site by UNESCO in 1981, the seemingly undiscovered ruins of Alise Sainte Reine, and the enchanting village of Flavigny sur Ozerain whose recent claim to fame is the movie *Chocolat*. Before heading south to the capital wine town of Beaune, the trail sweeps west to include Vézelay, an idyllic medieval village sitting high atop a hill and the scenic Vallée du Cousin and then journeys along the Route des Grands Crus. Exploring the area is like traveling through a wine list, for the region covers half the famous names in French wine.

Recommended Pacing: Spend at least two nights in northern Burgundy staying in the vicinity of the magnificent town of Vézelay; two nights in the neighborhood of Beaune so that you have time to spontaneously explore the narrow roads that spoke off the main roads and weave through the vineyards, and a night in southern Burgundy with a possible conclusion in the grand city of Lyon or the hilltown village of Pérouges. (Recommendations for places to stay can also be found in our France hotel guide.)

Before you embark on this itinerary—since wine is the underlying attraction—it seems best to provide you with some basic information to enhance your understanding and appreciation of the region's bounty that you will sample. From Chablis in the north to Mâcon in the south, 25,000 hectares of vineyards represent Burgundy's five wine districts which boast an incredible diversity, evidenced by the amazing 98 distinct appellations. Grouped into four categories, the appellations, Regional, Communal, Premiers Crus and Grands Crus, define the quality and origin of the grape. The general rule is the higher the quality, the more precisely identified the origin of the grape.

Four key factors influence the quality of great wines: The soil, the grape, the climate and the talent of the vintner. Because Burgundy is a tapestry of different soil types that distinguish the wines, vineyards are often sectioned off by stone walls from one soil variation to the next and are referred to as *terroirs*. Understandably the variety of grape or *cépage* selected is based on which best compliments the soil. In spite of the diversity of soil, with a few minor exceptions, the wines of Burgundy are from two supreme varietals: Chardonnay for the white wines and Pinot Noir for the red grape. So conveniently close to Paris, it is puzzling that Burgundy is not considered a year-round destination until one experiences the cold, dry winters that influence the wine.

Leave Paris to the southeast and take the A6 autoroute for the 1½-hour drive to the *Auxerre Sud* exit where you take the D965 for the 12-kilometer drive into **Chablis**, a busy little town synonymous with the elegant, dry white wine of Burgundy. (Note: You might also want to consider taking the TGV to Dijon and beginning your journey at the heart of the region.) Chablis wine roads travel into the surrounding hills, with the finest vineyards being found just northeast of the town. Cross the River Serein and turn left on the D91, a small road that leads you to the region's seven *grand crus*, which lie side by side: Bougros, Les Preuses, Vaudésir, Les Clos, Grenouilles, Valmur, and Blanchot. Vineyards cover over 1,300 hectares with the principal grape being the Chardonnay.

Returning to Chablis, take the D45 and follow the Serein upstream to **Noyers**, a charming little walled town of timbered houses. From Noyers take the D956 east 21 km to the junction of D905 and then south 10 km to **Montbard**. From Montbard it is just a few kilometers further to one of France's most wonderful monuments and attractions, **L'Abbaye de Fontenay**. Set against a backdrop of forest, this beautiful abbaye, its fountains and gardens will prove a highlight of your trip. (*Tel: 03.80.92.15.00, www.abbayedefontenay.com.*) Founded in 1118 by St Bernard this is a perfect example of a Cistercian abbey. It has endured dramatic changes with each century. It became the Royal Abbey in 1269, was pillaged by Edward III in 1553, during the French Revolution saw the last eight monks leave in 1790, and then was sold by the revolutionaries to an industrialist who installed a paper mill. It was then purchased by the Montgolfier family whose descendent in 1906 decided to dismantle the industrial buildings and bring the abbey back to its original medieval glory. You can tour—on your own or with a guide—and visit everything from the bakery to the dormitory and the Cloister, which remains one of the most wonderful examples of Romanesque architecture. (*Open all year, tel: 03.80.92.15.00.*)

Abbaye de Fontenay

Returning to Montbard, it is just a short journey south on the D905 to Venarey les Laumes. From here a circle detour on the D103 will take you to **Alise Sainte Reine**, a quiet hilltown with Roman ties. This fortified town is the scene of the last stand of the Gauls against Caesar. Follow signs to Mont Auxois which is located above the village and was the site of Caesar's final victory over the heroic Gaulic chieftain Vercingetorix in 52 B.C. after a six-week siege. The first excavations were undertaken in the mid 19th century, and they uncovered the remains of a thriving Gallo-Roman town, Alise, complete with a theater, forum, and a well-laid street plan. The Musée Alise has a collection of artifacts, jewelry, and bronze figures from the site.

From Alise continue the journey on to the picturesque village of **Flavigny sur Ozerain**, whose most recent fame is due to the fact it was used as the stage set for the film *Chocolat*. With its ancient narrow streets, fortified gates and religious and architectural heritage this is a wonderful old city to explore on foot. It is also famous for the production of anise balls and sweets made by the Abbaye since 1591. They accept visitors each day from 8:30 to 10:30 am. You might also want to plan a meal at La Grange les Quatre Heures where local farmers offer an à la carte menu featuring their own produce. (*Open July through August every day except Mondays, 12:30 to 5:00, tel: 03 80 96 20 62.*)

From Flavigny traveling the D954 west it is a pretty drive to the medieval town of **Semur en Auxois**. Nestled on the loop of the river Armançon, this is a very picturesque walled village with its massive stone towers, numerous bridges, church or Notre Dame and maze of houses all straddling the river on either side of the rocky spur.

Continuing east from Semur it is a beautiful drive through farmland past the Château at **Epoisses** and then on to connect with the N6 where you will turn north in the direction of Avallon. With its narrow cobbled streets **Avallon** is a larger town with cozy old houses at its center. Journey down through the old city, following signs to Pontaubert and then continue on to the magical pilgrimage site of **Vézelay.** Sitting high on its hilltop above the surrounding countryside and for many people the highlight of a visit to Burgundy, this little town of Vézelay is full of narrow streets lined with old houses with sculptured doorways and mullioned windows leading up to the 12th-century **Basilica Sainte Madeleine**, the enormous building that sits above the village. This extraordinarily long church is beautiful in its simplicity with its soaring columns and paved floor and when religious pilgrimages were the fashion, it was an important stop on the pilgrimage route to Santiago de Compostela in Spain. Take note of the brass coquille saint Jacques, the pilgrimage sign of welcome and hospitality that are still embedded in the cobbled streets. From Vézelay retrace your path to Pontaubert where you will cross the river, and turn immediately right, signposted **Vallée du Cousin.**

This is a very scenic drive on a country road that follows the picturesque, narrow, wooded valley of the rushing River Cousin and will deliver you back to Avallon. From Avallon follow signposts for the autoroute A6, which you take to the A38 towards Dijon.

Note: If time allows or if you use **Vézelay** as a base, be sure to travel the 10 km south on the D958 to a wonderful privately owned 12th century château, it is gorgeous in its furnishings and regal setting. The medieval stronghold of **Château Bazoches-du-Morvan** enjoys a bucolic setting on the site of a former Roman base and makes for a delightful and interesting excursion. (*Open all year, Nov 6 to Mar 24 by reservation only, tel: 03.86.22.10.22.*)

Semur

If you like bustling cities, follow the A38 all the way to **Dijon** where sprawling suburbs hide a historic core. Rue des Forges is the most outstanding of the old streets. Even if you are not a museum lover, you will enjoy the **Musée des Beaux Arts** in the palace of Charles de Valois. It is one of France's most popular museums, with some wonderful old woodcarvings and paintings. (*Open all year except Tuesdays, tel: 03.80.74.52.70.*) The aperitif Kir (cassis and white wine) was named after Canon Kir, the city's mayor and wartime resistance leader. Food note: There are plenty of opportunities to purchase Dijon mustard and, if you visit in November, you can attend the superb gastronomic fair.

From Dijon begins the wine region of the prestigious Côte de Nuits. The wine estates date back to 10th-century abbeys whose monks first planted vineyards predominately with the Pinot Noir grapes. Much of the 3,000 hectares are enclosed behind stone walls and the vineyards are referred to as *Clos*. Chambertin, Clos de Vougeot, and Romanée Conti represent Burgundy's Grands Crus and are located here. Further up the slopes, 550 hectares producing fine Burgundies are referred to as Hautes-Côtes de Nuits.

Outside Dijon, for a greater dose of the countryside, leave the autoroute after Sombernon at the village of Pont de Pany, pass the large hotel on your right, cross the canal, and turn right on the D35, signposted Urcy and Nuits Saint Georges. This scenic little country road winds steeply up a rocky limestone escarpment past the Château Montclust and through rolling farmland to **Urcy**, a tight cluster of cottages set around a church. After passing through Quemigny Poisot, turn left for Chamboef and left again in the village for Gevrey Chambertin. Down the limestone escarpment you go through a rocky tunnel around a couple of precipitous bends and you're in the vineyards.

Turn right and follow the D122 into Gevrey Chambertin where you join the great wine and tourist route, **Route des Grands Crus**, winding you through the villages that produce the premier Burgundian wines. As you drive around, look for the Flemish-style colored tiles arranged in patterns that decorate the roofs of the region—a reminder of the time when the Dukes of Burgundy's duchy stretched into the Low Countries. There are very few large estates in this region, most of the land belonging to small farmers who live and make wine in the villages and go out to work in their vineyards. Fields are called *climats* and every *climat* has a name. Some *climats* produce better wines, which are identified by their own name; others are identified by the name of the village. This is fine for the larger centers such as Beaune and Pommard, but the little villages—searching for an identity—have incorporated the name of their best-known vineyard into the village name. Thus Gevrey became Gevrey Chambertin, Saint Georges became Nuits Saint Georges, and Vougeot became Clos de Vougeot. **Gevrey Chambertin** is one of the region's most delightful villages, with narrow streets lined with gray-stone houses and numerous vintners' signs inviting you in to sample their wares.

Arriving at **Morey-Saint-Denis**, park in the large car park before the village and walk along its narrow streets.

The vineyards of **Chambolle–Musigny** produce some spectacular wines and you can learn about them at the wine museum housed in the cellars of the **Château-Hôtel André Ziltener** (also a hotel and recommended in our France hotel guide). This informative tour includes a tasting of the four grades of wine produced in the area. Madame Ballois, who is in charge, is a charming hostess, extremely knowledgeable and proud of the fact that the six red wines they offer for tasting are all, impressively, *première* and *grands crus*. The price of the tour is quite reasonable, or free to guests of the hotel.

The hillsides of **Clos de Vougeot** were first planted by Cistercian monks in the 14th century and a stone wall was built to encircle the vineyards and protect them from raiders in the One Hundred Years' War. An organization called **Chevaliers du Tastevin**, now recognized worldwide, chose the 16th-century **Château de Vougeot** in 1944 as a base from which to publicize Burgundy wines. You can see the courtyard, the great pillared hall where banquets take place, and the impressive cellars and 12th-century wine presses.

Nuits Saint Georges is somewhat larger than the other towns along the route. A great deal of wine is blended here under the town's name. After Nuits Saint Georges the Route des Grands Crus continues along the N74 to end at Corgoloin. The Côte de Beaune begins virtually where the Côte de Nuits ends.

After the Route des Grands Crus the first great commune is **Aloxe Corton** whose vineyards were once owned by Charlemagne. Legend states that Aloxe Corton is known for both its red and white wines because, during the time that Charlemagne owned the vineyards, his wife claimed that red wine stained his white beard and so he ordered the production of white wine too. He is commemorated by the white wine Corton-Charlemagne.

Hôtel Dieu

Arriving in **Beaune**, do not follow signs for *Centre Ville* but stay on the ring road that circles the city's walls in a counterclockwise direction. Park in one of the car parks adjacent to the ring road and walk into the narrow old streets of the wine capital of Burgundy. Today the most important landowner in the region is the Hospices de Beaune, a charitable organization founded in 1443 by Nicolas Rolin, chancellor of the Duke of Burgundy. Every year they hold a wine auction at the Hôtel Dieu—it is one of the wine trade's most important events. Built as a hospital, the **Hôtel Dieu** is so elegantly decorated that it seems more like a palace. You will want to take a guided tour of this lovely building which is an exceptional example of medieval architecture whose rooms house an incredible collection of furnishings, art, tapestries, and the incredible exhibit, the *Last Judgement* by Rogier van der Weyden. (*Open all year, tel: 03.80.24.45.00, www.hospices-de-beaune.tm.fr.*)

You can also visit the **Musée du Vin de Bourgogne** in the Hôtel des Ducs de Bourgogne. (*Closed Tues, Dec to Apr, tel: 03.80.22.08.19.*) There are delightful shops, restaurants, and cafés aplenty. Wine lovers may want to visit one of the *négotiant-éleveurs* who buy wines of the same *appellation* from growers and blend and nurture them to produce an "elevated" superior wine. At the heart of the wine region, Beaune serves as a wonderful base from which to explore the region. The wine capital, it reigns over 5,000 hectares of the Côte de Beaune whose wines are as diverse in character as they are high in quality. Full bodied reds as well as rich and complex whites are produced by vineyards known the world over: Pommard, Meursault and Puligny-Montrachet. When following the *Route des Vins* don't overlook the 650 hectares of the Hautes-Côtes de Beaune which wind up the slopes and are recognized for their red and white Burgundies.

Leave Beaune on the A74 in the direction of Chagny. After a short distance take the D973 to **Pommard** where tasting is offered at the château on the outskirts, as well as at other enticing vintners in the crowded confines of the village. (*Tel: 03.80.22.12.59, www.chateaudepommard.com.*) From Pommard continue into **Meursault**, a larger village that offers tasting at small vintners and at the larger Domaine du Château de Meursault. (*Tel: 03.80.26.22.75.*)

From Meursault, the D973 brings you into Auxley Duresses. At the far end of the village turn right following the brown signs indicating **Haute Côte de Beaune**. This wine route takes you on a narrow country lane up through the steeply sloping village of **Saint Romain**, high above the vineyards and back down to vineyards in **Orches**, a village clinging to the limestone cliffs, through **Baubigny** and into the wine center of **La Rochepot**. On the approach to the charming village of La Rochepot, visible on the horizon is its intricate, fairy-tale castle with its multi-tiled roof in vibrant colors of yellow, olive, red, black, and ochres, which has stood on its rocky peak since the 13th century. You can also see the ruins of the original castle that occupied the site, built in the 11th century by Alexander of Burgundy.

During the 15th century, the **Château de la Rochepot** became the home of the Lords Régnier and Philippe Pot, both Knights of the Golden Fleece and counselors to the Dukes of Burgundy. At the end of the 19th century Colonel Sadi Carnot carefully restored the castle, which had been destroyed during the French Revolution. Today a visit to the château (complete with drawbridge) gives you a glimpse of what life was like for the several hundred lords, ladies, guards, servants, and soldiers who called La Rochepot home. A tour of the castle shows you the dining room, kitchen, guards' chambers, and watch wall. *(Open Apr to Nov, closed Tuesday, tel: 03.80.21.71.37.)*

A short drive from Rochepot brings you to the intersection of the N6, which when followed south will take you past the vineyards of Puligny-Montrachet and then deliver you to the very scenic and historical wine region of the Chalonnais and the Mâconnais. The Côte Chalonnais is a geographic extension of the Côte de Beaune with its four thousand hectares of grapes planted from Chagny in the north to just north of Tournus. Leading vineyards of the Chalonnaise are Rully, Mercurey, Givry, and Montagny.

With its narrow streets winding down to the banks of the Saône, **Tournus** was once a prominent fishing town and the curious horizontal stones that pierce many of the town roofs are testament to that history. Fishing nets were draped on poles that were suspended between the stones, left to dry in the sun. Today the **Saint Philibert Abbey** (oldest of the great Romanesque churches of Burgundy), the **Perrin-de-Puycousin Museum** with its collections of traditional costumes and Bresse furniture, and the art museum dedicated to the local painter Jean-Baptiste Greuze are worth a visit. Tournus is also the northern geographic marker for the region of the Mâconnais. This is the largest and southernmost of the Burgundy wine districts with over 6,500 planted hectares. Chardonnay and Gamay grapes yield great fruity whites and rich reds and are distributed under famous labels such as **Mâcon**, Mâcon-Villages, and Pouilly-Fuissé.

From Tournus, we suggest you make a loop east and then south for an adventure that will include both architectural history and wine. From Tournus traveling the D14, it is approximately a 12-kilometer scenic drive to the medieval-walled town of **Brancion**. With a history that goes back to the 10th century, it was once considered one of the most strategic strongholds in southern Burgundy. It is necessary to park outside town and then venture by foot to explore this village where time seems almost to have stood still. It is interesting to visit the church with its lovely frescoes and the ruins of the old castle.

Brancion is situated almost equally distant from Tournus and the lovely **Château de Cormatin**. Surrounded by gorgeous gardens and heralded as having some of the most magnificent Louis XIII apartments left in France with its wonderful furnishings and tapestries, it is also famous as the site for many international meetings hosting heads of state from all over the world. (*Open Apr 1 to Jul 13, Aug 16 to Nov 11, Tel: 03 85 50 16 55.*)

From Cormatin, follow the well-signed 13 kilometers south along the D981 to **Cluny** and its famous Benedictine abbey, Saint-Pierre and Saint-Paul. Founded in 910, its abbots were considered as powerful and influencial as the kings or pope for the role they played in the ecclesiastical reform movement that reached to over 2000 monastaries throughout Western Europe. The present abbaye was built in 1089, and although much of it was destroyed during the French Revolution, its ruins embrace the narrow streets of town and stand proud on the horizon.

From Cluny travel 5 kilometers south on the D980 and then take the scenic D17 east (that parallels the N79), a road that wends its way through the charming hillside villages of **Berzé le Châtel, La Croix Blanche** and then **Berzé le Ville**. Built on a rocky outcrop just below the village of Berze le Ville is a lovely 12th-century chapel, **Chapelle des Moines**. Commissioned by the abbot of Cluny, its first structure was destroyed by a storm but then rebuilt by Italians. Intimate with a Byzantine-influence architecture, it is especially worth visiting for the gorgeous paintings that cover its vaulted walls. Their intensity of color is remarkable due to the fact that they were covered up by stucco and not discovered or exposed until the 19th century.

From Berzé la Ville cross over and pick up N79 traveling southeast until you see signs for small country towns are synonomous with the world's finest wines–Pouilly, Fuissé and Saint-Véran. A maze of country roads cross back and forth and journey through the vineyards that embrace these charming wine villages of Mâconnais. There are numerous wineries where one can stop and sample the liquid gold of the region, but we especially liked our visit at the **Château de Fuissé**, located at the heart of the town of the same name. Operated by Jean-Jacques Vincent and family, a visit here includes a tour of the cellars, the vineyards, and sampling their vintages. They are also set up to ship wines worldwide. (*www.chateau-fuisse.fr, tel: 03.85.35.61.44.*)

After exploring the wine towns it is a short distance on to Mâcon travel. From here one can catch the TGV on to other destinations or pick up the autoroute south to Lyon–one of France's most regal and gastronomique centers. A large city, you need to be armed with patience and a good map to negotiate to its historic center.

To the northwest of Lyon is the magical medieval village of **Pérouges**. Settled by the Romans and sentimentally named for the village they left, Perugia, this is an enchanting, walled, medieval village with cobbled streets, a few craft shops, restaurants (one must sample the local tarte) and a hotel. This medieval village was once home to farmers, craftsmen and weavers and although not rich in architecture, it remains much as it was in the middle ages. To visit is like stepping back in time. In fact we have the owners of the Ostellerie du Vieux Pérouges, (recommended in our France hotel guide), to thank for its preservation. At a time when all but a handful of residents had abandoned the town for more modern conveniences and appreciation for what was historic was forgotten, the town was slated for destruction. But the Thibaut Family started a foundation to preserve and restore Pérouges.

Pérouges is recommended as either a perfect end to this wine country journey or a convenient stopover before continuing on to explore our French Alps itinerary.

Wine Country Alsace

Strasbourg

Molsheim

A352

A35

Haut-ottrott

Obernai

Ottrott

Barr

Mittelbergheim

Andlau

Itterswiller

Colroy
la Roche

Blienschwiller

Dambach-la-Ville

Dieffenthal

Haut Koenigsbourg

D35

Scherwiller

Bergheim

N59

Sélestat

Ribeauvillé

GERMANY

Hunawihr

Col de Calvair
D48

Riquewihr

Zellenberg

Kaysersberg

D10

Kientzheim

Ammerschwihr

Route des Crêtes

D417

Col de la
Schlucht

Turckheim

Colmar

Munster

Eguisheim

Husseren

N83

A35

Hattstatt

Pfaffenheim

Rouffach

Paris

Thann

Mulhouse

A36

Basel

O Orientation

● Sightseeing

■■■ Itinerary route

SWITZERLAND

149

Wine Country–Alsace

Alsace borders Germany—in fact, from the Franco-Prussian war to the end of World War I Alsace was part of Germany. After World War II the district began to market its white wines sold in distinctive long, thin, green or brown bottles. The vineyards are at the foot of the Vosges mountains on east-facing hills set back from the broad Rhine river valley. The hills are never particularly steep or spectacular but are laced by narrow roads that wind along the vineyards from one picturesque village to the next. Villages such as Riquewihr and Kaysersberg are picture-book perfect with their painted eaves and gables, narrow cobbled streets, archways, and window boxes brimming with colorful geraniums.

Riquewihr

Recommended Pacing: Select a property in the wine region and use it as a base for your explorations of the area—two nights minimum. Finish your tour with a night or more in Strasbourg, a beautiful city. (Recommendations for places to stay can also be found in our France hotel guide.)

In Alsace, the wines are known by the names of the vineyards or villages and are identified by the type of grape from which they are made: Riesling, Gewürtztraminer, Muscat, or Pinot Gris, and sometimes by the phrase *réserve exceptionelle,* which indicates a higher price and premier wine. The grapes are similar to those used for German wines but the majority are used to make dry wines, not dessert wines.

Just before Mulhouse, a sprawling industrial city, leave the autoroute (exit 6) and take the N83, following signposts for Thann, around the outskirts of Cernay (signposted Colmar) to **Rouffach**. Nestled at the foot of the vineyards, this is a delightful town that is known in the region for its Festival of Witches, held the evening of the third Saturday of July, in

recognition of the sorcerers held captive in the tower so many centuries ago. Rouffach also has a wonderful park dedicated to the preservation of storks. As recently as the 1950s there were just seven breeding pairs, and as a direct result of efforts such as the protective park in Rouffach, there are now more than 250 pairs that are known to migrate from France to the African shores. Babies born here are kept in protective custody for three years until they are strong enough to sustain the long, arduous journey.

Surprisingly, altering their natural cycle in youth does not seem to influence or negate their natural instinct to migrate when released after maturity.

Just north of Rouffach is **Pfaffenheim**, a tiny wine village, where you leave the busy N83 to weave through the narrow village streets and into the vineyards to join the **Route du Vin**, a signposted routing that follows a winding itinerary through the vineyards. You soon arrive at **Gueberschwihr**, a cluster of gaily painted houses where, as you reach the village square, intricate painted signs advertise wine tasting in cobbled courtyards.

From the square, turn right and drive 2 kilometers to Hattstat, and on to Obermorschwir where the narrow road climbs steeply to **Husseren les Châteaux**, a cluster of homes with its castle perched high above the village.

Plan on spending some time in **Eguisheim**, a trim little medieval walled town complete with dungeon, lovely old timbered houses, shops, and restaurants set along narrow cobbled lanes. From Eguisheim the road drops down to the busy N83, which quickly brings you into Colmar.

Colmar is the largest town along the wine road and an important center for wine trade. Beyond the suburbs lies a pedestrian zone—an interesting mix of French and German culture and architecture. Short streets wind round old buildings between the plazas and lead you to the town's old quarter, with its intricately carved and leaning houses, known as **Petite Venise** because a shallow canal weaves its way through the narrow streets. Enterprising students offer gondola rides along the waterways, reminiscent of Venice.

Although Colmar is an easy city to explore on foot, with many streets restricted to pedestrians only, another option for touring the heart of the old town is a fun ride on the colorful train that chatters along the cobbled streets and offers an interesting commentary of the city's highlights. There are numerous craft, antique, and boutique shops, and a full offering of restaurants. When sightseeing, be sure to visit the Dominican monastery, now the **Unterlinden Museum** with an excellent collection of portraits and an exhibition of crafts and customs. One room is a re-created Alsatian vintner's cellar complete with wine presses. (*Closed Tues, Nov to Mar, tel: 03.89.20.15.50.*)

Colmar is an intimate city and one you will want to explore but it can also be used as a base from which to explore Strasbourg. It is a short commute by train between the two cities, and Strasbourg, a truly large city, is not as overwhelming to negotiate when you arrive conveniently *sans auto* at its center.

Just west of Colmar is the charming Alsatian village of **Turckheim**. Park outside the town walls and then venture inside to explore a maze of cobbled streets that boast numerous shops and restaurants—a wonderful town.

From Turckheim, make a detour off the Route du Vin up the D417. As the vineyards wane, the valley narrows and pine trees decorate the heights as you drive the 15 kilometers to **Munster**, situated at the foot of the Vosges. Munster is famous for being the home of the celebrated cheese, rather than for its picturesque streets.

From Munster, the D417 climbs and twists through green Alpine fields dotted with farms. Climbing higher, you enter a vast pine and oak forest to emerge at the summit, **Col de la Schlucht**, which offers spectacular views across the wild slopes of the Vosges mountains. Turn right on **Route des Crêtes** (D61), a skyline road constructed by the French during World War I to ensure communications between the different valleys. Now the route presents a scenic trip and signposts lead you to several beautiful spots that you can walk to before coming to **Col de Calvair**, a tiny ski resort. At Col du Bonhomme, join the D415, which travels down the ever-widening valley to Kaysersberg.

Kaysersberg rivals its neighbors as being one of the most appealing towns in Alsace. Vineyards tumble down to the town from its ancient keep and 16th-century houses line narrow roads along the rushing River Weiss. **Albert Schweitzer** was born here and his house is open as a small museum. (*Open May to Oct.*)

Leave Kaysersberg on the narrow D28 in the direction of Ribeauvillé and pass **Kientzheim**, a picture-perfect little village encircled by a high wall and surrounded by vineyards. Ammerschwihr, another charming town, and Riquewihr, the finest walled town and a gem of Alsace, lie just a few kilometers farther on, one to the south and one to the north.

Turn south from Kientzheim to the lovely walled town of **Ammerschwihr**, worth a detour if only to seek out its Porte Haute Cigognes, one of the entry towers, where each year storks nest—it is from here that their young test their first flight.

Just to the north of Kientzheim, **Riquewihr,** one of the most beautiful villages in Alsace, is completely enclosed by tall, protective walls and encircled by vineyards. It is easy to understand why this picturesque spot is a magnet for visitors. This picture-book village is a pedestrian area, its narrow streets lined with half-timbered houses. Signs beckon you into cobbled courtyards to sample the vintners' produce, and cafés and restaurants spill onto the streets. The local museum is housed in the tall square stone-and-timber tower **Dolder Gate** and **Tour des Voleurs** (Thieves' Tower), which exhibits grisly instruments of torture. (*Open Jul and Aug, closed Oct to Easter, open weekends rest of year, tel: 03.89.49.08.40.*)

Just beyond Riquewihr is another charming, picturesque town, **Zellenberg**, worth a detour off the Route du Vin, if only to circle up through its medieval streets and back down—here you find nothing commercial, just a pretty village.

Nearby **Hunawihr** boasts a much-photographed fortified church sitting on a little hill among the vineyards beside the village and the **Center for the Reintroduction of Storks**. Just a few years ago the roofs of the picture-book villages of Alsace were topped with shaggy storks' nests. Alas, in recent years fewer and fewer storks have returned from their winter migration to Africa and the center is dedicated to their reintroduction into the area. Concentrated within the boundary of the park are seemingly hundreds of the birds who build their nests on the multitude of frameworks provided. Storks born in the park are protected and kept until the age of three to establish the instinct of the park being a migratory base to which to return, season after season.

It is wonderful that the storks are returning in greater numbers each season and it is truly captivating to travel the region and look up to see the nests and pairs of large white, long-legged birds atop many of the region's rooftops. (*Closed Nov 11 to Apr, tel: 03.89.73.72.62.*)

Wine Country–Alsace

Rising behind the attractive town of **Ribeauvillé** are the three castles of Ribeaupierre, a much-photographed landmark of the region. The shady side streets with their beamed houses are quieter and contain some lovely buildings.

Continuing on the Route du Vin, just a few kilometers to the north is the charming town of **Bergheim**. Protected by its walls, Bergheim lies just off the main road and is a much quieter village than many along the wine route.

Haut Koenigsbourg

Continuing north from Bergheim, make a sharp left on the D1-bis at the medieval village of **Saint Hippolyte** and climb steeply up from the vineyards to **Haut Koenigsbourg**, the mighty fortress that sits high above the town. This massive castle was rather overzealously restored by Kaiser Wilhelm II in the early part of this century to reflect his concept of what a medieval fortress should look like, complete with massive walls, towering gates, a drawbridge, a keep, a bear pit, towers, a baronial great hall, and an armory. From the walls the view of vineyards tumbling to a sky-wide patchwork of fields that stretches to the Rhine river valley is superb. On especially clear days you can see the very distant outline of the Black Forest. (*Closed in Jan.*)

Leave the castle in the direction of Kintzheim and turn left on the D35 for **Chatenois**. Take the narrow entry into the town square and continue straight across the busy N59 on the D35 through **Scherwiller**, dominated by the ruined castles of Ortenbourg and Ramstein high on the hill above, through the vineyards to **Dieffenthal**, **Dambach la Ville**, where a bear clutching a flagon of wine between its paws decorates the fountain in front of the Renaissance town hall, and the wine village of **Blienschwiller** before arriving in the hillside village of Itterswiller.

Itterswiller has its attractive, timbered houses strung along the ridge facing south to the vineyards. This is a lovely village with lovely shops and lovely views.

Continuing north along the Route du Vin from Itterswiller, the road travels through a number of wine towns crowned by the ruins of their castles, **Château d'Haute Andlau**, **Château de Landsberg** above the larger wine town, **Barr**, and the **Château d'Ottrott** above the charming village of **Ottrott**. Between Andlau and Barr, it is worth the short detour off the wine road to drive up and through the village of **Mittelbergheim**, designated as one of France's Most Beautiful Villages. Although there are not many stores, Mittelbergheim boasts some of the region's best winemakers and many of their cellars are located along the village streets and are open to visitors.

From Ottrott, follow the road as it winds back toward the main road and the larger city of **Obernai**. If you like to shop, park on the main street through town and then investigate the maze of pedestrian streets with their enticing shops and restaurants.

Strasbourg, the *grande dame* of the region and one of France's most beautiful cities, is just a short distance northeast of Obernai on the border with Germany. Although, personally, I usually avoid large cities, Strasbourg is gorgeous and well worth the effort to navigate its miles of urban surround to penetrate its old quarter. Begin armed with a good map and take the time to chart a route before you begin the journey.

Set on the banks of the River Rhine where it meets the Ill, Strasbourg's city center is full of charm. The old quarter is an island banded by the River Ill, with the Place Kléber and the lacy pink-sandstone **Nôtre Dame Cathedral** at its core. It is filled with interesting little streets of shops, restaurants, and hotels and leads to the footbridges that span the River Ill. The nearby **Petite France** quarter, where craftsmen plied their trades in the 16th and 17th centuries, is full of old timbered houses, most notably the fine **Maison des Tanneurs** with its intricate wooden galleries. Many of the craftsmen's old workshops are now delightful restaurants.

From Strasbourg, you can cross into Germany's Black Forest, journey on into Switzerland, or travel a 350-kilometer drive (four hours) on the autoroute to Reims where you can join the Champagne wine route. It is also approximately a 300-kilometer drive (three and a half hours) from Strasbourg to the heart of the Burgundy region and Beaune, reputed to be the capital of the wine industry.

Old Strasbourg, Petite France

Wine Country–Alsace

Wine Country Champagne

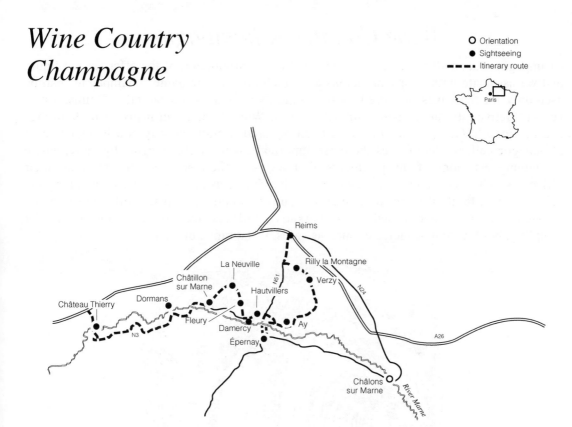

Wine Country–Champagne

Champagne is a small wine district dedicated to the production of the effervescent liquid that we associate with happy occasions and celebrations. The name "champagne" can be used only for the wines produced by this region's vineyards. Its capital is Reims, a not-very-attractive city due to being almost razed in World War I, but many of its buildings and its fine old Gothic cathedral have been restored. Below the city is a honeycomb of champagne cellars. Nearby lies the most important town for champagne, Épernay, where the mighty mansions of the producers alternate with their *maisons* (the term for their offices, warehouses, cellars, and factories). The vineyards are south of Reims, along the valley of the Marne. It is not particularly beautiful countryside, just gentle slopes facing towards the sun, interspersed with workaday villages that offer opportunities for sampling, but few tourist facilities such as cafés, restaurants, or shops.

Épernay, Mercier Champagne Cellar

Recommended Pacing: Our Champagne itinerary covers a very small geographic area. We suggest you spend two or three nights in the region. Any of the properties we recommend in the region would serve as a convenient base from which to explore and sample the bounty of Champagne.

Unlike wines from Burgundy, the quality of champagne is not derived solely from the area but also from the manufacturing process. It is the dose of sugar or "bead" that makes the bubbles, and the smaller the bead, the better the champagne. The essence of champagne is the blending of several different grapes; a branded wine, it is known by the maker and not by the vineyard. There are three distinct zones in the 55,000 acres in Champagne: the *Montagne de Reims*, the *Vallée de la Marne*, and *Côte des Blancs*. This itinerary visits the champagne houses in Reims and Épernay and drives round the Mountain of Reims and along the Valley of the Marne before returning you to Paris.

This journey begins in **Reims**, once the capital of France (4th to 9th centuries) and now one of the capitals of the Champagne district. The **Nôtre Dame Cathedral** dates from the 12th century and is where the kings of France used to be crowned (follow signs for *Centre Ville*). Begun in 1211, it is one of the oldest examples of Gothic architecture in France, and while it suffered heavy damage in World War I, it was beautifully restored in 1938. Traffic around the cathedral is terribly congested.

You may want to save your cellar tours until Épernay, but if you like to visit a house in each city, several invite you to come by without appointment. While the basic procedures and methods used to produce champagne are similar, the grand names for champagne all have their own history and interesting stories to tell. Tours are available in English and take about an hour. Except in July and August the houses are usually closed between 11:30 am and 2 pm.

Mumm, 34 Rue de Champ de Mar, offers a film, guided tour of the cellars, and tasting. (*Closed weekends in winter, tel: 03.26.49.59.70.*)

At **Piper-Hiedsieck**, 51 Blvd. Henry Vasnier, visitors tour the galleries in six-passenger cars that take you on a Disney-like tour of the cellars with giant dioramas of grapes and interesting explanations on the production of champagne from harvest to disgorging. (*Open Mar to Jan, tel: 03.26.84.43.44.*)

Pommery, 5 Place du Général Gourard, offers a film, guided tour of the cellars, and tasting. (*Closed Christmas to New Years, tel: 03.26.61.62.56.*)

Taittinger, 9 Place Saint-Nicaise, offers a film, guided tour of the cellars, and tasting. (*Open all year, tel: 03.26.85.84.33.*)

Leave Reims south in the direction of Épernay (N51). After leaving the suburbs and light industrial areas behind, when you're among the fields and vineyards, take the first left turn signposted **Route du Champagne**, which charts a very pleasant horseshoe-shaped drive around the **Montagne de Reims** to Épernay. Above, the vineyards end in

Faux de Verzy

woodlands and below, they cascade to the vast plain, the scene of so much fighting during World War I.

The first small village you come to on the D26 is **Villers Allerand**, which leads you to **Rilly la Montagne**, a larger village which offers the opportunity for a stroll and a drink in a café as well as the chance to sip champagne. As you drive along, look for the peculiar-looking tractors with their high bodies and wheels set at a width that enables them to pass through the rows of vines and meander down the little lanes.

As the route nears **Mailly Champagne** and **Verzy**, you pass some of the most superior vineyards for the production of champagne grapes. The picturesque windmill found between the two villages was used as an observation post during World War I.

The wine route rounds the mountain at Verzy where a short detour up into the woodlands brings you to **Faux de Verzy**, an unusual forest of gnarled, stunted, and twisted beech trees hundreds of years old. Return to Verzy and continue along the D26, turning south through **Villers Marmery**, **Trépail**, and **Ambonnay** to **Bouzy**, a community famous not only for its champagne grapes but also for its red wine. At Bouzy the wine route splits and our route follows signposts into nearby Épernay.

Traffic is much less of a problem in **Épernay** than Reims. While much of the damage has been repaired, there are still several scars from the severe bombing that Épernay suffered in World War I. Follow signposts for *Centre Ville* and particularly *Office de Tourisme,* which brings you to your destination in this sprawling town, the Rue de Champagne, a long street lined with the *maisons* and mansions of the premier champagne producers Möet et Chandon, Perrier Jouët, Charbaut, De Venoge Pol Roger, and Mercier.

Try to allow time to take both the Möet et Chandon and Mercier cellar tours. **Möet et Chandon**, founded in 1743, is across the street from the tourist office. They offer a very sophisticated tour of their visitors' center (where Napoleon's hat is displayed), a walk through one of the largest champagne cellars in the world, and an excellent explanation on how champagne is made. (*Open all year, tel: 03.26.51.20.00.*)

Just as the Rue de Champagne leaves behind its grand mansions, you come to **Mercier's** modern visitors' center where the world's largest wine cask sits center stage. Holding the equivalent of 200,000 bottles of champagne, it was made to advertise Mercier at the World Trade Fair in Paris in 1889 and proved as great an attraction as the Eiffel Tower. Houses that interrupted its progress to Paris had to be razed. Mercier's tour gives you an upbeat movie history of Mercier champagne, then whisks you down to the galleries in a glass-sided elevator past a diorama of the founders ballooning over their estate. An electric train weaves you through the vast cellars past some interesting carvings and boundless bottles of bubbly. (*Closed Tues and Wed, Nov to Mar, tel: 03.26.51.22.22.*)

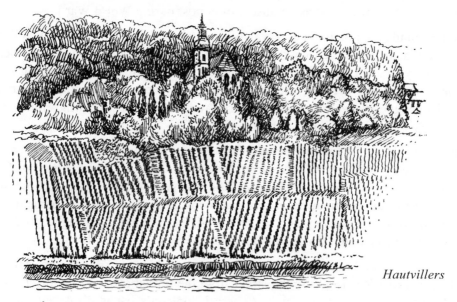

Hautvillers

Leaving Épernay, follow signposts for Reims until you see the Route de Champagne signpost to both the left and right. Turn left to **Ay** and follow the route along the Vallée de la Marne to **Hautvillers**, the prettiest of Champagne's villages with its spic-and-span homes and broad swatch of cobbles decorating the center of its streets. It was in the village basilica that Dom Perignon performed his miracle and discovered how to make still wine sparkling by the *méthode champenoise*. He also introduced the use of cork stoppers (tied down to stop them from popping out as pressure built up in the bottles) and blended different wines from around the region to form a wine with a superior character than that produced by a single vineyard. The abbey is now owned by Möet et Chandon and contains a private museum. However, you can enjoy the lovely view of the valley from the abbey terrace.

From Hautvillers, descend through the vineyards to **Cumièrs**, a workaday village known for its red wine, and on to **Damery** with its pretty 12th- and 16th-century church. Climbing through vineyards, you have lovely views across the River Marne to the villages and vineyards strung along the opposite bank.

Pass through **Venteul** and **Arty** and on to the more attractive village of **Fleury**, which offers tasting in the large building decorated with murals. As you climb through pretty countryside to **Belval**, vineyards give way to fields. Passing through woodland, you come to **La Neuville aux Larris** with its enormous champagne bottle sitting next to the church, and return to the River Marne at **Châtillon-sur-Marne**. A huge statue overlooking the river proclaims this village as the birthplace of Pope Urban II.

At **Verneuil** cross the river and continue on the N3 into **Dormans**, which saw fierce fighting in World War I and was badly damaged. Set in a large green park, the **Chapelle de la Reconnaissance** (Chapel of Gratitude) commemorates those killed in the battles of the Marne in 1914 and 1918 and offers splendid views over the valley. You can quickly return to Épernay on the N3 or continue to Paris via **Château Thierry**, set on the River Marne against a lovely wooded backdrop. The English claimed the town as theirs in 1421 then Joan of Arc recaptured it for France. The gates through which she entered the city still stand—**Porte Saint Pierre**. Napoleon defended the city against Russian and Prussian troops in 1814.

Wine Country–Champagne

The French Alps

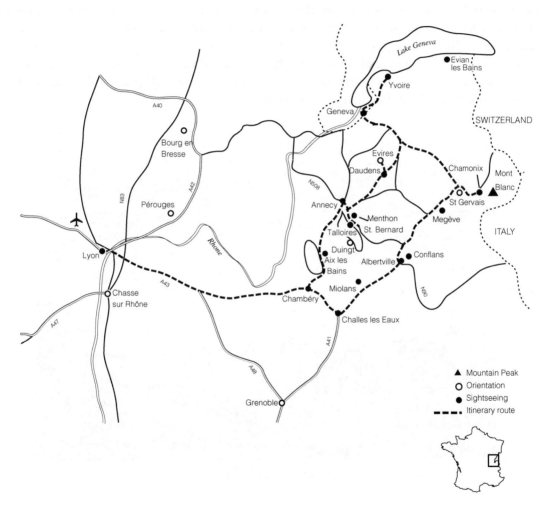

Mountain Peak ▲
Orientation ○
Sightseeing ●
Itinerary route

167

The French Alps

The French Alps encompasses a beautiful region tucked to the south of the shores of Lake Geneva with majestic peaks establishing a natural border between Italy, France, and Switzerland. This is a region of towering mountains, Alpine valleys, lakes, and rivers, a region that will be appreciated by all who share a love of nature and the mountains—both the sportsman and the photographer. It is a region to be enjoyed year round, but a chameleon with its dramatic changes in seasonal dress.

Mont Blanc, Chamonix

The French Alps

Recommended pacing: This itinerary assumes your travels will both begin and end in Geneva. However, it is important to note that if you are traveling along the Rhône Valley, it is also easy to make an itinerary loop of this region with Lyon as the originating city. If your travels begin in Geneva, you will most definitely want to spend a few nights here to enjoy this elegant city just across the Swiss border. With a beautiful waterfront setting, gardens, fountains, and bridges spanning the river that weaves through the city, Geneva is intimate in size. It is easy to walk and explore its many distinctive districts, from the elegant shopping streets and regal residential quarters to the cobbled streets of its old quarter. (For recommendations of places to stay in Geneva, either refer to our guide, *Switzerland: Charming Inns & Itineraries* or visit our website, *www.karenbrown.com.*) Once you leave Geneva, it is recommended that you select one place to stay for a minimum of two nights in one of the key mountain towns such as Chamonix or Megève, and then select a base for two nights for exploring the lake region of Annecy. Before returning to Geneva, we strongly recommend an excursion to medieval Yvoire, a little way beyond the city on the shores of Lake Geneva. If your trip originates in Lyon, again we would recommend two nights near Lake Annecy, two nights in the mountains near Mont Blanc, and then a night in Geneva as well as a visit to the charming village of Yvoire on the edge of Lake Geneva.

From **Geneva**, travel a gorgeous, narrow valley shadowed by towering peaks in the direction of Chamonix and Mont Blanc. If you're in a rush you could take the autoroute, but the N205 parallels the autoroute and seems just as efficient and perhaps prettier as it travels through the villages. This area is absolutely gorgeous in spring and summer, with a dramatic backdrop of high snow-covered peaks that contrast with lush green pastures dotted with chalets, grazing cattle, and an abundance of wildflowers. The many ski lifts and gondolas that climb from the villages indicate that this is definitely a winter sport destination, but in other seasons, parachutes color the skies and mountain trails, waterfalls, and mountain peaks beckon and challenge all abilities.

The resort town of **Chamonix** is nestled in a valley of the same name that stretches 20 kilometers between the towering Mont Blanc range to the south and the Aiguilles Rouges

Mountains to the north. Considered the ultimate winter and summer resort, Chamonix was home to the first Winter Olympics in 1924 and boasts the highest summit in Europe, the towering peak of **Mont Blanc**. Although of international renown and acclaim, Chamonix retains the ambiance of a small mountain town, especially in the pedestrian village of Chamonix Sud with its charming, weathered *chalets chamoniards* individualized by their elegantly painted façades, shopping arcades, an intimate town square, and the delightful Rue du Moulins.

From Chamonix, retrace your path traveling west and then turn south toward the charming Alpine village of **Megève**. Described as the "essence of rustic chic," the town was conceived in the 1920s to be France's version of Switzerland's St. Moritz. Ideally located for visiting many of the region's exclusive resorts (St. Gervais, Combloux, Les Contamines, and Chamonix), Megève boasts a number of gourmet restaurants, luxury boutique hotels, and gorgeous shops. At its core, a pedestrian zone preserves its character and minimizes the impact of crowds, who are forced to utilize one of the many parking garages on the perimeter.

In the shadow of Mont Blanc, all the Haute Savoie villages offer the sportsman both a winter and summer paradise. In winter you can enjoy: paragliding, hot springs, downhill skiing, cross-country skiing, helicopter skiing, snowmobiling, Turkish-bath saunas, ice-skating, curling, and Megève's casino. Summer attractions include: spa treatments, mountain biking, walking, tennis, golf, archery, paragliding, lake and river fishing, rafting, swimming, the summer luge, horse-back riding, mountaineering, and the tramway.

From Megève, it is a beautiful drive following the Arly River as it cuts a path through a rugged, narrow mountain canyon to the city of **Albertville**. Albertville, built on the valley floor after flood channels were dug to eliminate flooding, became the area's new commercial center. Its predecessor, the old walled town of Conflans, still remains, strategically positioned on the hillside above the city and the confluence of the Arly and Isère rivers. Dating back to Roman times, the town is fun to explore with its ancient fortifications, buildings, and cobbled streets.

A bustling city, Albertville was home to the 1992 Olympic Winter Games. The year marked the first Olympics since the reunification of Germany in 1990 and the breakup of the Soviet Union in 1991, and resulted in a record 2,174 athletes from 65 countries. This was also the last time the Winter Games were held in the same year as the Summer Games. Only 18 of the 57 events were held in Albertville itself, while nearby resorts hosted the rest.

Continuing south along the Isère, the beauty of the region wanes a bit past Albertville until the silhouette of castle ruins appears at **Miolans**. In the 10th century this impressive fortress was commissioned by the Miolans family on the site of an ancient settlement. It was later confiscated by the Dukes of Savoy who used the fortress as a prison. Over a period of 200 years it served to confine 192 prisoners, the most famous of whom was the Marquis de Sade, who managed to escape. The château overlooks the Combe de Savoie valley, a rich wine-growing region that extends from Miolans, dips south at Montmeilian, and then continues north to Calles les Eaux. The various varietals grown in the region include Pinot, Gamay, Mondeuse, Chardonnay, and Altesse.

Chambéry, the capital of the counts and dukes of Savoy during the 14th century, is located just south of the **Lac du Bourget**, in the heart of the French Alps. Dominated by the castle, the remarkable old town is preserved as a pedestrian area and has lovely old mansions, dramatic fountains, and intriguing alleys lined with cafés.

It is just a short drive on to the Lac du Bourget and **Aix les Bains,** its principal resort town, which is very touristy and full of sun-worshipers. However, I much prefer the lovely **Lac d'Annecy** to the northeast. Nestled on its northern shore is the beautiful city of **Annecy**, crowned by its silhouetted castle. The city enjoys a lovely old pedestrian district transected by waterways and gardens along the waterfront, a magnet in warm weather for sun seekers who blanket its lawn. Numerous boat excursions originate from its harbor to explore the lake and Alpine setting.

Château de Miolans

From Annecy, roads depart along both the west and east banks of Lac d'Annecy. The drive along the east bank is definitely the prettiest, with little villages whose homes and hotels cluster along the waterfront. Detour just off the riverfront to visit the ornate turreted château above **Menthon St. Bernard.** Far away from the workaday hustle, nestling in a vast park, the stone towers of Menthon St. Bernard's castle dominate the lake. A baronial residence, it has passed down to descendants of the same family since the 11th century.

Talloires, a lovely village with one of the prettiest settings along the lake, is found about a third of the way south from Annecy along the eastern shore. Nestled in a serene alcove on the lakeshore, this would be a lovely place to lunch at one of its terrace restaurants. From Talloires you can also enjoy views across the narrow stretch of lake to the decorative towers of Duingt.

If you are fond of pottery, travel northeast from Annecy following the N203 (in the direction of Chamonix and Thonon les Bains) and turn off at Daudens, following signs to **Evires**. After crossing the railroad tracks, turn right just before town to find the pottery workshop and museum, housed in an old farm, of master potter Jean Christophe Hermann, considered the best in the region. Founded in 1981, the museum enjoys a rich collection of over two million pieces. This is considered one of the finest collections of Savoyard pottery in the world. (*L'Atelier de Poterie. Visits by reservation only, tel: 04.50.62.01.90*)

Before circling back to Geneva, head to the lakeshore just to the northeast of the city, to the picturesque village of **Yvoire**. With its 700-year-old castle, ramparts, and tower gates, Yvoire is an enchanting medieval village situated on the French side of Lake Geneva. Cars are not permitted within the walls and so wandering the narrow cobbled streets and the paths along its shore and harbor is both peaceful and scenic. Although it is a convenient half-hour drive back to Geneva from Yvoire, you can also travel the distance by train or boat (one hour). Numerous lake excursions are offered from the port.

The French Alps

Bed & Breakfast Descriptions

As you first enter the driveway of Domaine de la Brillane, you'll pass through a peaceful vineyard: a fitting entrance to this enchanting experience. After twenty years in the financial world, Rupert, who's English, decided to change his career. He bought the vineyard and Mary, who's Belgian, joined him. Together they built their dream: a vineyard first, and then a handsome and intimate bed and breakfast. Your charming hosts do their best to make your stay unforgettable. And it's clear that they achieve that goal, because staying in such a delightful bed and breakfast is an experience equaled only by the adventure of discovering new wines through the passion of your hosts. Guestrooms are in a separate part of the house, so privacy is never an issue. Each of the five rooms (all named after a vine) is spacious and comfortable, with contemporary furnishings and up-to-date conveniences. The Cabernet Sauvignon was my favorite, with breathtaking views over the Sainte Victoire mountain (the source of inspiration to Cézanne and many others). In the morning, enjoy a wonderful breakfast surrounded by pine and oak trees, and afterward why not go for a wine tour with Rupert? *Directions:* From Aix, take direction Gap/Sisteron, A51. Drive to the N296 and exit N12 Aix les Platanes. On your left is Le Puy St. Reparade. After a few miles you'll see a sign on your left for Couteron. Follow the sign to Domaine de la Brillane.

DOMAINE DE LA BRILLANE
Hosts: Mary & Rupert Birch Mertens
195 Route de Couteron
13100 Aix en Provence, France
Tel: 04.42.54.21.44, Fax: 04.42.54.31.25
5 Rooms, Double: €120–€160
Open: all year, Credit cards: MC, VS
Other Languages: English, Spanish
Region: Provence-Alps-Côte d'Azur, Michelin Map: 528

Set in the center of the sweet town of Amboise, within walking distance of the famous château, Le Vieux Manoir is almost too pretty to be real. At first glance it looks like a painting of a storybook-perfect little French manor house, enhanced by lush lawns, carefully trimmed shrubbery, lovely trees, and beautiful flowers in perfectly manicured gardens. A high wall shields the property from the street so it is not until you enter the gates that you see the creamy-white home with pretty blue shutters and a steep slate mansard roof accented by perky dormer windows. Gloria and Bob Belknap (who previously owned one of Boston's most elegant bed and breakfasts, the Terrace Townhouse) saw the property while visiting friends in the Loire and, with a dream of someday moving to France, looked beyond the dilapidated exterior and saw a potentially lovely home. Skillful renovations have transformed the house and now it is beautifully decorated and as perfect inside as out. You come into a charming, comfortable salon with a beautiful handcrafted copy of a 19th-century conservatory, which looks out to another exquisite little garden. Gloria has decorated the cute bedrooms with loving care and great taste, using wonderful antique pieces. If you are staying at least three days, you can one of the two 17th-century cottages on the grounds. Each one has a living room, kitchen and garden setting. *Directions:* Ask for driving directions.

LE VIEUX MANOIR
Hosts: Gloria & Bob Belknap
13, Rue Rabelais
37400 Amboise, France
Tel & Fax: 02.47.30.41.27
6 Rooms, Double: €130–€195
1 Cottage: €210 daily
Open: all year, Credit cards: MC, VS
Other Languages: fluent English
Region: Center, Michelin Map: 518

A country lane delivers you to the doorstep of Les Aubépines, an old restored working farm nestled on lush acreage. This cozy and intimate timbered brick farmhouse has a fairy-tale appearance—windows are shuttered, dormers pop through the angles and pitches of the second-story roof, and the front façade is stacked high with firewood. When we arrived, Yves was mowing his vast lawn but was not too busy to give us a warm welcome and an offer of refreshing cider. We found Françoise inside and settled with her in front of the open fire in the main salon, a very inviting room with windows opening on to the surrounding greenery and heavy old beams hung with a mélange of pottery, copper pots, and fresh flowers. The Closson Mazes offer table d'hôte to guests on a pre-arranged basis, using regional as well as many homegrown products. An open stairwell climbs from the main room to a comfy loft sitting area and two guestrooms. Both are attractive: the pink room has a shower and the yellow room enjoys the privacy of its own back stair and has a private bath. At the other end of the hallway is a suite of rooms, which affords a family with private, comfortable living space. A swimming pool is also available to guests. *Directions:* 13 km southeast of Pont Audemer. Coming from Paris, take the A13 to exit 26 towards Pont Audemer. After 3 km, at the Medine roundabout, take D89 towards Evreux. Turn left immediately after the Les Marettes sign then Chambres d'Hôtes signs.

LES AUBÉPINES AUX CHAUFFOURNIERS
Hosts: Françoise & Yves Closson Maze
5 Chemin de la Bergerie, Les Chauffourniers
27290 Appeville–Annebault, France
Tel & Fax: 02.32.56.14.25
2 Rooms, Double: €65–€70, 1 Suite: €65–€105
Minimum Stay Required, Table d'hôte: €25
Open: Mar to Sep & off season by reservation
Credit cards: none
Other Languages: fluent English, Spanish
Region: Upper Normandy, Michelin Map: 513

This pleasant property is located just five minutes away from the bustling town of Uzès, which dates back to Roman times. Your friendly hosts, Clive and Diane, both from England and passionate Francophiles, spent 18 months restoring this stone Provençal farmhouse into the wonder that it is today. Each of the four spacious guestrooms has its own entrance off the heavily antique-accented living room and library. On the ground floor is the "figuier" guestroom (all are named after trees), furnished with Louis Philippe pieces, stone walls, and a gorgeous tiled floor. This room, our favorite for its stylish and cozy ambiance, has the added bonus of a terrace with a river view. The three other rooms located upstairs all have lovely wood floors, comfortable furnishings, and of course, en-suite bathrooms. The "cherry" room has a dazzling view over the pool and the grounds. Outside there's a charming courtyard where, under the shade of wisterias, a bountiful breakfast is served in the mornings and delicious beverages in the evenings. Enjoy a soak in the refreshing pool or take a stroll through the well-tended gardens, surrounded by colorful flowers. And don't forget to visit the enchanting Uzès, which has numerous antique shops, cafes, and a must-see outdoor market on Wednesdays and Saturdays. *Directions:* From Uzès, follow the D982 to Arpaillargues. On the right you'll see the signpost for Le Mas du Moulin, just before the River Les Seynes.

LE MAS DU MOULIN   **New**
Route d'Uzès
30700 Arpaillargues, France
Tel & Fax: 04.66.58.46.42
4 Rooms, Double: €80–€110
1 Apartment: €350–€550 weekly
Table d'hote: €25
Open: Mar to Oct, Credit cards: none
Region: Languedoc-Roussillon, Michelin Map: 526

Enter through a dramatic old gate and continue to the end of a peaceful lane bordered by plane and olive trees, as well as vineyards, and you are rewarded with Le Vallon. If you're fortunate, Michèle and Fred will be present to greet you. A charming couple, they extend a warm and gracious welcome. After living many years in the Basque country, Michèle and Fred decided to change their life and bought this 18th-century mansion. They dedicated five years to renovations and the result is an absolute jewel. They have preserved many original elements such as stone walls, ceiling beams, floor tile and even the built-in old armoire in the living room. This elegant two-story house offers three spacious bedrooms and one suite—all decorated with fine antiques and Provencal fabrics. Each room has a bathtub and shower and all very luxurious in their amenities. They all enjoy magnificent views. Surrounded by four acres of park, the inviting pool is a restful place to lounge and take advantage of the adjacent fully equipped summer kitchen. As an added bonus, you are welcome to help yourself to the bounty of their vegetable and fruit garden. Le Vallon is a dream come true for your hosts, whose passion and love for their intimate home is contagious. *Directions:* From Avignon take D942 and exit at Loriol du Comtat. At the roundabout take the 3rd exit and continue on D107. Then turn right on D126, and Chemin des Serres will be on your left. Continue on until the blue sign "Le Vallon".

LE VALLON   **New**
Hosts: Michèle & Fred Vogt
Domaine le Vallon, Chemin De Serres
84810 Aubignan, France
Tel: 04.90.62.71.27
3 Rooms, 1 Suite, Double: €140–€200
Minimum Stay Required: 2 nights
Open: Apr to Oct, Credit cards: all major
Other Languages: English, French, German, Italian
Region: Provence-Alps-Côte d'Azur, Michelin Map: 528

A breathtakingly lovely Renaissance castle, the Château de la Verrerie offers the comfort and refinement of an English country home coupled with incomparable French flair for artful decoration and fine cuisine. Each guest bedroom is spacious and unique, with its own color scheme and special charm. Laguiche is a gorgeous room decorated in colors of blue and yellow and its bathroom boasts two tubs—one for the parent and one for the child. Marquise was Count Béraud's great-grandmother's room and it was in a small sitting alcove in the turret off her bedroom that she used to mesmerize her grandchildren with stories of old. Rooms vary in price depending on their size but they are all lovely and some of the smallest are most charming. All enjoy views out to the well-manicured lawns and gardens, which extend to nearby woods or across to the serene lake. An inviting guest sitting room combines warmth and elegance to a perfect degree. Relax in this esthetically beautiful setting, tour the historic chapel and Renaissance gallery and enjoy gourmet lunches and dinners served in the neighboring La Maison d'Helène. This restaurant, in a cozy, beamed 18th-century cottage, features regional dishes and fine wines. *Directions:* Located 44 km northeast of Bourges. From Bourges travel north on the D940 for 34 km. At La Chapelle d'Angillon travel northeast on D926 for 6 km to Le Grand Rond. La Verrerie, 4 km north, is reached by the D39 and D89.

CHÂTEAU DE LA VERRERIE
Host: Comte Béraud de Vogüé
Oizon, 18700 Aubigny sur Nère, France
Tel: 02.48.81.51.60, Fax: 02.48.58.21.25
10 Rooms, Double: €160–€270, 2 Suites: €370*
*Breakfast not included: €14
Table d'hôte: €35 & Restaurant
Closed: Christmas, Jan 15 to Feb 14
Credit cards: all major, Other Languages: fluent English
Châteaux & Hôtels Collection
Region: Center, Michelin Map: 518

About halfway between Meursault and the village of Rochepot, just past Auxey-Duresses, you find the hamlet of Melin and a family-owned château converted to B&B. Turn at the gîte sign and you will be rewarded by the peacefulness of the setting as soon as you pass through the main gates. A side passage delivers you into the courtyard and the B&B office. Very successful as vintners, it might be necessary to search for your hosts—they are often in the tasting room offering samples of their award winning labels. A staircase off the graveled courtyard climbs to the Maranges (named for their 1er Cru), a charming, intimate room with a view over the courtyard and a bathroom off to the side with an open, tiled shower which can communicate by a side door with the Gevrey Chambertin suite. The suite enjoys a large bedroom with sitting area and a small side twin-bedded room. Climbing the turret stair once again leads to the Meursault suite. Decorated with beige and pastel blue colors with a king size bed, this also has a sitting room overlooking both the courtyard and the rooftops of the neighboring village and a small second twin-bedded room with a background hue of soft violet. Pommard is handsome with wonderful old wood floors whose décor incorporates reds and leather. Breakfast is served whenever guests want it in a beautiful large dining room or on the terrace. *Directions:* From Beaune, take the N74 towards Châlon; just south of town, take the D973 for Rochepot.

CHÂTEAU DE MELIN
Hosts: Hélène & Arnaud Derats
Hameau de Melin
21190 Auxey-Duresses, France
Tel: 03.80.21.21.19, Fax: 03.80.21.21.72
4 Rooms, Double: €95–€125
2 Suites: €120–€195
Open: all year, Credit cards: none
Other Languages: good English
Region: Burgundy, Michelin Map: 519

La Bihourderie was once home to the Bohor, who trained the knights at jousting tournaments during the Middle Ages. La Bihourderie is a long, low farmhouse draped in ivy and full of character. White shuttered windows peek out from this picturesque one-story home, further enhanced by a very steep roof which is prettily accented by gabled windows. La Bihourderie is a family home and is extremely appealing. The tidy front courtyard abounds with beautifully tended, colorful flower gardens. There is a separate section of the house with a private parlor just for guests, off which you find the five bedrooms, named after works of art by Van Gogh. Les Iris is attractively decorated with fabrics blending with the framed copy of Van Gogh's painting of the iris and Les Blés Jaunes has clever touches of tied wheat bunches. When the days are warm, breakfast is served at tables set outside on the lawn behind the house, so wonderfully close to the fields. Crops alternate with each year from wheat to sunflowers. I hope you're there when the sunflowers are in full bloom coloring the landscape yellow. *Directions:* From Tours, take the N143 towards Loches. Go through Cormery, then turn left 10 km after Cormery in the direction of Azay-sur-Indre. The Chambres d'Hôtes sign is on your left.

LA BIHOURDERIE
Host: Naomi Berthonneau
37310 Azay-sur-Indre, France
Tel: 02.47.92.58.58
4 Rooms, Double: €53–€58
1 Suite: €70
Table d'hôte: €20
Open: all year, Credit cards: all major
Other Languages: fluent English
Region: Center, Michelin Map: 518

In the hills near Toulon, the Zerbibs opened their lovely home as a bed and breakfast. Marceau Zerbib, a talented architect, completely renovated the house so that there are now four attractive guest bedrooms, a separate studio, all tastefully appointed in a quiet, elegant manner with country antiques enhanced by lovely fabrics. The home (a traditional Provençal-style structure with a heavy tiled roof and green shutters) has a parklike setting that is captivating. The gardens are spectacular, with a lush lawn sweeping away behind the house to steps leading down to a lower terrace with a large pool surrounded by comfortable lounge chairs. Overlooking the pool is a protected terrace and a cheerful blue-and-white tiled outdoor kitchen where guests may prepare a light meal. Well-tended gardens abound—the display of flowers everywhere is magnificent. In the background the property extends to a setting of pine and olive trees. Neither Charlotte nor Marceau speaks English, but their hospitality is so genuine that language barriers are quickly overcome. *Directions:* From the A50 (about 11 km west of Toulon), take the Bandol exit and follow signs to Le Beausset on the D559. Go through the village and take the second right at the roundabout. In about a block, turn right on the tiny road beside the bakery (Chemin de Cinq-Sous) and continue for 1.1 km. Turn left at a small lane signposted Les Cancades.

LES CANCADES
Hosts: Charlotte & Marceau Zerbib
1195, Chemin Fontaine de 5 Sous
83330 Le Beausset, France
Tel: 04.94.98.76.93
4 Rooms, Double: €75–€85
2 Suites: €130–€140
Studio: €150 daily; €750 weekly (Jul & Aug)
Open: all year, Credit cards: none
Other Languages: no English
Region: Provence-Alps-Côte d'Azur, Michelin Map: 527

The Villa le Goëland is spectacular; the setting, accommodations, and your hosts, Paul and Elizabeth. On a hilltop embraced by the ocean, this lovely, turreted villa displays a sweeping panorama from the coast of Spain, across the old port, intimate fishing harbor, beach, casino, and lighthouse-to the Bay of Gascony. A regal, yet intimate, home; the first floor entry has gorgeous paneling and a dramatic staircase climbing to a balustrade above. Just off the entry is a lovely salon that serves as the reception. Pass through the glass double doors to a large room that runs the length of the villa and accommodates a dining room and living room and then opens onto an expanse of wrap-around porch. Breakfast is an opportunity to meet other guests and partake of freshly baked goods, yogurt, juices, and Paul's own homemade strawberry jam. On warm days, breakfast is served on the terrace with the glistening, blue sea as the backdrop. The balustered walkway accesses the three guestrooms; each with its own unique charm and corner location and double views. "Ravize" is the smallest with Juliette balconies and a multi-jet shower. "Goëland" spacious in a blue and white décor, enjoys the luxury of a terrace. And "Montebello" exceptionally large, offers wonderful views and an enormous bathroom with a deep, claw-foot tub. *Directions:* Plateau de l'Atalaya is located above the heart of town between Plage du Port Vieux and Port des Pecheurs.

VILLA LE GOËLAND
Hosts: Paul & Elisabeth Daraignez
12 Plateau de l'Atalaye
64200 Biarritz, France
Tel: 05.59.24.25.76
4 Suites: €150–€270
Open: all year, Credit cards: MC, VS
Region: Aquitaine, Michelin Map: 524

Named for the 8 hectares of grand cru vineyards that stretch above the town, the Hotel Winzenberg is a simple, clean little hotel offering good value for money and a warm welcome. The Dresch family, involved in the wine business for many generations, have now achieved great success in the hospitality business. Alexia competently and graciously oversees the welcome and comfort of guests. The building's dark-orange gabled façade is easy to spot on the village's main street, a location that means there is a fair amount of traffic noise during the day, though very little at night. The entrance is set back off its own small courtyard and just off the entry a large room with soft-yellow walls and exposed beams is the gathering spot for the hearty breakfast buffet. Guestrooms are similar in decor, with just the color scheme varying. Three of the bedrooms have balconies and they would definitely be the ones to request—especially in the summer when it is nice to sit out for an afternoon glass of wine. Adding a special touch to the decor are the pretty painted murals of Alsatian town and vineyard scenes commissioned specifically for the hotel, which are attractively painted on many of the headboards and dresser tables. While the hotel does not serve evening meals, a popular winestube, Le Pressoir de Bacchus, is just two doors away. *Directions:* Blienschwiller is located on the Route du Vin between Barr and Dambach la Ville.

HOTEL WINZENBERG
Host: Alexia Horning
58, Route des Vins
67650 Blienschwiller, France
Tel: 03.88.92.62.77, Fax: 03.88.92.45.22
13 Rooms, Double: €45–€53*
*Breakfast not included: €6,90
Open: Feb 20 to Jan 3, Credit cards: all major
Other Languages: good English
Region: Alsace, Michelin Map: 516

Le Clos des Saunières, located just a few miles away from Beaune, makes an excellent base from which to explore the area. Fabienne and Bruno bought this 18th-century property in 2005, and spent a full year of renovations. This property has a very special feel to it, and with its two-acre garden and vineyards, the setting is gorgeous. The five bedrooms are all very charming, each named after a grape variety; three are located on the main floor and two suites are on the first floor. All are decorated with care and detail by Fabienne. Furnishings are rustic antiques. They have brand new bathrooms and some rooms have beamed ceilings and exposed stones on the walls. Located in a peaceful hamlet, you will enjoy breakfast on the grounds where tables are set on the grass or in the middle of the vineyards and next to the 17th-century Pigeon Tower. And then, enjoy their swimming pool with never-ending vineyards and nature views. You will enjoy the offer of an aperitif and a taste of their property wine. For more comfort, two cottages have been built so you might want to stay longer and enjoy the place and its surroundings. *Directions:* From Lyon, freeway A6, take exit 24-1 Hospices les Beaune, at the first roundabout take Chalon-Autun direction D18; before the bridge, take the small road on your right indicated Bligny les Beaune to the end and turn right. Then you will see the sign "Le Clos des Saunières" and the house will be the first one on your right.

LE CLOS DES SAUNIÈRES   ***New***
Hosts: Fabienne & Bruno Guillemin
2, Rue De La Cardine, Hameau de Curtil
21200 Bligny Les Beaune, France
Tel: 03.80.22.38.89, Fax: 03.80.24.73.09
5 Rooms, Double: €120–€180, 1 Suite: €180–€200
2 Cottages: €300 daily, €2000 weekly
Table d'hôte: €35
Open: all year, Credit cards: all major
Other Languages: English, French
Region: Burgundy, Michelin Map: 519

Le Clos du Buis is an incredibly lovely bed and breakfast with room rates that are amazingly low for the quality and charm of this little jewel. This delightful 200-year-old stone building is right in the heart of the lovely town of Bonnieux. When you first see Le Clos du Buis you would never dream that there is a sweet garden and a pretty swimming pool nestled behind the house and that the prime rooms have a splendid view. Pierre Maurin, who grew up right in Bonnieux, spent many years as a chef for the French embassy, then returned to his village and bought a derelict bakery that had lain abandoned for over 50 years. The Maurins have very cleverly retained the adorable façade of the old bakery and you might walk right by thinking it is a "real" shop. Old-fashioned, handmade-lace curtains decorate the windows behind which the pastries formerly were displayed. On either side are groomed potted trees. Protecting the entrance is an overhanging roof with an intricate border made in a fancy, wrought-iron design. The same sensitivity and excellent taste that motivated the Maurins to recreate the exterior is apparent in every detail within. Pierre and his wife Lydia did the decorating and it is exactly right. The fabrics, the colors, the antiques, the fresh flowers, and the way it is all put together are most appealing. *Directions:* Located on the bottom edge of Bonnieux, just one block up the hill from the Eglise Neuve (the lower church).

LE CLOS DU BUIS
Hosts: Lydia & Pierre Maurin
Rue Victor Hugo
84480 Bonnieux, France
Tel: 04.90.75.88.48, Fax: 04.90.75.88.57
6 Rooms, Double: €84–€120
1 Cottage: €500 weekly
Table d'hôte: €25
Closed: Dec & Jan, Credit cards: MC, VS
Other Languages: good English
Region: Provence-Alps-Côte d'Azur, Michelin Map: 527

Located where mulberry trees were once grown to feed silkworms, Les Trois Sources, nestled among lavender fields, vineyards, and cherry trees. Just a short drive from the village of Bonnieux, is an 18th-century fortified farmhouse with Renaissance parts wrapped around a large graveled courtyard, softened by potted plants and an old mulberry tree under which cheerful tables are set for breakfast. In its early history Les Trois Sources might have been a priory but today you find accommodations brimming with character. Your hosts, Caroline and Paul, bought the abandoned house and totally renovated it, with the goal of disturbing the architectural features as little as possible while adding all the amenities of a modern bed and breakfast. They have succeeded admirably. An awesome, wide, ancient stone spiral staircase leads to the bedrooms, four of which are huge (the fifth is also spacious by normal standards). The decorating complements to perfection the rustic nature of the very old structure: there is a rugged, natural, uncluttered look accented by some antique pieces, handsome white homespun bedspreads, original tiled floors, beamed ceilings, and thick castle-like walls. As an added bonus, there is a swimming pool in the garden. *Directions:* From Avignon, take N100 toward Apt then turn right on D36 toward Bonnieux. After crossing the road to Lacoste, continue for 1 km.

LES TROIS SOURCES
Hosts: Caroline Guinard & Paul Jeannet
Chemin de la Chaîne
84480 Bonnieux, France
Tel: 04.90.75.95.58, Fax: 04.90.75.89.95
4 Rooms, Double: €80–€140
1 Suite: €140–€200
Open: all year, Credit cards: MC, VS
Other Languages: good English
Region: Provence-Alps-Côte d'Azur, Michelin Map: 527

Madame Christiane Bordes gives Maison Trille heart. She opened rooms in her house to outside guests not for the income but because she truly loves what she does: to make guests feel welcome, comfortable, and at home; as well as cook and provide bountiful breakfasts and gourmet table d'hôte dinners. Christiane delights in spoiling her guests with both the presentation and quality of her regional specialties. I could dedicate this entire description to Christiane but Maison Trille is charming in its own right. Typical of homes in this area of Bearn, this beautiful wisteria-draped farm complex, dating back to 1701, wraps round a central courtyard. Guests enjoy their own private entry to the wing that houses a living room and five bedrooms decorated with lots of accents around each one's special theme. La Poule, a lovely room with twin beds, opens to its own outdoor patio. I loved our small and cozy room, translated as Batchelor Button, whose shuttered windows open to the sounds of cowbells and the morning chant of birds. This home has a long history of hospitality, including overnight lodging to people traveling along the pilgrimage route. If you are interested in a longer stay, Christiane has converted her wonderful old barn to a long-term rental. *Directions:* Take N134 south from Pau for 10 km. At Gan continue a little farther south on D934 to a sign for the B&B to the left off the main road. Note: Maison Trille is not actually in the town of Bosdarros or Gan.

MAISON TRILLE
Host: Christiane Bordes
Chemin Labau, Rte de Rébénacq
64290 Bosdarros, France
Tel: 05.59.21.79.51, Fax: 05.59.21.57.54
5 Rooms, Double: €72–€75
1 Cottage: €975 weekly
Table d'hôte: €35
Open: all year, Credit cards: none
Other Languages: some English
Region: Aquitaine, Michelin Map: 524

It is hard to know where to begin with a description of the Château de Goville as it has so many wonderful and unique characteristics. It has endless collections—a hallway of over 60 dollhouses; incredible displays of prized porcelain; antique dolls; magnificent pottery; massive display of buttons—family heirlooms and possessions that span the 300 years the château has been in the family. Public rooms are as diverse and as numerous as the collections. A delightful and inviting Louis XIII bar whose walls are hung with an incredible collection of watercolors displaying Normandy costumes also boasts numerous vintage game sets ready for you to master at intimate settings for two. Distinct color schemes and decor distinguish the elegant public rooms, all overlooking the surrounding gardens through marvelous floor-to-ceiling windows. The grand salon is decadent and elegantly dressed in rich reds, greens, and golds, while the main dining room, in contrast, is very pretty with walls and fabrics of soft blues, yellows, and greens. A bountiful breakfast is delivered to the guestrooms, which are as varied and diverse as the public rooms. I especially loved Adeleine, a back corner room enjoying four windows, decorated in warm reds and creams with a pretty floral frieze. *Directions:* From the Bayeux ring road, take the D5 southwest towards the town of Le Molay Littry. The Château de Goville is located on the left side just before Le Molay Littry.

CHÂTEAU DE GOVILLE
Host: Jean-Jacques Vallée
Route D5-La Coliberderie
14330 Le Breuil-en-Bessin, France
Tel: 02.31.22.19.28, Fax: 02.31.22.68.74
10 Rooms, Double: €115–€180*
*Breakfast not included: €13
Table d'hôte: €33, Thur through Mon
Open: all year, Credit cards: all major
Region: Lower Normandy, Michelin Map: 513

Corinne and Régis Burckel de Tell bought a characterful 15th-century stone house facing directly onto the main street in the center of Calvisson, a very old village surrounded by vineyards just west of Nîmes, and began the tremendous task of restoration. Corinne (an art historian) and Régis (an artist) were passionately committed to preserving the architecture and culture of the area. Ceilings were stripped back to expose original beams, floors covered with stone slabs or terracotta tiles, and fireplaces brought back to working order. They then furnished the house with a charming rustic simplicity, country antiques and natural fabrics. In the heart of the house is a romantic courtyard garden, which is a true delight, with flowers and greenery setting off the stone walls. It is here under the stars that dinner is usually served. When the weather is chilly, guests eat family-style at one large table in a wonderful room with stone walls and arched ceiling. The bedrooms, reached by a stone-slab circular staircase, are individually furnished and display the same tasteful, understated beauty. Régis, whose paintings highlight the walls throughout the house, offers week-long art classes for small groups. *Directions:* From A9, take the Gallargues exit then the N113 towards Nîmes. Take the D1 to Calvisson just after the Bas Rhône Canal. Once in the village follow the signs to the house, which is two doors from the town hall going up the hill.

CHEZ BURCKEL DE TELL
Hosts: Corinne & Régis Burckel de Tell
Grand Rue 48
30420 Calvisson, France
Tel: 04.66.01.23.91
5 Rooms, Double: €55–€60
2 Suites: €70–€75
Table d'hôte: €20
Open: Mar 1 to Nov 1, Credit cards: none
Other Languages: good English, Italian, Spanish
Region: Midi-Pyrénées, Michelin Map: 526

Villa Panko, a most attractive, pale-pink villa accented by light-green shutters and tiled roof, is very special. Located in a secluded but extremely convenient area of Cap d'Antibes, this intimate bed and breakfast is truly a delight. When you step into the living room, there is a homelike, informal ambiance, and then you meet your hostess, Clarisse Bourgade, whose radiant smile and genuine warmth make guests feel instantly at ease. Although there are just two guestrooms, Villa Panko is run with great professionalism. Bedrooms and bathrooms are decorated with loving care, down to the tiniest detail such as the designs on the towels matching the stenciling on the wall. The bedrooms have lovely linens and appealing fabrics. Bouquets of fresh flowers, teapots with all the tea makings, and an information packet are all thoughtful touches. One of the bedrooms has recently been converted to a mini-apartment wit its own kitchen. Breakfast is a beautiful presentation of delicious pastries and breads, fresh fruit, orange juice, cheeses, yogurt, and jam. In warm weather, breakfast is served out in the stunning, English-style garden with its quiet nooks, pretty trees, and gorgeous flowerbeds. *Directions:* From Antibes center, follow signs for Cap d'Antibes. At the roundabout, go toward Cap d'Antibes; at the next intersection continue on Blvd du Cap. Take first right on Chem. du Crouton; take the first left. Go to the end, then turn left on the private lane.

VILLA PANKO
Host: Clarisse Bourgade
17, Chemin du Parc Saramartel
06160 Cap d'Antibes, France
Tel: 04.93.67.92.49, Fax: 04.93.61.29.32
2 Rooms, Double: €80–€110
Minimum Stay Required
Closed: Aug & Christmas, Credit cards: none
Other Languages: good English, Italian
Region: Provence-Alps-Côte d'Azur, Michelin Map: 527

We received a compelling letter imploring us to visit Bastide Sainte Agnes—"...our favorite bed and breakfast in all of France". We visited and were shown around the beautiful estate by the charming owners, Maryse and Michel Pinbouen. The Bastide Sainte Agnes, a 19th-century farmhouse gracefully restored to its original beauty, creates its own environment of peace and tranquility. It is hard to imagine that other houses are nearby and that Carpentras is only 3 kilometers away—high walls and many trees totally insulate it from the outside world. One part of the house is built of stone and another of stucco and the façade is painted a rich shade of yellow set off to perfection by pretty red doors and shutters. The guestrooms are all attractively decorated, but it is the gardens that will capture your heart. Immaculately tended lawns, exotic trees, and fragrant flowers exude beauty and tranquility. Adding to guests' enjoyment are a large swimming pool, a romantic trellised niche where breakfast is served, and a "summer kitchen" where guests can fix themselves a light supper or lunch. Your hosts are extremely gracious and professional—always there to help if you have a question, yet never intruding on your privacy. *Directions:* From Carpentras go east on D974 toward Bédoin. Turn left toward Carombe then after 300 meters, turn left again. The Bastide Sainte Agnes is on your right after 200 meters.

BASTIDE SAINTE AGNES
Hosts: Maryse & Michel Pinbouen
Route de Carombe, Chemin de la Fourtrouse
84200 Carpentras, France
Tel: 04.90.60.03.01, Fax: 04.90.60.02.53
5 Rooms, Double: €76–€120
1 Apartment: €160 daily, €900 weekly
Open: all year, Credit cards: MC, VS
Other Languages: good English
Region: Provence-Alps-Côte d'Azur, Michelin Map: 527

The Château du Foulon, built in 1840, is a beautiful small château, owned by Vicomte and Vicomtesse de Baritault du Carpia. The home is surrounded by a 100-acre park, complete with 25 handsome peacocks and one naughty swan. Inside, the rooms, without exception, are furnished with exquisite antiques, many dating back to the 17th century. The essence within is of a fine home, elegant, yet very comfortable, with an appealing, lived-in ambiance—photographs of beautiful children and grandchildren show that indeed a family lives here. The guestrooms, each nicely decorated with pretty wallpapers and attractive fabrics, look out over the gardens from large casement windows. In addition to the three bedrooms and one suite, there is a charming apartment, with its own little kitchen, bedroom, and living room. The apartment or spacious suite would make an excellent choice for accommodation if you plan to stay for an extended time. There are few homes in the Médoc that open their doors for bed and breakfast, so it is a pleasure to recommend the Château du Foulon. If you want to explore the glorious Médoc (which produces some of the world's finest wines) or just enjoy an interlude in the French countryside, this lovely château makes an excellent choice. *Directions:* Take D1 north from Bordeaux for about 28 km. In Castelnau de Médoc, at the first traffic light turn left and almost immediately you see the sign for the château on your left.

CHÂTEAU DU FOULON
Hosts: Vicomte & Vicomtesse de Baritault du Carpia
33480 Castelnau de Médoc, France
Tel: 05.56.58.20.18, Fax: 05.56.58.23.43
3 Rooms, Double: €80
1 Apartment, €100, 1 Suite, €100
Open: all year, Credit cards: none
Other Languages: some English
Region: Aquitaine, Michelin Maps: 521, 524

The de Valbrays are a charming, friendly, enthusiastic, and artistic young couple who truly make their visitors feel like invited guests. Their grand home dates from 1773 and has been in François's family since 1820 when his great-great-great-grandfather, the Comte de Valbray, resided here. Old family photos and portraits abound in the gracious salons. It is hard to pick a favorite bedroom, as all are furnished in keeping with the style and mood of the château; however, the Rose Room is very special: feminine in decor, it was once inhabited by François's grandmother. Also very special in their furnishings and outlook are the Lake Room and the Charles X Room. Downstairs, the parquet floors, grand chandeliers, and marble fireplaces in the public rooms attest to a very rich and elegant heritage. The elegance of a bygone era continues as guests dine at small candlelit tables dressed with family silver and china. There are billiards in the library and a swimming pool and tennis court in the park available to guests. A stay of at least two days is recommended to fully appreciate the de Valbrays' hospitality and the ambiance of this aristocratic setting. The renovated cottage offers quiet and privacy and is ideal for those who want to settle for a week or more. *Directions:* From Angers (25 km) take the D107 north towards Cantenay Epinard, then take D768 in the direction of Feneu to Champigné. The château is signposted from Champigné, located on the D190.

CHÂTEAU DES BRIOTTIÈRES
Hosts: Hedwige & François de Valbray
Les Briottières, 49330 Champigné, France
Tel: 02.41.42.00.02, Fax: 02.41.42.01.55
15 Rooms, Double: €160–€250, 3 Suites: €320–€350*
1 Cottage: €900 daily, €4500 weekly*
*Breakfast not included: €15
Table d'hôte: €50
Open: all year, Credit cards: all major
Châteaux & Hôtels Collection
Region: Loire Valley, Michelin Map: 517

The Manoir de Ponsay is a superb country farm estate surrounded by rolling pastures, fields of wheat, and pockets of woodlands. As you drive up the winding lane and arrive in front of the stately stone manor, you will be warmly greeted by your charming host, Monsieur de Ponsay, who has proudly taken over innkeeping duties from his parents. Upon entering their spacious home, you notice an abundance of handsome antiques, old prints, and family portraits. Nothing looks contrived or chosen by a fancy decorator to fit the space—everything looks as if it has been there forever. It has. This lovely home has been passed down through 12 generations, from father to son, since 1644. A stone staircase spirals up to the bedrooms. Four are extremely large and beautifully decorated in antiques (my favorite, Chambre Fleur, has pale-pink wallpaper setting off pretty pink-and-green floral fabric used on the bedcovers and repeated on the draperies). There are three very pleasant less expensive bedrooms—just not as regal in size or decor. If it is an evening when table d'hôte is offered, by all means accept: the meals are outstanding. *Directions:* From the A83 (Nantes-Niort) take exit 6 and go northeast 11 km to Chantonnay. From Chantonnay take the D949b east in the direction of Poitiers. Just a few kilometers beyond Chantonnay, turn left in Saint Mars-des-Prés on a small road towards Puybelliard and follow signs.

MANOIR DE PONSAY
Host: Aurelia et Laurent de Ponsay
Saint Mars-des-Prés
85110 Chantonnay, France
Tel: 02.51.46.96.71, Fax: 02.51.46.80.07
7 Rooms, Double: €62–€120, 1 Suite: €120*
*Breakfast not included: €9, Table d'hôte: €32
Open: all year, Credit cards: none
Other Languages: good English, Spanish
Châteaux & Hôtels Collection
Region: Loire Valley, Michelin Map: 521

The Domaine de Gorneton, as a property, and Jacqueline and Jean Fleitou, as superb hosts, both exceeded our expectations. The Fleitous, in search of a place outside of Lyon to raise their family, found the house of their dreams—a huge estate in the countryside, surrounded by 5 hectares of parklike grounds. Built around a central courtyard, the romantic, ivy-draped, combined stone and stucco home abounds with character. The oldest part dates to 1646 and there is even a secret passageway that leads from the house down to the river. On the grounds you find a swimming pool, tennis court, refreshment kitchen, ping-pong and small billiard table, large pond, fountains, splendid gardens, forests, horses, dogs, and a cat. When the Fleitous' five children grew up, the house was really too big for two people, so they decided to take in guests. Jean, who is retired, dons his chef's apron and prepares delicious dinners, served family-style at one large table. When the weather is warm, guests dine outside; when it is chilly, they gather in the cozy dining room that oozes charm with its low-beamed ceiling, antique table, soft lighting, and massive fireplace. *Directions:* From A7 exit at Chasse sur Rhône. Take the first right, then the next left (near a McDonalds). Go under the railroad track, turn left, then right at the next street. Go up the hill, following signs to Trembas. The Domaine is on the right, marked by a small sign.

DOMAINE DE GORNETON
Hosts: Jacqueline & Jean Fleitou
Hameau de Trembas, 712 Chemin de Violans
38670 Chasse sur Rhône, France
Tel: 04.72.24.19.15, Fax: 04.78.07.93.62
4 Rooms, Double: €120–€180
1 Apartment: €800 weekly
Table d'hôte: €40
Open: all year, Credit cards: none
Other Languages: good English
Region: Rhône-Alpes, Michelin Map: 523

When the Lamberts were looking for a home close to Avignon, they fell in love with a charming, 18th-century manor, but it was much larger than they needed for their small family. Happily, they considered the recommendation of a friend, a perfect solution—open a bed and breakfast. The Lamberts renovated the home, making five spacious bedrooms for guests, each with a king-sized bed and a large bathroom. Knickknacks, dolls, and family memorabilia give all the rooms a homey, lived-in ambiance. My favorite guestroom, La Cigale, is especially appealing, with windows looking down to a lovely, secluded pine forest. The heart of the home, the charming kitchen, has a large fireplace, a multicolored tile floor, and fragrant sprigs of lavender draped from the open-beamed ceiling, all combining to make this a cozy setting for breakfast. However, in warm weather breakfast is often served outside in the delightful walled garden. Guests are welcome to use the pool, a relaxing spot after a day of touring the countryside. The Lamberts are extremely gracious hosts who spent five years in the USA and speak excellent English. *Directions:* Take exit 23 (Avignon Nord) from the A7, following signs on D6 to Vedène. Continue on D6 through Saint Saturnin to Jonquerettes. Turn right in the village center on D97 and go up the hill. As the road starts down the hill, the entrance is on the left side of the road, opposite a "road narrows" sign.

LE CLOS DES SAUMANES
Host: Elisabeth Lambert
519 Chemin des Saumanes
84470 Châteauneuf de Gadagne, France
Tel: 04.90.22.30.86, Fax: 04.90.83.19.42
5 Rooms, Double: €80–€190
Minimum Stay Required
Open: Easter to Nov & off season by reservation
Credit cards: none
Other Languages: fluent English
Region: Provence-Alps-Côte d'Azur, Michelin Map: 527

Châteauneuf en Auxois has been designated as one of France's most beautiful villages and so we were thrilled to learn from Lisa of the Lady A (moored in the town below the village) that she works very closely with a charming bed and breakfast located in the village itself. While her husband works in Dijon, Annie runs Chez Bagatelle and is present to welcome guests. The four guestrooms, all with their own entrance, are named for a color of fabric used in the room: Blue, Maroon, Yellow, and Rose. Blue is simple and sweet with the color introduced in the beige-and-blue lampshades and drapes. Rose and Maroon are both two-story units with a sitting area on the first level and bath and bed on the landing above. Yellow is handsome with an old (non-working) fireplace and is popular as it has the luxury of its own private garden niche tucked just off its entrance. Guestrooms are very simple, with furnishings set on earthen-colored tiled floors, but are all spotless and enjoy little touches such as a single daffodil on the bathroom counter. All have their own bathroom with toilet and shower. Breakfast is served in a charming front room with wooden tables decked out with a pretty red-print fabric and fresh posies of flowers. *Directions:* Located at the top/back of the village. Turn right just after passing under the arched gateway, before the woods and look for the Gîtes sign on the right.

CHEZ BAGATELLE
Host: Annie Bagatelle
Rue des Moutons
21320 Châteauneuf en Auxois, France
Tel & Fax: 03.80.49.21.00
4 Rooms, Double: €55–€65
Table d'hôte: €25
Closed: Feb 17 to Mar 3, Credit cards: none
Other Languages: some English
Region: Burgundy, Michelin Map: 519

Ideally located at the heart of the Loire Valley and tucked off the main road in the village of Mesvres, you will find the charming La Marmittière. With just three comfortable rooms in a quiet setting, they are conscientious of every detail of your stay. In an old wine estate, guestrooms are located in a building all to themselves and each enjoys a private, outside entrance. Named after the color selected for their décor, "La Suite" offers a little kitchenette, dining area and two guestrooms (one twin, one queen)—perfect accommodation for a family. Apricot is a sweet room with a double bed, and my favorite, Chambre Bleue, is accessed off an end stair and enjoys its own private terrace. Rooms are pretty but simple in their décor, clean and fresh in their modern appointments. Cross over the graveled drive to the main house and you will discover the lovely dining room where breakfast and table d'hôte are offered. A long trestle table is set in front of a large open fireplace and on the opposite wall a bright mural, a copy of a Gaughin, painted by your host, Yves, introduces a splash of color. On the day of our visit the table was adorned by a cloth, hand embroidered (by your hostess, Marie) with Pierre de Ronsard's Sonnet to Helene—a very romantic poem to set a very romantic mood. *Directions:* After Amboise, take the D31 towards Blère to La Croix en Touraine. Then take D40 towards Chenonceaux. After 1,5 km, turn left for Vallée de Mesvres.

LA MARMITTIÈRE
Hosts: M & Mme Boblet
22, Vallée des Mesvres
37150 Civray de Touraine, France
Tel: 02.47.23.51.04
2 Rooms, Double: €60
4 Suites: €105
Table d'hôte: €23
Open: Mar 15 to Nov 15, Credit cards: none
Region: Center, Michelin Map: 518

La Rabouillère, has a wonderful ambiance of old, with 400 year old woods and beams incorporated into its construction. The home was designed by the owner, Jean Marie, who actually built it himself on weekends. There is a storybook quality to this brick-and-timbered bed and breakfast with its steeply pitched roof accentuated by perky gables. You enter into a large family room where guests gather before the open fire in the winter. Antiques abound, and with the beamed ceiling, timber, and exposed brick walls, the mood is certainly old-world. This family/living room is where Martine serves breakfast on chilly mornings, although when the days are balmy guests frequently prefer to eat outside. Martine lovingly decorated each bedroom with Laura-Ashley-type fabrics and antique accent pieces. The rooms are all named after flowers. My favorite, Les Jonquilles, is decorated in soft yellows. All of the bathrooms are spacious and offer special amenities such as built-in hairdryers. In addition to the five bedrooms, there is a two-bedroom apartment. The setting too is superb: a 17-acre wooded estate with a small pond in front. For those who are château-sightseeing, La Rabouillère offers a great base right in the heart of the Loire Valley. *Directions:* Go south from Blois on D765 for about 9 km to Cour-Cheverny then take D102 towards Contres. About 6 km beyond Cheverny, turn left following the La Rabouillère signs.

LA RABOUILLÈRE
Host: Martine Thimonnier
Chemin de Marçon
41700 Contres, France
Tel: 02.54.79.05.14, Fax: 02.54.79.59.39
2 Rooms, Double: €90, 2 Suites: €100–€160
1 Apartment: €145 daily
Open: Apr to Nov & off season by reservation
Credit cards: MC, VS
Other Languages: some English
Region: Loire Valley, Michelin Map: 518

This character-filled 13th-century watchtower, with farmhouse and dovecote added in 1693, was converted for bed and breakfast accommodation and is run by Ian and Penelope Wanklyn, who hail from England. Aurifat enjoys an extraordinary setting on a slope just below Cordes-sur-Ciel, classified as one of France's most beautiful villages, looking out to a sweeping view of the valley. Capturing the same view, set just below the home, is a very large, attractive swimming pool. All of the sweetly decorated guestrooms have their own entrance and flowered balcony or patio. Cordes has many restaurants, but for those who prefer to "eat in" there is a fully-equipped kitchen and a barbecue where guests may fix a meal. Next to the kitchen is a garden sitting room with an extensive library and internet access. For such reasonably priced accommodations, the amenities are outstanding. We were so pleased to have an opportunity to meet the Wanklyns—they are a very handsome couple and extremely charming. It is easy to understand why we have received so much praise of their genuine hospitality from many of our readers. *Directions:* Upon arrival in lower Cordes, take the cobbled street up the hill at the Cité sign. After 400 meters, take the left fork down the hill, marked with two small signs, "Le Bouysset" and "Aurifat." After 500 meters take a left on a hairpin curve (Rte de St. Jean) and Aurifat is 200 meters along on the right.

🖥 🏊 @ P 🚭 ≈ 🚶 👫 🏇 🍇

AURIFAT
Hosts: Penelope & Ian Wanklyn
Aurifat
81170 Cordes-sur-Ciel, France
Tel & Fax: 05.63.56.07.03
4 Rooms, Double: €75
Open: mid-Feb to mid-Dec, Credit cards: none
Other Languages: fluent English
Region: Midi-Pyrénées, Michelin Maps: 525, 526

Véronique realized her dream—to convert her family home into a B&B. Véronique was born and fondly spent her family vacations in this grand 18th century manor on over 5 hectares of lawn bordered by river La Loire and covered with orchards. A feeling of grandeur pervades this two-story building made of soft cream stone with wedgewood blue shutters outside and high ceilings with elegant furnishings inside. Although the décor is regal, Véronique has managed to achieve a comfortable, inviting ambiance. There are seven guestrooms including a large room set on old stone floors in what was once the Orangerie. Another that Véronique terms a "family unit" is located in an independent building just off the parking. My favorite rooms are the five in the manor, all named for famous women. Cassandra, on the third floor under a ceiling mural of an illusory sky, is decorated in rich creams and beiges in the bedroom and bath. The cozy Mme Seveigne (Louis XIV's mistress) is decorated in a warm rust and cream fabric. Her clawfoot tub and sink are cleverly curtained off. A central window opens to the sound of songbirds nesting in the back garden. Settle in and enjoy the tranquil setting with a picnic on the river's edge, or explore the region's magnificent châteaux. As Véronique invites: Let my home be your home for a night, a weekend, or longer. *Directions:* From Blois travel N152 north to Orleans. In Cour sur Loire, the Château is posted off the road to the right.

CHÂTEAU DE LA RUE
Host: Véronique de Caix
Cour-sur-Loire, 41500 Suèvres, France
Tel: 02.54.46.82.47, Fax: 02.54.46.88.17
7 Rooms, Double: €92–€158
Table d'hôte: €35
Open: all year, Credit cards: none
Other Languages: good English
Region: Center, Michelin Map: 518

Facing directly onto the street, Le Beguinage is an appealing, 18th-century, one-story house with a series of cute gables and perky chimneys accenting the steep roof. Enhancing the country-cottage look are green shutters, tall windows with white frames, and a heavy cloak of ivy. You would never guess from the front that the back of the house opens up to a marvelous garden. Here you see large sweeps of lawn, several ponds, mature shade trees, meandering paths, well-kept beds of flowers, and even a small river. There are plenty of lounge chairs thoughtfully placed so guests can relax and listen to the birds while enjoying the tranquility. Your hosts are Patricia and Brice Deloison, who lived in Paris before deciding to move to the countryside. Brice is a balloon pilot and can arrange to pick up guests in the back garden for a ride. This is a simple property, so if you are looking for top-of-the-line quality and a decorator-perfect interior, this might not be your cup of tea, but everything is spotlessly clean and well maintained. If you want a reasonably priced place to stay and a genuinely warm welcome, Le Beguinage is a very good choice. Be sure to ask for one of the rooms in the main house: these are more attractive. From Le Beguinage you can walk to Château de Cheverny and into town for dinner. *Directions:* From Blois take the D765 south to Cour-Cheverny. Turn into town at the first entrance—the bed and breakfast is on your right.

LE BEGUINAGE
Hosts: Patricia & Brice Deloison
41700 Cour–Cheverny, France
Tel: 02.54.79.29.92, Fax: 02.54.79.94.59
6 Rooms, Double: €52–€85
1 Cottage: €160 daily
Open: all year, Credit cards: MC, VS
Other Languages: good English
Region: Center, Michelin Map: 518

Manoir de la Brunie, an intimate, 14th-century home made of pretty honey-tone stone, accented with white shutters, is located on the "road of the châteaux of the Valley of the Dordogne" just on the outskirts of Le Coux, a small town near the River Dordogne. This bed and breakfast is a real beauty, exuding great warmth and charm. There is a happy mood throughout, and the day we visited, the interior seemed to glow as if the sun were shining, even though it was a rainy day—an effect perhaps achieved by all the warm colors used throughout. The lounge and room, where guests eat breakfast and Table d'hôte dinners are attractively decorated with a comfortable homelike ambiance. Upstairs, the guestrooms are beautifully decorated and have especially glamorous bathrooms. I thought my favorite was Comarque, with its restful creamy tones and canopy bed, until I saw Fayrac, an exceptionally spacious, ever-so-pretty room decorated in blue toile fabric. If you are traveling with children, Castelnaud, with its adjoining children's room, would be an ideal choice and the property has recently added a pool. *Directions:* From Sarlat, take D57 west to Beynac, continuing on D703 toward Bergerac. At Siorac, go across the bridge, then up the hill to Le Coux. Go through the village, turn left at the first street after the town hall and go a little over 1 km. The Manoir is signposted on your right.

MANOIR DE LA BRUNIE
Host: Joyce Vinnemur
Le Coux, 24220 Bigaroque, France
Tel & Fax: 05.53.31.95.62
4 Rooms, Double: €62–€97
1 Suite: €117–€127
Table d'hôte: €27
Open: all year, Credit cards: VS
Other Languages: some English, Spanish
Region: Aquitaine, Michelin Map: 524

A lovely stone manor house surrounded by lawn and embraced by its own stone walls, sitting in the quiet village of Crépon just minutes from the coast and D-Day beaches, the Manoir de Crépon has achieved Gîtes de France's highest rating. These merits are in themselves impressive, but when I met the owner, Mme Poisson, I was reminded of what is most important—genuine warmth of welcome. Though we arrived on her doorstep at a busy time, we were welcomed with a warm, sincere smile and no hint of inconvenience. She loves her home and sharing it with her guests. Bedrooms, all with garden and lawn views, are found upstairs off a grand hallway. One guestroom suite boasts a lovely bedroom and a small side room with a dear twin iron bed (perfect for a child) and gorgeous tiled basin. At the other end of the hall, a bedroom with double bed and a lovely corner back room with two double beds share a bath. There are in addition two standard double rooms, one with a decor of lime green and a bird print, and my favorite, a lovely twin-bedded (or king) room decorated in reds and creams. On the entry level there are two salons and an inviting kitchen where guests settle in the mornings at a long trestle table in front of a magnificent fireplace (lit in winters) to enjoy a hearty breakfast. *Directions:* Crépon is located inland from Arromanches approximately 10 km traveling the D65. The manor is located just past the war memorial statue.

MANOIR DE CRÉPON
Host: Mme Anne-Marie Poisson
Route de Caen-Arromanches
14480 Crépon, France
Tel: 02.31.22.21.27, Fax: 02.31.22.88.80
4 Rooms, Double: €80
2 Suites: €95–€115
Open: all year, Credit cards: MC, VS
Other Languages: some English
Region: Lower Normandy, Michelin Map: 513

It is not often that you can actually reside in a historical monument, but you can do just that at Le Prieuré Saint Michel. The complex has been authentically restored and is truly a masterpiece. The granary is now used for various exhibitions and concerts, the giant press where the monks produced the Calvados brandy is still intact, and the lovely little chapel is now an art gallery featuring the sketches of many French artists. Equally outstanding are the splendid, meticulously tended gardens. There is an old-fashioned rose garden featuring an incredible variety of fragrant roses since days of yore. In contrast there is the "new" rose garden, the iris garden, the herbal gardens, and on and on. Each is laid out as it would have been long ago. Two ponds with ducks and swans complete the idyllic scene. In summer, the grounds are open to the public, but guests are assured of their privacy with their own intimate little garden. Each of the cottages is handsomely decorated. This is a gorgeous property and I was thrilled to meet Viviane and Jean-Pierre, who ventured here from a corporate life in Paris, were captivated by the setting, and now very graciously share their enchanting home with guests. *Directions:* Take D916 west from Vimoutiers through Argentan. Just a few kilometers after leaving Vimoutiers, turn right at the sign for Crouttes (D703). Go through town following signs for Le Prieuré Saint Michel.

LE PRIEURÉ SAINT MICHEL
Hosts: Viviane & Jean-Pierre Ulrich
61120 Crouttes (Vimoutiers), France
Tel: 02.33.39.15.15, Fax: 02.33.36.15.16
2 Rooms, Double: €95–€120
2 Suites: €125–€135
2 Cottages: €420–€650 weekly
Open: all year, Credit cards: MC, VS
Other Languages: good English
Region: Lower Normandy, Michelin Map: 513

Le Logis du Jerzual is well located for enjoying the medieval city of Dinan. Housed within the walls of a traditional maison bourgeoise, the logis has its own character and ambiance. Dating from the 15th and 18th centuries, the rooms aren't overly large, but comfortable, and Madame Ronsseray extends a warm welcome. The cozy house is just up a narrow passage from the main street, set behind its own gate and in a terraced garden. The four guestrooms are staggered on different levels and open onto a small staircase. Guestrooms and bathrooms were recently redone and redecorated, and the guestrooms boast many handsome antique pieces passed down through the family. Breakfast is served inside in one of two small, cozy rooms—a back room with a beautiful old Breton clock and gorgeous sideboard or the other overlooking the front garden. In warm weather breakfast is offered at tables in the garden. Note: The location halfway up a cobbled street requires a lot of walking. On first arrival you can actually drive from the port right up the street amongst the pedestrians and park at the narrow passage to the bed and breakfast. Afterwards, Madame will direct you to a free parking lot for residents (which you are considered as an overnight guest). *Directions:* Follow signs to Le Port, cross the old bridge, and continue straight across from the bridge up Rue du Petit Fort (also referred to as Le Jerzual). Le Logis du Jerzual is on the right.

LE LOGIS DU JERZUAL
Host: Sylvie Ronsseray
25–27, Rue du Petit Fort
22100 Dinan, France
Tel: 02.96.85.46.54, Fax: 02.96.39.46.94
5 Rooms, Double: €75–€90
Open: all year, Credit cards: MC, VS
Other Languages: good English
Region: Brittany, Michelin Map: 512

Le Prieuré is a charming bed and breakfast snuggling up to a beautiful church in the small village of Dissay sous Courcillon. Amazingly, both the church and the priory date all the way back to 1180. Additions were made to the priory in the Renaissance era but it retains many of its 12th-century features and exudes great charm. It took years to make Le Prieuré the jewel you see today, though luckily all the basic ingredients were already in place: a stone house abounding with character, a beautiful church next door, a large enclosed garden, mature shade trees, and even fish ponds in the back. Marie-France is very talented and has decorated the house in great taste. She and Christophe already owned many fine family paintings and gorgeous heirloom furniture to use in the rooms, giving the house the feeling of a private home. The 12th-century guest lounge with its stone walls and massive arched stone ceiling is architecturally stunning. This is where breakfast is served, although when the weather is balmy, most guests prefer to eat outside in the garden. There are three extremely spacious, attractively decorated bedrooms, all overlooking the pretty back garden. My favorite is the pink room, which is especially lovely with appealing fabrics and antique furniture that create a charming country ambiance. *Directions:* Located in the center of Dissay sous Courcillon (N 138) next to the church. From Le Mans take A28, exit 26. From Tours take A28 to exit 27.

LE PRIEURÉ
Hosts: Marie-France & Christophe Calla
1, Rue de la Gare
72500 Dissay sous Courcillon, France
Tel: 02.43.44.09.09
3 Rooms, Double: €100–€130
Open: Mar to Nov, Credit cards: none
Other Languages: good English
Region: Loire Valley, Michelin Map: 517

A long drive leads through the forest, which opens out to a sweeping expanse of lawn dominated by Le Mésangeau, a splendid stone mansion reflecting somewhat the Italian style with its stone façade and red-tiled roof. When Brigitte and Gérard bought the home, it was a disaster; but after ten years of restoration, the result is an exceptional bed and breakfast with guests' comfort uppermost in the planning. A whole wing has been allotted to guests; which, in addition to five bedrooms, also has a large lounge with a sitting area, two billiard tables, game tables, and even a piano. All of the individually decorated bedrooms overlook the lovely back garden with its 350-year-old oak tree and have names to reflect their style of decor. My favorite, Brittany, has pretty, country antique furniture. Upon prior request, the Migons happily prepare dinner—they say it gives them the perfect opportunity to get to know their guests better. When the weather is nice, guests dine outside, otherwise the meal is served in a charming dining room with beamed ceiling and a huge open fireplace where a fire blazes on chilly days. The grounds have been transformed into a park with a small lake overlooked by a romantic gazebo. Gérard also has an incredible collection of 20 French antique cars. *Directions:* From the church in Drain, take D154 toward St. Laurent des Autels. Go about 3.5 km and turn left at the sign.

LE MÉSANGEAU
Hosts: Brigitte & Gérard Migon
49530 Drain, France
Tel: 02.40.98.21.57, Fax: 02.40.98.28.62
3 Rooms, Double: €90–€110
2 Suites: €160–€220
Table d'hôte: €35
Open: all year, Credit cards: none
Other Languages: good English
Region: Loire Valley, Michelin Map: 517

You will fall under the spell of the enchanting Domaine du Haut Baran much as Americans William and Rosalie did a few years ago while visiting William's French family. They purchased the estate, convinced that this gorgeous piece of paradise was to be their home and business. With her use of colors, special wall textures, hand-painted motifs, fine linens, and luxurious appointments, Rosalie has created very elegant guestrooms. The Rose Room, with a king bed dressed in crisp white linen set under old wooden beams and looking out through large-paned windows to a private terrace and bucolic views, is definitely the choice room. At this end of the house the Sunflower and Wisteria rooms are very pretty with their flower themes, but are much smaller and furnished with just a bed and side chairs. Off the front cobbled yard are the Wheat and the Cala Lily rooms, which can interconnect. An end room, Lavender, has lovely corner windows. The only room with an interior access is the Pine room, located at the top of a spiral staircase off the living room. Breakfast and table d'hôte dinners are a memorable experience, whether served by flickering candlelight under the beams of the old barn or on the terrace overlooking the spring-fed ponds and the valley beyond. *Directions:* From Cahors take the D811 west, towards Villeneuve sur Lot. Approximately 2.5 km after Puy l'Eveque, watch for a small sign for the Domaine on the right before Duravel.

DOMAINE DU HAUT BARAN
Hosts: William & Rosalie Haas
46700 Duravel par Puy l'Evêque, France
Tel: 05.65.24.63.24, Fax: 05.65.36.59.05
7 Rooms, Double: €165–€220
Minimum Stay Required
Table d'hôte: €50
Open: all year, Credit cards: none
Other Languages: fluent English
Region: Aquitaine, Michelin Map: 524

Tucked at the edge of the village, at the base of the vineyards, Les Feuilles d'Or, with a four épis rating from Gîtes de France, offers travelers a comfortable and quiet haven from which to explore the Alsatian wine region. Of new construction, in the charming Alsatian style with wooden shutters, the property has a wonderful mural of a family enjoying a vineyard picnic on the wall by the entry. One guestroom has handicapped-access and a side ramp affords access to the upper floor, terrace, and breakfast room. Follow the suggestion of the storks painted on the wall of the entry stairway, one with suitcase in hand and the other with a welcome sign, both pointing upwards, and climb upstairs to the landing. Here or on the outdoor terrace is where guests relax as well as enjoy the bountiful breakfast. On this floor you find two guestrooms, Chambre Tendresse with a double bed and Chambre Câline with a king bed, each mirroring the other in terms of size and bathroom. On the next floor are two family suites, Suite Forêt to the front and Suite Vignoble on the back. The suites each have two bedrooms (twin and double beds) and a shared bathroom. All the rooms are spacious, modern in furnishings, and equipped with thoughtful luxuries such as robes, soaps, cotton balls, and hairdryers. *Directions:* The scenic D35 wine road passes right by Eichhoffen, approximately 4 km south of Barr. Les Feuilles d'Or, located on the south side of the village, is well signed.

LES FEUILLES D'OR
Hosts: Renée & Francis Kuss
52, Rue du Vignoble
67140 Eichhoffen, France
Tel & Fax: 03.88.08.49.80
5 Rooms, Double: €75–€130
Table d'hôte: Fri & Sat
Open: all year, Credit cards: none
Other Languages: little English, German
Region: Alsace, Michelin Map: 516

The enchanting Moulins des Vontes with its storybook setting is a gem and is convenient for visiting the châteaux of the Loire. The magic begins as the automatic green, iron gates open and you catch your first glimpse of an adorable, ivy-laced, stone mill with white shutters snuggled on a tiny island in the middle of the River Indre. Closer inspection shows that this isn't just one mill, but three, on a necklace of little islands that span the river, connected by picturesque medieval stone bridges. The largest mill is the home of your charming hosts, Odile and "J.J." Degail, who lived for eight years in the United States; the second mill is a small museum showing how mills operate; and the third one is your home. Above the waterwheel are three individually decorated bedrooms with large tiled bathrooms. Each is exceptionally spacious and takes up an entire floor. My favorite, the Oriental, has its theme set by a splendid antique Chinese painting. All the rooms have windows on three sides overlooking the romantic river and at night you are lulled to sleep by the gurgle of the stream flowing below your window. Little wooden rowboats offer the opportunity to explore the river and if you are into fishing, rods are available for your pleasure. *Directions:* From Tours take D943 (formerly N143) towards Loches for 12 km. Turn right on D17, go 1.3 km, turn left to Vontes, and make another left to Bas-Vontes. The house is at the end of the road.

LES MOULINS DES VONTES
Hosts: Odile & Jean-Jacques Degail
Vontes
37320 Esvres sur Indre, France
Tel: 02.47.26.45.72, Fax: 02.47.26.45.35
3 Rooms, Double: €130
Minimum Stay Required
Open: Apr to Sep, Credit cards: none
Other Languages: good English
Region: Loire Valley, Michelin Map: 518

The 17th-century Château de la Flocellière is irresistible—truly one of the treasures in this guide. The stunning, cream-colored, fairy-tale stone château has a steep slate roof, round towers at each end, and dormer windows embellished with intricately carved stone. Lending the scene an even greater romantic appeal are the crumbling stone walls and towers of the oldest part of the castle, dating back to the 11th century. Stretching out behind the château there is a charming, sheltered terrace, enhanced by colorful flowers, a trellis laced with climbing roses, and an old well, from which you have expansive views of an idyllic landscape of gently rolling hills, woodlands, pastures, old stone houses, cultivated fields, and even an ancient tower or two. The interior of the castle is also sensational, with room after room furnished with family antiques and exuding a refined, understated elegance. Of special merit is L'Orangerie, where breakfast is served, with the sun streaming in through tall, vaulted, windows that run the length of two facing walls. The bedrooms continue the same standard of excellence with decorator-perfect fabrics, antique furniture, fine linens, and top-quality bathrooms. The final ingredient of perfection are your hosts, Vicomte and Vicomtesse Vignial, who genuinely love to share their home with guests. *Directions:* From the church in La Flocellière, turn on Rue du Château and follow signs to the château.

CHÂTEAU DE LA FLOCELLIÈRE
Hosts: Vicomte & Vicomtesse Patrice Vignial
30, Rue du Château, 85700 La Flocellière, France
Tel: 02.51.57.22.03, Fax: 02.51.57.75.21
6 Rooms, Double: €125–€205*
2 Cottages: €550–€600 daily, €1900 weekly*
*Breakfast not included: €12, Table d'hôte: €54
Open: all year, Credit cards: all major
Other Languages: good English
Châteaux & Hôtels Collection
Schlosshotels & Herrenhäuser
Region: Loire Valley, Michelin Map: 518

Le Domaine de Mestré, a former agricultural estate belonging to the Fontevraud Abbey, dates back to the 12th century and stones in the courtyard evidence an ancient Roman road. You enter through gates into the courtyard. Immediately to your left is a pretty barn, which now houses a boutique featuring beautifully packaged soaps and bath oils manufactured right on the property by three generations of the Dauge family. Because all their products are without any artificial coloring, fragrances, or chemicals, they are very popular. Across the courtyard from the boutique, the 12th-century chapel has been converted into the dining room, attractively decorated with yellow walls and small tables set with yellow linens. Also facing the courtyard, the bedrooms are in two separate stone buildings. All are attractive and most have antique furniture and feature Laura Ashley fabrics, and we were thrilled to see the new family suite that has been converted from the girls' childhood bedrooms. The gracious Dauge family strives to make each guest feel welcome in their home. The Dauge's daughter, Marie Amélie is taking over the management of this lovely property so that her parents can retire. She prepares lovely meals using ingredients from the estate farm. *Directions:* Take the N152 (Tours to Samur) and cross the river to Montsoreau. From Montsoreau take D947 towards Fontevraud l'Abbaye. Before reaching town, there is a sign to the right for the Domaine.

LE DOMAINE DE MESTRÉ
Owners: Rosine & Dominique Dauge
Host: Marie Amélie Dauge de Courcy
49590 Fontevraud l'Abbaye, France
Tel: 02.41.51.75.87, Fax: 02.41.51.71.90
12 Rooms, Double: €75–€150*
*Breakfast not included: €9
Table d'hôte: €25, not offered Thur & Sun
Open: Apr to Dec 14, Credit cards: none
Other Languages: good English
Region: Loire Valley, Michelin Map: 517

Since the 15th century the splendid Château de Garrevaques has passed down through the generations in the same family. It was continuously used as the family's home until the charming, effervescent Marie-Christine persuaded her mother to open the château as a bed and breakfast. In fact, the creative Marie-Christine originated the concept (which quickly spread) of owners of beautiful private manors opening their doors and hearts to paying guests. Marie-Christine, a retired purser with Air France, and her husband, Claude Combes, live at the château, where she helps her mother run their successful business. The château is lovingly decorated with heirlooms, beautiful antiques, and fabric-covered walls and exudes great warmth, elegance, and genuine hospitality. If you have heard the French are aloof, a visit to Château de Garrevaques will quickly dispel that myth. After a day of sightseeing, a swimming pool and a tennis court are yours to enjoy. For dining, consider walking next door to the neighboring Le Pavillon du Chateau (owned by the same family and recommended in our guide to France Hotels) with its restaurant—convenient and excellent. You might also want to take advantage of the Pavillon's spa facilities. *Directions:* From Toulouse take the D2/D622 about 45 km to Revel. In Revel, at the traffic lights, turn onto the D1 and then opposite the Gendarmerie, take the D79F to Garrevaques.

❄ 🏂 ♨ CREDIT ☎ 🐕 🏨 @ W P ⊘ ❀ ≈ 🚶 🖼 ⛷ ♿ 🏌 🚶‍♂️ 🐎 🚣 🍇

CHÂTEAU DE GARREVAQUES
Hosts: Marie-Christine Combes & Andrée Barande
81700 Garrevaques, France
Tel: 05.63.75.04.54, Fax: 05.63.70.26.44
20 Rooms, Double: €180–€220*
1 Cottage: €450 daily, €2450 weekly*
*Breakfast not included: €12
Open: all year, Credit cards: AX, VS
Other Languages: good English, Spanish
Châteaux & Hôtels Collection
Region: Midi-Pyrénées, Michelin Maps: 525, 526

La Closerie is a lovely pale-salmon-colored home offering five charming guestrooms. We were greeted warmly by Sandrine, an artist, who gave us a personal tour of her home. Just off the entry is the breakfast room, which leads to Chambertin, a pretty bedroom with a spacious bathroom and large corner tub. Climb the stairs from the entry to three more guestrooms. At the top of the first landing is my favorite, Romaneé, a very spacious room with a pair of twin iron beds set on an old creaking floor against a backdrop of very pretty floral and pinstriped paper. An enormous, handsome mirror, original to the home, dominates one wall. Views through two large windows are of the central courtyard and garden. Vougeot is a cozy room with a double bed that can connect with Romaneé next door or be accessed off its own back staircase. It also boasts a twin bed set in an alcove off the bathroom. On the other side of the hallway is Corton, a simple room with a double bed set under exposed beams which spans the width of the house. On the top floor is another favorite, Chambolle, decorated in soft yellow with a pretty floral frieze. A lovely pool is set in the garden up against the neighbor's wall. For stays of at least one week, you might want to settle in to the charming one bedroom, garden level gîte with kitchenette. *Directions:* From the N74 about 16 km south of Dijon, turn east on the D25 towards Gilly-les-Citeaux. La Closerie is just off the D25 to the south.

LA CLOSERIE DE GILLY
Hosts: Sandrine & André Lanaud
16, Avenue Bouchard
21640 Gilly-les-Citeaux, France
Tel & Fax: 03.80.62.87.74
5 Rooms, Double: €75–€90
1 Cottage: €350–€400 weekly
Open: all year, Credit cards: MC, VS
Other Languages: some English, Spanish
Region: Burgundy, Michelin Map: 519

In a tranquil setting of pasture, orchard, and forest, La Réserve is a beautiful amber-washed, two-story manor just a short drive from Giverny, whose owners offer guests a genuine welcome. Unbelievably, the building is of new construction—with much hard work and love, Marie Lorraine and Didier built it themselves, repaired furniture, and made all the bedspreads and curtains. The result is a gorgeous, elegant place to stay with exceptional accommodation. On the ground floor you find a beautiful salon with fireplace and old pool table, a gorgeous dining room, and an adorable guestroom tucked just below the stairs looking out through large windows across to orchards and fields grazed by cattle. Upstairs, guestrooms under high, beamed ceilings are magnificent. Twin or queen beds are set on creaking wooden floors topped with attractive throw rugs, while large, shuttered windows open onto greenery and seem almost to frame a painting worthy of Monet. Just 90 minutes from CDG airport, the Brunets recommend a minimum of two nights' stay so that you can explore Normandy, and spend at least a day lazing in the countryside. *Directions:* Depending on the approach, traveling the main pedestrian street, either turn right past the American Museum or left past the church at the charcuterie, and travel uphill (C3) 1200 meters until you see white painted arrows. Turn left, follow the lane, then go left again just past the orchard.

🏠 🛒 @ W P ♿ 🚶 🐎 ⚓

LA RÉSERVE
Hosts: Marie Lorraine & Didier Brunet
27620 Giverny, France
Tel & Fax: 02.32.21.99.09
7 Rooms, Double: €100–€160
Entire house: €1300 daily, €6000 weekly
Open: Apr to Oct & winter by reservation
Credit cards: none
Other Languages: good English
Region: Upper Normandy, Michelin Map: 513

The Moulin de Fresquet is truly a jewel, with the heart of the old stone mill dating back to the 17th century. The millstream still flows right beneath the house—in fact, from several of the guestrooms you can look out the casement windows and watch the gurgling waters. The family room where guests gather for breakfast is filled with beautiful antiques that Gérard inherited from his grandmother. The ambiance is one of rustic beauty with handsome stone walls accented by family portraits and 200-year-old tapestries, heavy beamed ceiling, bouquets of fresh flowers, and a massive stone fireplace. A narrow staircase leads down to the attractive bedrooms, which have color-coordinated draperies and bedspreads, and French doors opening onto private patios. One of my favorites, Les Meules, is a large room with windows overlooking the stream, and a door onto the garden. Le Meunier enjoys a lovely sitting room and terrace near the mill. Claude, so pretty with sparkling brown eyes, is a fabulous cook, and dinner, served in a newly renovated building whose expanse of windows expose the lushness and peacefulness of the idyllic setting, is an event not to be missed. This lovely mill is located in one of the most beautiful regions of the southwest and convenient to the beautiful towns and villages of both the Dordogne and Lot river valleys. *Directions:* From Gramat take D840 south towards Figeac. 500 meters after Gramat, at the roundabout, take the lane on the left signposted to the mill.

MOULIN DE FRESQUET
Hosts: Claude & Gérard Ramelot
46500 Gramat, France
Tel: 05.65.38.70.60, Fax: 05.65.33.60.13
5 Rooms, Double: €64–€97
1 Suite: €110
Table d'hôte: €25
Open: Apr to Nov, Credit cards: none
Other Languages: some English
Region: Midi-Pyrénées, Michelin Map: 524

A road winds up from the village of Le Grand Bornand to Le Chalet des Troncs through a high, narrow Alpine valley whose pastures are dotted with picture-perfect Swiss chalets in the shadow of towering, majestic peaks. With a real love and respect for the local architecture, Jean-François Charbonnier has completely rebuilt a clustering of weathered mountain chalets terraced up a hillside of flowers, masterfully outfitting them with all the comforts and modern conveniences without compromising the ambiance. Two guestrooms, individually housed in their own cottage, enjoy their own entrances off a private garden terrace and are especially cozy and romantically rustic, with lovely old furnishings and beautiful Alpine fabrics set against a backdrop of exposed stone walls and hand-hewn beams and planks used for ceilings, floors, and clever partitions between bedroom and bathroom. Since my last visit they have added two handsome suites and a covered pool. Le Chalet des Troncs' dining room receives well-deserved accolades for its cuisine and intimate ambiance, whether on the garden terrace or in one of the three cozy dining rooms. Christine and Jean-François live life with a passion and their love of the region is infectious. *Directions:* From Annecy take the D909 east for Thones and just before La Clusaz turn north on the D4 towards Le Grand Bornand. From the north side of the village follow the Route du Bouchet and travel 5 km to its end and Les Troncs.

LE CHALET DES TRONCS
Hosts: Christine & Jean- François Charbonnier
Vallée du Bouchet, Les Troncs
74450 Le Grand Bornand, France
Tel: 04.50.02.28.50, Fax: 04.50.63.25.28
4 Rooms, Double: €140–€180*
*Breakfast not included: €15
Table d'hôte: €35
Open: all year, Credit cards: all major
Other Languages: good English
Region: Rhône-Alpes, Michelin Map: 527

If you are looking for a tranquil little hideaway while exploring the beautiful area of Provence, the Domaine du Bois Vert is truly a gem. Although the construction is only a few years old, the clever owners, Jean Peter and Véronique Richard, have tastefully achieved the ambiance of an old farmhouse by incorporating a typical rosy-tan stuccoed exterior, light-blue wooden shutters, and a heavy tiled roof. The mood of antiquity continues within where dark-beamed ceilings, tiled floors, dark wooden doors, and white walls enhance a few carefully chosen country-style Provençal pieces of furniture and country-print fabrics. There are three bedrooms, each immaculately tidy and prettily decorated. The bedroom to the back of the house is especially enticing, with windows looking out onto the oak trees. Meals are not served on a regular basis, but Véronique treats guests who stay a week to a dinner featuring typical regional specialties. The swimming pool is a most refreshing bonus. *Directions:* Grans is approximately 40 km southeast of Arles and 6 km from Salon de Provence. From Grans, go south on D19 (signposted to Lançon-Provence). About 1 km after you pass Grans, turn left on a small road where you will see a Gîtes sign. In a few minutes turn left again at another Gîtes sign and take the lane to the Domaine du Bois Vert.

■✗@P⊘≋⊥🏌🐎🍇

DOMAINE DU BOIS VERT
Hosts: Véronique & Jean Peter Richard
Quartier Montauban
13450 Grans, France
Tel & Fax: 04.90.55.82.98
3 Rooms, Double: €72–€79
Minimum Stay Required
Closed: Jan 5 to Mar, Credit cards: none
Other Languages: good English
Region: Provence-Alps-Côte d'Azur, Michelin Map: 527

The Bastide Saint Mathieu is a beautiful property. Entry through he huge olivewood door transports you back to years ago. Converting the property from a state of ruin, fortunately, many original elements were preserved, contributing to its romantic ambiance and character. This elegant two-story house offers five spacious suites, Provencal in their decor: fine antiques, wooden floors, fire places, and high-beamed ceilings. My favorite room was the red one with a canopy bed and its own terrace. You will be indulged by the fine linen, drinks tray, a bathroom with separate shower and bath tub including products from the perfumeries de Grasse. Then in the morning enjoy a bountiful breakfast served on the terrace. Weather permitting, afterward relax at the large pool overlooking an acre of olive and fruits trees and colorful flowers. This splendid property offers warmth and charm enhanced by the amenities of a fine small hotel (air-conditioning, satellite TV, internet, elevator) while preserving "ultimate privacy." *Directions:* From A8 exit Grasse sud, turn right. At large roundabout take 2nd right. Next roundabout turn left and then right to the Blue Elephant roundabout. Take exit St. Mathieu-St. Jean. At T junction turn left, follow direction St. Jean; La Bastide is on your left.

❄ ☕ 🏃 💳 ☎ 🚻 @ W P ≈ 🖼 ⚓ 🚶 ⛷ 🎣

BASTIDE SAINT MATHIEU
Hosts: Soraya & Bill Colegrave
35 Chemin de Blumenthal
06130 Grasse, France
Tel: 04.97.01.10.00, Fax: 04.97.01.10.09
5 Rooms, Double: €290–€330
2 Suites: €330–€380
Open: all year, Credit cards: all major
Châteaux & Hôtels Collection
Region: Provence-Alps-Côte d'Azur, Michelin Map: 527

Jacqueline and Auguste Bahuaud purchased a handsome manor dating from the mid-1800s and, with great love and labor, meticulously restored the house to its original splendor. Throughout the home everything is fresh, new, and beautifully decorated. The bedrooms are especially outstanding: each has its own personality, each is very inviting. My particular favorite is the Blue Room, which has a prime corner location, affording windows on two walls looking out to the rear garden and the river. One of the very nicest aspects of La Croix d'Etain is its setting: the parklike grounds stretch behind the house with terraced lawns shaded by mature trees. A romantic path through the garden leads down to Grez-Neuville, a real gem of a small village nestled on the banks of the Mayenne river. There are many boats along the Mayenne that can be rented by the day or week for exploring the picturesque countryside. Your gracious hosts, Jacqueline and Auguste, warmly open their home and hearts to their guests. *Directions:* From Angers, take N162 north for about 17 km and take a right onto the Grez-Neuville exit. Go into the village and find the old church. As you go down towards the river, you see on your left a beautiful old stone church, and just adjacent to it, the Chambres d'Hôtes sign on the gate of the Bahuauds' home.

LA CROIX D'ETAIN
Hosts: Jacqueline & Auguste Bahuaud
2, Rue de l'Ecluse
49220 Grez–Neuville, France
Tel: 02.41.95.68.49, Fax: 02.41.18.02.72
5 Rooms, Double: €75–€100
1 Cottage: €250–€450 weekly
Table d'hôte: €30, not Sun
Open: all year, Credit cards: MC, VS
Other Languages: some English
Region: Loire Valley, Michelin Map: 517

I cannot imagine why Guérande is not better known: it is a stunning medieval town with its walls intact and even the moat still filled with water. Happily the town also has a lovely bed and breakfast, making a visit to Guérande even more special. Le Tricot, a stately, cream-colored, 18th-century mansion, is hidden behind stone walls at the end of a small lane. It has been in the de Champsavin family for seven generations. When your charming hosts, Andrea and Loïc de Champsavin, took over the home, it had lain empty for ten years and time had taken its toll: the mansion needed to be totally renovated. With great love and labor, the de Champsavins have made amazing progress in bringing the property back to its original beauty, both inside and out. It is especially astounding to see all the work that Andrea has accomplished. Not only has she made all of the drapes and bedspreads, but also reupholstered chairs and sofas. All of the bedrooms are now as pretty as can be and all have top-notch, tiled bathrooms. One of the most enchanting features of Le Tricot is its gorgeous garden, which stretches out behind the home to be enclosed by the medieval stone wall of the town. The garden, which has an informal English air, is impeccably kept and its beds of colorful flowers are so beautiful that it seems ready for a photo shoot from a gardening magazine. *Directions:* Enter Guérande through the Bizienne gate—the road on the right by the church is Rue du Tricot.

LE TRICOT
Hosts: Andrea & Loïc de Champsavin
8, Rue du Tricot
44350 Guérande, France
Tel: 02.40.24.90.72, Fax: 02.40.24.72.53
4 Rooms, Double: €100–€145
1 Suite: €175–€200
Open: May to Sep & off season by reservation
Credit cards: none
Other Languages: good English, German
Region: Brittany, Michelin Map: 512

Dana and Robert Ornsteen, your charming American hosts, lived for many years in Paris before purchasing L'Enclos, an enchanting hamlet in the heart of the idyllic Périgord. The complex (once the estate of the Count de Souffron) encloses a courtyard, on one side of which sits the manor, a creamy-beige, two-story home, prettily accented by white shutters. Also facing the courtyard is a cluster of stone cottages, which exude a whimsical, storybook character with their jumble of steep, weathered, interconnecting rooflines and perky gables. Two guestrooms are found in the manor house—the others occupy the hamlet's ivy-laced, yellow-hued stone cottages. The cottages are named for their "past": La Boulangerie still has its bread ovens; La Chapelle occupies the old church; romantic Rose Cottage has thick stone walls, painted furniture, and Provençal fabrics. Two cottages have full kitchens. The gardens are outstanding, with impeccably manicured lawns, weathered stone walls, and gorgeous flowerbeds. A swimming pool nestles in a lush grassy oasis. Everything is absolute perfection, and the price is incredible for such superb quality. You will love it. *Directions:* From Périgueux take D5 east towards Hautefort. At Tourtoirac turn left on D67, cross the bridge, keep right at the Y, and continue for 1.4 km. Turn left into the lane signposted Pragelier, go down the hill and through the gates to L'Enclos.

L' ENCLOS
Hosts: Dana & Robert Ornsteen
Pragelier
24390 Hautefort, France
Tel: 05.53.51.11.40, Fax: 32.03.41.70.03
2 Rooms, 7 Cottages: Double: €70–€160*
*Breakfast not included: €10
Minimum Stay Required, Table d'hôte: €40
Open: May to Oct 1, Credit cards: none
Other Languages: fluent English, Spanish
Region: Aquitaine, Michelin Maps: 521, 522, 524

This charming roadside inn, by origin part presbytery, part farm, offers reasonably priced, simple accommodation paired with a lovely countryside restaurant. Windows trimmed in a dusty blue, dressed with window boxes overflowing with geraniums, are set in the cream stucco of the exterior under the undulating tile roof. The reception area with its heavy old beams and antique circular table is cozy, warmed by an old oven sitting against a backdrop of hand-painted tiles. To the right, off the reception is the inn's delightful restaurant, which offers four incredible menus. To the left of the entry is the breakfast room, which opens onto a side garden terrace. Climb a small staircase off the breakfast room to a two-tiered sitting room, which was cozily renovated for the Duke of Windsor who stayed here on occasion. Three guestrooms are accessed off the entry stair. Room 1 is set behind a low door and takes up the area that once was the presbytery. In what was the farm, room 2 is the largest while room 3 is intimate and can open to the neighboring room 4. When rented individually, room 4 has an independent entrance off an outside staircase. Room 5, accessed off the back courtyard, enjoys its own terrace and a more lavish bath. *Directions:* Driving south from Boulogne-sur-Mer, turn off the N1 and travel east on D147 (a small country road) to Beaussent where you turn south on the D1 towards Inxent. The inn is on the right side of the road with parking on the left.

AUBERGE D'INXENT
Hosts: Laurence & Jean-Marc Six
La Vallée de la Course, 318, Rue de la Vallée
62170 Inxent, France
Tel: 03.21.90.71.19, Fax: 03.21.86.31.67
5 Rooms, Double: €65–€72*
*Breakfast not included: €9
Closed: mid-Dec to mid-Jan, first week of Jul
Credit cards: MC, VS
Region: North Calais, Michelin Map: 511

This magnificent 17th century house is in the center of L'Isle sur la Sorgue, a city well known for antique stores and surrounded by the river "La Sorgue." La Maison sur la Sorgue is a dream come true for your charming hosts who spent a year to find it and another year of restoration. Beyond the old antique door you arrive in a dramatic, glass-roofed courtyard opening to the sky, with stone floor, where you will be met by your young hosts. They make it evident that their gigantic home is really your home. Going up a few stairs an old stained glass will brighten your path leading to the four spacious guests rooms. You will feel as though you are a world traveler as the decor of each room comes mainly from India and Vietnam. My favorite room is "The Room on the Loggia"; a big room with an open shower, decorated in burgundy, with a beamed ceiling and a large terrace overlooking the pool. Another room with a smaller terrace is the "Attic Suite", with a little salon, a mezzanine modern bathroom, and a view facing the Chapel of the Virgin. Then two other rooms offer charm, one with a canopy bed; the other hiding the surprise of the shadows! Each suite displays special mementos they have brought back from their travels. To share even more, they have opened a shop next door, "Retour de Voyages". *Directions:* From Cavaillon, follow signs to L'Isle sur la Sorgue; in the center go straight until you pass a bank, and make a left on a little bridge to Place Goudard.

LA MAISON SUR LA SORGUE
Hosts: Fréderic Dol & Marie-Claude Marseille
6 Rue Rose Goudard
84800 L'Isle sur la Sorgue, France
Tel: 04.90.20.74.86, Fax: 04.90.20.72.66
2 Rooms, Double: €200–€240
2 Suites: €240–€290
Table d'hôte: €30
Open: all year, Credit cards: all major
Region: Provence-Alps-Côte d'Azur, Michelin Map: 527

Take a picture-perfect château set in a splendid forest, add an owner who is a professional decorator and a family who welcomes guests as friends, and you have all the ingredients for a perfect bed and breakfast. The exceptional Château d'Ivoy is the artistic creation of Marie France Gouëffon-de Vaivre. She and her husband purchased the property from a famous ethnologist who was using it as a laboratory and even had chickens living in the majestic reception hall! After years of intensive renovation, this handsome château once again glows with the splendor of the 16th century. The Gouëffon-de Vaivre family has private living quarters, but the rest of the home is open to guests who are free to wander from one incredible room to the next. Each is a showplace displaying Marie France's great flair for decorating along with many whimsical touches that make you smile. Every room has its own distinct personality, running the gamut from the masculine hunting room with plaid fabric on the walls to the alluringly romantic parlor. I loved them all, but my very favorite was the Lord Drummond room with its gorgeous canopy bed, rich paisley fabrics, and tall windows capturing a marvelous view of the beautiful park behind the house. *Directions:* From Bourges go north on D940 to la Chapelle d'Angillon then take D12 to Ivoy le Pré. Go through town. The château is located on the right as you leave Ivoy le Pré on D12 toward Henrichemont.

CHÂTEAU D'IVOY
Host: Marie France Gouëffon-de Vaivre
18380 Ivoy le Pré, France
Tel: 02.48.58.85.01, Fax: 02.48.58.85.02
4 Rooms, Double: €195
1 Suite: €310
Open: all year, Credit cards: MC, VS
Other Languages: good English
Region: Loire Valley, Michelin Map: 518

The Château du Plessis is a lovely, aristocratic country home. The Plessis has been in Valerie Benoist-Renoul's family since well before the Revolution, but the antiques throughout the home are later acquisitions of her great-great-great-great-grandfather. The original furnishings were burned on the front lawn by revolutionaries in 1793. Furnishings throughout the home are elegant, yet the Renouls have established an atmosphere of homey comfort. Artistic fresh-flower arrangements abound and you can see the cutting garden from the French doors in the salon that open onto the lush grounds. The well-worn turret steps lead to the beautifully furnished accommodations. In the evening a large oval table in the dining room provides an opportunity to enjoy the company of other guests and the country-fresh cuisine. Dinner is a wonderful four-course meal. Advance reservations must be made. Valerie, along with her husband Laurent, take great pride in her home and the welcome they extend to their guests. Valerie and Laurent are pleased to carry on the tradition of service and welcome established by her parents. *Directions:* Travel north of Angers on N162. At the town of Le Lion d'Angers travel towards Chateau Gontier and travel 11 km farther north to an intersection, Carrefour Fleur de Lys. Turn east and travel 2.5 km to La Jaille-Yvon and its southern edge.

CHÂTEAU DU PLESSIS
Host: Valerie Renoul
49220 La Jaille-Yvon, France
Tel: 02.41.95.12.75
5 Rooms, Double: €120–€220, 2 Suites: €220*
*Breakfast not included: €12
Table d'hôte: €48
Open: all year, Credit cards: all major
Other Languages: good English, Spanish
Châteaux & Hôtels Collection
Region: Loire Valley, Michelin Map: 517

Lacoste is such a beautiful village tucked into the hills of Provence that we felt so lucky to find an exceptionally outstanding place to stay. The Domaine de Layaude Basse, a charming, 18th-century stone farmhouse nestled in the trees just outside Lacoste, has been in the Mazel family for many generations. With loving care and exceptionally good taste, Lydia and Olivier Mazel, your gracious hosts, totally renovated the family home as a bed and breakfast, adding bathrooms for all the guestrooms, a cheerful, glass-enclosed dining room, a splendid swimming pool, and attractive landscaping. They have been sensitive to the nature of the house and not only preserved the wonderful architectural features of the house, but also kept many of the old farm tools, now artistically displayed on the walls. One of my favorite rooms just oozes charm with a huge stone fireplace, tiled floors, beamed ceiling, yokes for oxen on the walls, dried flowers hanging from the ceiling, a marvelous hanging cupboard, and antique plates. The bedrooms are not large, but as sweet as can be, with pretty Provençal fabrics used throughout. Three new rooms have just been added and are equally lovely. The swimming pool is nestled on a terrace with an incredible view out over the beautiful countryside. The Domaine de Layaude Basse is a marvelous value—a reasonably priced place to stay that offers great charm. *Directions:* Located about 40 km northwest of Aix-en-Provence, just outside Lacoste on D108.

DOMAINE DE LAYAUDE BASSE
Hosts: Lydia & Olivier Mazel
84480 Lacoste, France
Tel: 04.90.75.90.06, Fax: 04.90.75.99.03
5 Rooms, Double: €75–€95
Table d'hôte: €27
Open: all year, Credit cards: none
Other Languages: some English
Region: Provence-Alps-Côte d'Azur, Michelin Map: 527

The enchanting Château du Guilguiffin is a gorgeous stone manor accented by white shutters, steeply pitched slate roof, perky dormers, and a profusion of chimneys. A circular drive sweeps to the entrance facing onto a lawn enclosed by three circular walls interrupted by three 18th-century columns with unique Oriental motifs, which make this 1400-acre property a "historic site." The elegant decor is outstanding, with beamed ceilings, mellow wood paneling, and heirloom antiques. In contrast to the formal parlor, the breakfast room is delightfully casual—a happy room with pretty yellow walls, blue doors, blue-and-white tiles, and a "walk-in" stone fireplace. Guests enjoy breakfast at one large table topped by a gay Provençal-print cloth. The bedrooms are exquisitely furnished with antiques accented by fabric-covered walls and color-coordinating draperies and bedspreads. The garden too is equally stunning. Early spring presents an unbelievable spectacle of 350,000 daffodils followed by thousands of azaleas and rhododendrons. Barbecues are available so that guests can grill fresh fish from the local market and enjoy dinner in the parklike grounds. Restaurants are just ten minutes away. Philippe Davy is an exceptional host and the château has been in his family for over 900 years. Stay at least a week to explore the best of Brittany. *Directions:* From Quimper, go west on D784 towards Audierne. The château is on the left, 3 km before Landudec.

CHÂTEAU DU GUILGUIFFIN
Hosts: Angelica & Philippe Davy
Guilguiffin, 29710 Landudec, France
Tel: 02.98.91.52.11, Fax: 02.98.91.52.52
8 Rooms, Double: €135–€220
1 Cottage: €150–€770 weekly
Open: Apr to Nov 15, off season by reservation
Credit cards: all major
Other Languages: fluent English, German
Châteaux & Hôtels Collection
Region: Brittany, Michelin Map: 512

Quercy Blanc is a relatively untouristed region south of Le Lot where charming, little villages are built with the region's beautiful, cream limestone and hug the quiet river or nestle in the lush farmland. A gorgeous, 60-hectare complex of farmland and forest, Domaine de Saint Géry resembles a small village with a collection of buildings housing dining room, guestrooms, spa, and factory for Domaine's wonderful foie gras—all set off from the central courtyard. The large, outdoor pool enjoys views of the countryside complete with grazing horses. The property was in a state of ruin when Patrick's parents returned searching for his mother's family history. (Saint Géry is a name associated with nobility since the 11th century.) They purchased the home, but it wasn't until Patrick and his wife, Pascale, decided to settle here that his mother's dream was realized. The home is beautifully decorated in warm colors with handsome furnishings and antiques, oriental carpets, tile floors, and modern bathrooms. While the price is high, the exclusivity and solitude will appeal to those seeking this atmosphere. Dinner is table d'hôte for resident guests at tables set before a large fireplace. Under Patrick's artful direction, the experience is incredible; if you love foie gras—they are masters! *Directions:* Exit the A20 at Cahors Sud-58; take N20 towards Cahors, then Montcuq for 500 meters. Turn left on D7 (direction of Labastide Marnhac) and to the outskirts Lascabanes.

DOMAINE DE SAINT GÉRY
Hosts: Patrick & Pascale Duler
46800 Lascabanes, France
Tel: 05.65.31.82.51, Fax: 05.65.22.92.89
4 Rooms, Double: €224–€345*
1 Suite: €480–€622*
*Breakfast not included: €28
Table d'hôte: €96
Closed: Jan 1 to May 15, Credit cards: all major
Region: Midi-Pyrénées, Michelin Map: 525

Pass under the stone archway draped in honeysuckle into the garden of the Maison Rancèsamy and you will be captured by its spell and understand why Isabelle and Simon settled here after much traveling. Everything was in bloom in early summer when we visited: the wisteria, the jasmine, the lavender, the roses, and the honeysuckle whose scent filled the entire garden. There is a wonderful herb garden whose bounty enhances the delicious table d'hôte dinners. In fine weather, dinner is served in the garden—otherwise, guests eat in the dining room. There are five tastefully decorated guestrooms, all named for flowers found in the garden. Each room enjoys a private bathroom. Guests enjoy the amenities of a lounge, and a swimming pool. Around the house and garden are many art works made by a friend: the artistically carved and painted dining-room table, the large entry bench with the cleverly placed game board at its center, and the totem pole on the deck. The spectacular views over the hills and vineyards will take your breath away. As Isabelle mentioned, she has been told that her home has soul and that is the best compliment she could ever receive. *Directions:* From Pau head south on the N134. At Gan, after the pharmacy, take the D24 for 9 km to Lasseube. Turn left on the D324 and then right after the farmhouse. Follow the road over two bridges to the home signed on the left.

MAISON RANCÈSAMY
Hosts: Isabelle & Simon Browne
Quartier Rey
64290 Lasseube, France
Tel & Fax: 05.59.04.26.37
5 Rooms, Double: €75–€90
Minimum Stay Required
Table d'hôte: €32
Open: all year, Credit cards: none
Other Languages: fluent English
Region: Aquitaine, Michelin Map: 524

L'Aubèle is a lovely Bearnese-style home in a small village that looks across fields to the Pyrénées. The stone and plaster home is attractive with its shuttered windows and third-floor dormers peeking through the slate roof. Typical of the houses in this region, the courtyard is central to the home and barn and is enclosed behind a front wall. Although L'Aubèle had been abandoned for 25 years, it was tightly boarded up, so while the Desbonnets had to add modern conveniences such as plumbing, the interior cabinetry, the staircase, and the old windows were all in great condition. A seating arrangement in front of the large, open fireplace is a wonderful place to settle and an intimate dining area overlooks the park. Upstairs, you find the guestrooms and a cozy sitting area with bookshelves packed with novels and information on the region. La Rose, named for its color scheme, is a pretty room with a double bed and en suite bathroom, while the second, very handsome bedroom has an old sleigh bed and an enormous bathroom. With just two bedrooms this is perfect for family or friends traveling together. *Directions:* Located west of Pau, from Navarrenx, take the D2 towards Monein then at Jasses take the D27 towards Oloron Ste. Marie. In Lay-Lamidou turn left, then first right, and L'Aubèle is the second house on the right. (A small brass plaque displays the Desbonnet name.)

L' AUBÈLE
Host: Marie-France Desbonnet
4, Rue de la Hauti
64190 Lay-Lamidou, France
Tel & Fax: 05.59.66.00.44
2 Rooms, Double: €65
Open: all year, Credit cards: none
Other Languages: some English
Region: Aquitaine, Michelin Map: 524

La Mozardière is a charming, 18th-century farmhouse with an idyllic setting on the outskirts of Legé, offering total tranquility, yet only 39 kilometers south of Nantes. Christine and Gérard lived for many years in Paris, but yearned for a quieter life. They honed their choice of the ideal place to live to somewhere near Nantes and eventually found the perfect house—La Mozardière. Just what they had been dreaming of! Gérard says they still wake up each morning loving their new way of life and the beauty of their surroundings. It is no wonder they are so happy here: you will be too. Just behind the home is a lovely garden stretching out to a romantic small lake, with many very old shade trees and well-kept flowerbeds enhancing the scene. There are just two guestrooms: the "green" room on the ground floor and the "blue" room upstairs. My favorite is the green room, which has French doors leading directly to the garden. There is nothing fancy or ostentatious about La Mozardière: it is simple, pretty, and exudes the warmth of a private home. Christine and Gérard are gracious hosts. Christine occasionally offers dinner, but she also has a second career as a potter and makes wonderful, whimsical ceramic ware (which you will see for sale as you enter) in a kiln in the old barn. *Directions:* From in front of the church in Legé, take the road for Touvois. Just before leaving town, turn left onto Richebonne and follow signs.

LA MOZARDIÈRE
Hosts: Christine & Gérard Desbrosses
9, Impasse de Richebonne
44650 Legé, France
Tel: 02.40.04.98.51, Fax: 02.40.26.31.61
3 Rooms, Double: €59
Table d'hôte: €28
Open: Mar to Oct, Credit cards: none
Other Languages: good English
Region: Loire Valley, Michelin Map: 517

Levernois is a country village located just five minutes by car on D970 from Beaune. Here the ivy-clad Hôtel le Parc offers a tranquil alternative to Beaune for those travelers who prefer the serenity of the countryside. This is a simple hotel which is comprised of a lovely ivy-covered home. Guests congregate in the evening in the convivial little bar, just off the entry salon or at tables in the lovely, shaded courtyard garden. (Note: The owners prefer that guests purchase beverages from them rather than bring their own, if they drink in public areas.) In the summer, breakfast is also offered in the courtyard; in winter guests are served in the attractive breakfast room. Breakfast is the only meal served. Wide, prettily papered hallways lead to the bedrooms. The rooms are attractive and simply decorated, and all but two have their own clean bath or shower. Although Le Parc is a hotel, it is so reasonably priced that I have decided to include it in the bed & breakfast guide. *Directions:* Travel 3 km southeast of Beaune on Route de Verdun-sur-le-Doubs D970 and D111.

HÔTEL LE PARC
Hosts: M & Mme Botigliero
Levernois, 21200 Beaune, France
Tel: 03.80.24.63.00, Fax: 03.80.24.21.19
17 Rooms, Double: €55–€70*
*Breakfast not included: €8
Closed: Dec 1 to Jan 15, Credit cards: MC
Other Languages: some English
Region: Burgundy, Michelin Map: 519

Several years ago Martine Descamps decided to change her lifestyle, moving from Paris to the Loire Valley where she and her husband bought a large 19th-century manor-farmhouse and opened a bed and breakfast. The house is set in a lovely agricultural region where vineyards stretch out in every direction. The two-story house forms one side of an enclosed courtyard full of flowers and trees. The Descamps created four spacious bedrooms with modern bathrooms for guests. Each bedroom is named after its former life, such as Le Pressoir, the room where the grapes used to be pressed. It has one wall of exposed stone, a large window at the opening through which the grapes were dumped, a king-sized bed, and a table cleverly made from the gears of the old pressing machine. Guests enjoy their own large lounge with a piano, billiard table, comfortable sitting area, and an open fireplace. Breakfast is served in a charming dining room with lovely terracotta floors, beamed ceiling, and a large open fireplace. Martine offers a delicious three-course dinner, by special request, served in the garden during summer months. Another bonus is a large pool in the garden behind the house and a barn converted to a fitness room. *Directions:* From Chinon, cross the River Vienne and take D749 toward Ile Bouchard. After 1 km, turn right at the sign "Ligré par le vignoble." Go 5 km, turn left at the hamlet of Le Rouilly, and follow signs to the bed and breakfast.

MANOIR LE CLOS DE LIGRÉ
Host: Martine Descamps
Hamlet of Le Rouilly
37500 Ligré, France
Tel: 02.47.93.95.59, Fax: 02.47.93.06.31
4 Rooms, Double: €100
Table d'hôte: €30
Open: all year, Credit cards: none
Other Languages: fluent English
Region: Center, Michelin Map: 517

From the moment you drive through the gates, you will be enchanted by the Manoir Saint-Gilles de la Cirottière, a storybook-perfect, 15th-century château accented by manicured lawns, clipped box hedges, and fragrant rose gardens. It is immediately obvious that the owners are perfectionists, for everything is tended immaculately. One wing of the house, a charming two-story stone building accented by a tall turret, is totally dedicated to guests. It has an inviting lounge where small tables with colorful Provençal tablecloths are set in front of a massive stone fireplace. The attractively decorated bedrooms are reached by the stone staircase that spirals up the tower. My favorite is room 3, the Typhaine, an exceptionally large room with windows capturing a view of the front garden and the wooded park behind. Your gracious hosts, Monsieur and Madame Naux, have a daughter who lives in the USA, and they seem especially to enjoy entertaining guests from abroad. *Directions:* Coming from Angers on the RN147, take D53 marked to Blou and Saint Philbert. Very soon after leaving the highway, D53 goes over the railroad tracks. At the first road after crossing the tracks, turn left at the dead end sign, then turn left again at the first road with the second dead end sign. Go about 300 meters and turn right at the first small lane (third dead end sign). The manor with its white gate is at the road's end.

MANOIR SAINT-GILLES DE LA CIROTTIÈRE
Hosts: M & Mme Naux
Saint Gilles de la Cirottière
49160 Longué, France
Tel: 02.41.38.77.45, Fax: 02.41.52.67.82
4 Rooms, Double: €82–€85
1 Suite: €130
Minimum Stay Required
Open: Apr to Nov, Credit cards: none
Other Languages: some English
Region: Center, Michelin Map: 517

My first trip to Europe with my parents included the Normandy coast and the D-Day beaches—a trip that brought my history books to life! I kept thinking of my own children when we discovered the Ferme de la Tourelle, and I couldn't help thinking that this would be a perfect spot to bring them. The price is incredible and accommodations, although very simple and basic, are clean and comfortable and three of the five guestrooms are equipped with both a double bed and bunk bed. Actually located in Fontenailles, a small hamlet on the outskirts of Longues-sur-Mer, Ferme de la Tourelle, true to its name, is a working farm. The main home is a handsome two-story farmhouse with one tall tower whose windows are dressed with boxes overflowing with geraniums. This is the Lecarpentiers' home and they welcome you here for a bountiful breakfast served at the long, handsome trestle table in their kitchen. Guestrooms are found in a separate building across the lawn. On the first floor guests enjoy their own sitting room and use of a kitchen. Four bedrooms are found on the second floor, with the fifth on the third floor under the roofline. This bed and breakfast is simple, clean, and an excellent value. *Directions:* Halfway between Port en Bessin and Arromanches. Travel the D514 and on the east side of Longues-sur-Mer watch for the sign to Fontenailles. Follow Gîtes signs to Ferme de la Tourelle (there are a couple of B&Bs in the village).

🛋 🚴 P ⚓

FERME DE LA TOURELLE
Hosts: J-Maurice & Janine Lecarpentier
Hameau de Fontenailles, Ferme de la Tourelle
14400 Longues-sur-Mer, France
Tel: 02.31.21.78.47, Fax: 02.31.21.84.84
5 Rooms, Double: €45
Open: all year, Credit cards: none
Other Languages: very little English
Region: Lower Normandy, Michelin Map: 513

Château Talaud is absolutely perfect. This splendid, 18th-century estate offers all the warmth, charm, and intimacy of a bed and breakfast, enhanced by the sophisticated amenities of the finest small hotel. Plan to stay as long as possible, making Château Talaud your home while exploring Provence. A long tree-lined lane leads up to the stately mansion, a beautiful, honey-colored, three-story home nestled in its own garden. Stretching away in every direction are immaculately kept fields of grapes that produce Côte de Ventoux wine. Your charming hosts, the Deiters-Kommers, are Dutch, but have lived throughout the world. Hein now produces fine wine while Conny operates the bed and breakfast. The château's comfortable yet elegant interior—combining gorgeous fabrics, fine antiques, and exquisite furnishings all chosen by Conny—is definitely Architectural Digest material. The bedrooms are spacious—some enormous—and all have cable TV, direct-dial phones, and splendid large bathrooms. I adored the Blue Room, which has pastel-blue walls, an incredibly high ceiling, wooden canopy bed, and a marble bathroom as large as many bedrooms. Conny is a gourmet chef and on Tuesday and Friday serves a superb dinner for her guests. *Directions:* From the A7, take the Avignon Nord exit 23. Go toward Carpentras on D942 for 10 km then turn left on D107 toward Loriol du Comtat. Château Talaud is on your left after 2 km.

CHÂTEAU TALAUD
Hosts: Conny & Hein Deiters-Kommer
D107, 84870 Loriol du Comtat, France
Tel: 04.90.65.71.00, Fax: 04.90.65.77.93
3 Rooms, Double: €190–€210, 2 Suites: €200–€230
1 Cottage & 2 Apartments: €1500–€1700 weekly
Minimum Stay Required
Table d'hôte: €50
Closed: Jan & Feb, Credit cards: MC, VS
Other Languages: fluent English
Region: Provence-Alps-Côte d'Azur, Michelin Map: 527

The Relais des Monts is a beautiful inn residing in an ivy-covered stone farmstead with a weathered slate roof and a central courtyard. Nestled in a high mountain valley, I was at first disappointed that we were distancing ourselves from the Tarn River, until we finally arrived in this tranquil paradise. The Relais des Monts has three guestrooms; all are private, spacious, unique, and have their own outside entrance. Two enjoy their own private garden and one has a balcony terrace. "Victoria" is accessed off the courtyard by walking across the lower, angled roof of an adjoining building, and then through a small door. The interior features treasures that Claudine and Jean brought back from their decades of living in Africa: a handsome four-poster bed is draped in netting, a jute bedspread is designed with a shield matching that on the headboard, a jungle helmet sits on a counter next to a photo of a hunter sporting the same, bath towels are hung on a bamboo ladder. A floor-to-ceiling arched window, framing a magnificent mountain valley view, opens onto a terrace. On the garden level, "Manon," with a separate sitting room, is very attractive in a décor of blue and yellow. Also on the garden level, "Estelle" became my favorite. Cheerful, cream-colored headboards painted with flowers compliment the red floral and checked fabrics that also enclose the angled window seat. *Directions:* From D907 turn up from the town of La Malène, direction Canourgue.

RELAIS DES MONTS
Hosts: Claudine & Jean Laboureur
Les Monts
48210 La Malène, France
Tel: 04.66.48.54.34, Fax: 04.66.48.59.25
3 Rooms, Double: €180–€210*
*Breakfast not included: €15
Open: Apr to Sep by reservation, Credit cards: MC, VS
Region: Midi-Pyrénées, Michelin Map: 526

La Grange de Jusalem is very special, intimate and charming. Travelers fortunate enough to stay will feel like guests in a private home. The drive up to the home is like a treasure hunt—you follow a series of discreet blue signs as the tiny lane winds through a sea of vineyards, ending at a pretty, 18th-century light-beige stone farmhouse with white trim and blue shutters built around a courtyard. There is no air of formality here at all: instead, it seems you are a friend of the family coming to visit. The five guestrooms, three of which were newly constructed for the 2003 season, are furnished with family antiques and have a personal, homelike ambiance. Another wonderful addition is a cozy reading/tea room just off the dining room where guests can settle and enjoy the surrounding views. Next to the house, bordered by endless vineyards, there is a delightful swimming pool. What makes this bed and breakfast so extraordinary is your hostess, Maryvonne. This pretty, gentle woman exudes such a genuine, unpretentious warmth that you will be captivated by her charm. Best of all, she is a gourmet chef and guests come to stay from far away to enjoy her fabulous home-cooked meals. In the summer, dinner is served by candlelight on the terrace with the vineyards almost at your fingertips. *Directions:* Mazan is about 7 km east of Carpentras. From Mazan take D163 south toward Malemort, watching for small directional signs on the right.

LA GRANGE DE JUSALEM
Host: Maryvonne du Lac
84380 Mazan, France
Tel: 04.90.69.83.48, Fax: 04.90.69.63.53
5 Rooms, Double: €75–€95*
*Breakfast not included: €7,50
Table d'hôte: €26
Open: all year, Credit cards: none
Other Languages: some English
Region: Provence-Alps-Côte d'Azur, Michelin Map: 527

Le Mas de Cante-Perdrix is situated in one of the loveliest parts of Provence, an area of picturesque hilltowns and endless fields of vineyards. Cante Perdrix means "song of the partridge" and the area where the property is located was at one time rich with partridges. Laraine (who is English) and Sean (who is American) took several years to find the perfect property for opening a bed and breakfast and when they finally discovered Le Mas de Cante-Perdrix, an old farmhouse dating back to 1846, it needed a tremendous amount of work. It didn't have electricity or running water but it had the ingredients that the Dunns felt important: good location, charming house, and sufficient space for an independent living area for guests. The house is sheltered from the street by a tall line of cypress trees. As you come down the driveway, the first things you see are the lovely garden and swimming pool. The Dunns are excellent gardeners and their well-kept lawns and beautifully tended flowers greatly enhance the property. There is also a splendid back garden with terrace. Guests have a separate entrance to the six bedrooms, all decorated by Laraine who also prepares a delicious table d'hôte dinner every night. The combination of Laraine and Sean's friendliness and fluent English makes Le Mas de Cante-Perdrix a haven. *Directions:* Mazan is about 7 km east of Carpentras. From Mazan, take D70 toward Caromb—Le Mas is on your right.

LE MAS DE CANTE-PERDRIX
Hosts: Laraine & Sean Dunn
690, Route de Caromb (D70)
84380 Mazan, France
Tel & Fax: 04.90.69.78.69
5 Rooms, Double: €115
Minimum Stay Required: 2 nights
Table d'hôte: €40
Open: all year, Credit cards: all major
Other Languages: fluent English
Region: Provence-Alps-Côte d'Azur, Michelin Map: 527

The Patrolins were pioneers in the French bed and breakfast field and over the years have truly professionalized the art of making guests welcome and comfortable. Located just outside Cahors in the beautiful Lot Valley, Le Mas Azemar looks up to the majestic Château de Mercuès. The decor in this lovely two-story, 18th-century country house is pretty, with soft, warm colors differentiating the various rooms—the entry is a soft cream, the hallway a soft pink with blue trim, the dining room a lovely yellow with a complementary yellow-and-white-striped wallpaper, the library a pretty blue, and the doors and exposed beams are stained in a light gray. The entry leads to the summer dining room, which opens onto a lovely living room leading to the back gardens and pool. The winter dining room, its beams hung with dried-flower arrangements, is very appealing, with a long table set in front of an old water trough on one side and a large open fireplace on the other. We were able to see only a few bedrooms but they were all lovely and while they varied in size, they were all comfortable in appointments and amenities. *Directions:* Traveling the N20 from Cahors, turn off on D811 and travel west 5 km to Mercuès. In the village turn left at a small sign on the D145 towards Caillac. Le Mas Azemar is just off the road on the right.

LE MAS AZEMAR
Hosts: Sabine & Claude Patrolin
Rue du Mas de Vinssou
46090 Mercuès, France
Tel: 05.65.30.96.85, Fax: 05.65.30.53.82
5 Rooms, Double: €95–€105
Table d'hôte: €32
Open: all year, Credit cards: none
Other Languages: fluent English
Region: Midi-Pyrénées, Michelin Maps: 524, 525

The famous gourmet chef, Philippe Monti, of the Hostellerie de Crillon le Brave, opened his bed and breakfast in 2003. Philippe and Isabelle have done a terrific job renovating this 18th-century house which they named for the region's oldest and rarest Noria waterwheel that is located in their garden. All of the charming and comfortable bedrooms are spacious and rustic and are furnished with wrought-iron beds and locally found antiques. Provencal fabrics and beamed ceilings enhance the ambiance. Some rooms enjoy a private terrace. The Pomme de Pin suite has a canopy bed, polished walls, a living room and a huge open bathroom with bathtub and shower. Well tended gardens abound, the display of flowers is gorgeous and a beautiful saltwater pool is set in the middle of the garden and includes a pool house. Even the wash-house has been transformed into an inviting summer living room so you can relax and enjoy the surrounding beauty. The Montis have a real passion for nature and they have planted a few fruit trees, so you can enjoy their excellent marmalade and fresh fruit when you attend their table d'hôte twice a week. Philippe was born in the area, and has traveled all around France as a chef, and he is eager to show you all that the region has to offer. *Directions:* In Carpentras follow signs toward Mont Ventoux and Bédouin on the D974. Then go toward Modène. At the entrance of the village (facing the church) turn left onto Rte de Mazan until you see the Villa's sign.

LA VILLA NORIA   **New**
Hosts: Isabelle & Philippe Monti
La Contadine
84330 Modène, France
Tel & Fax: 04 90 62 50 66
5 Rooms, Double: €70–€150
Table d'hote: €35
Open: all year, Credit cards: none
Region: Provence-Alps-Côte d'Azur, Michelin Map: 528

We knew nothing about this property other than the fact it had been awarded four épis by the Gîtes de France, so we were wonderfully surprised to find such a gorgeous place to stay. Located off a country lane just before the village of Sezanne, this property is the hamlet of Montgivroux and should be awarded a village rating of four fleuris for its profusion of beautiful flowers. We stayed in a room located above the spacious breakfast room, in one wing of the complex off a long, wide corridor at the top of the stairs. Our room was large, beautifully furnished with a mix of antiques and reproductions, had exposed beams, very pretty soft-yellow and peach floral paper on a few of the walls, great lighting and a desk at which I could work, a TV, and a large modern bathroom stocked with all the amenities, including large plush towels and even robes. I kept thinking, "This isn't a B&B: it rivals some of our finest hotels." Since our visit, the family has ambitiously added another 16 rooms. This is also an equestrian center, and horses enjoy accommodation in the barn behind the guest wing. Breakfast is a lavish buffet feast. A lovely large pool is set overlooking the landscape. Here guests can enjoy barbeques with their hosts as well as a poolhouse and terrace bar. Tennis courts are tucked away in the open fields. *Directions:* Drive south from Reims on the D51 and approximately 10 km after the intersection of R33 watch for a small sign to the east, to Mondement.

LE DOMAINE DE MONTGIVROUX
Host: Laurent Carbonaro Family
Domaine Équestre Montgivroux
51120 Mondement-Montgivroux, France
Tel: 03.26.42.06.93 or 95, Fax: 03.26.42.06.94
20 Rooms, Double: €80–€230
Open: all year, Credit cards: MC, VS
Other Languages: good English, Italian
Region: Champagne-Ardenne, Michelin Map: 515

The 18th-century Manoir de Clénord is a handsome manor in the heart of the Loire Valley, ideally situated for exploring the rich selection of châteaux in the region. The interior exudes an ambiance of lived-in comfort with handsome family heirlooms used throughout. The dining room—located in the oldest wing of the house—is especially appealing. It has a beamed ceiling, a huge fireplace, and, in the center of the room, a fabulous trestle table, mellowed with the patina of age, where guests sit down family-style for breakfast. A wooden staircase leads to the guestrooms, each individual in decor as in a private home. Quality wall-coverings color-coordinate with fabrics used on the drapes and beds. The suites are especially elegant. If you are on a tight budget, there is one lovely little room (barely big enough for a double bed) that offers a real bargain. In addition to the manicured formal gardens and expansive surrounding forest, guests can enjoy a large, beautiful swimming pool and tennis court. *Directions:* From Blois go south 10 km on D765 towards Cheverny and Romorantin. At Clénord, turn left at the sign for the Manoir de Clénord. The entrance is signposted on your left.

MANOIR DE CLÉNORD
Host: Renauld Family
Route de Clénord
41250 Mont Près Chambord, France
Tel: 02.54.70.41.62, Fax: 02.54.70.33.99
8 Rooms, Double: €69–€149
Table d'hôte: €35
Open: Mar to Nov or on request all year for groups
Credit cards: MC, VS
Other Languages: good English, Italian
Region: Center, Michelin Map: 518

Mont Saint Jean, located in the heart of Burgundy, is a perfect base from which to explore the area. After driving through the beautiful countryside and the hilltop medieval village, you are rewarded with views of this outstanding Norman-French manor house from the 19th century. It offers a picturesque and unusual setting. As soon as you enter the Château, your charming hosts will welcome you. On the ground floor, a cozy salon with fireplace, a library and a dining room are at your disposal. A wide wooden stairway leads you up to all the bedrooms. All are very spacious and benefit from high ceilings, contemporary furnishings with a few handsome antiques, fireplaces and gorgeous views. The "Enchanting View" room has a private balcony and a spectacular panorama over the valley. Tobias and Marco offer table d'hôte twice a week, using all fresh ingredients from the area. They are constantly improving the place and committed to making your stay memorable. Plans for the future include converting the vaulted cellar in for wine tasting as well as a fitness area. *Directions:* From A6 exit Pouilly en Auxois, stay on D977 for 25 km, and take D36 on your right to Mont St Jean. Drive through the village. Take right at restaurant "Le Medieval" and Chateau les Roches will be on your left behind a black gate.

*CHATEAU LES ROCHES   **New***
Hosts: Tobias Yang & Marco Stockmeyer
Rue de Glanot
21320 Mont-Saint-Jean, France
Tel & Fax: 03.80.84.32.71
6 Rooms, Double: €125–€150
1 Cottage: €900 weekly
Table d'hôte: €29 (Thur & Sat)
Open: Mar to Jan, Credit cards: all major
Other Languages: Fluent English, German, French
Region: Burgundy, Michelin Map: 519

The first impression of La Terre d'Or, from its exterior, is that it is simply a newly constructed house. But once you are greeted with an infectious smile by the owner himself and welcomed into the warmth and comfort of his home, your opinion will quickly change and you will succumb to its charms. Throughout, the Martins have effectively incorporated old tiles, mantels, and woods in the decor, which give it a lot of character. The main entry is warmed and scented by an open fire and a handsome table used for breakfast sits center stage. The decor is light and airy, with whitewashed walls setting off handsome accent pieces. There are five immaculate bedrooms in the main house, one just off the main entry behind a double set of doors to ensure privacy and quiet. This has a luxurious bathroom with two sinks, tub, and shower, and private toilet. Upstairs the other guestrooms include one with a bed tucked into an alcove under the windows with a backdrop of trees—it's just like being in a tree house. Next to the pool is a lovely suite, Les Orchidees Sauvages. In an adjacent garden cottage the Martins offer couples or a family fabulous accommodation: two bedrooms sharing a central living room and kitchenette. *Directions:* Travel west from Beaune on D970, towards Bouze. After 1.9 km watch for a small road that winds up to the right, signposted "La Montagne." From here, follow well-posted signs to the B&B.

LA TERRE D'OR
Hosts: Christine & Jean-Louis Martin
Rue Izembart
La Montagne, 21200 Beaune, France
Tel: 03.80.25.90.90, Fax: 08.21.47.99.67
5 Rooms, Double: €120–€205*
2 Cottages: €320–€390 daily, €2100–€2500 weekly*
*Breakfast not included: €12
Open: all year, Credit cards: MC, VS
Other Languages: good English
Region: Burgundy, Michelin Map: 519

L'Orangerie has a wonderful location in the heart of Burgundy, amidst a landscape of vineyards, gently rolling hills, pockets of woodlands, cultivated fields, and lush pastures. Built in the late 1800s, this large, handsome house exudes a stately charm, with tall French windows accented by white shutters; walls romantically laced with ivy; and dormer windows punctuating a steep mansard roof. L'Orangerie is thoughtfully organized for the comfort and privacy of guests and has a lounge exclusively for them. Light streaming in through tall arched windows, yellow walls with white trim, fine paintings, traditional furnishings, antique accents, and hardwood floors set a scene of tasteful, refined, homey comfort. The five guestrooms are similarly decorated in pastel colors, with lovely prints, artifacts from around the world, attractive furniture, and white tiled bathrooms. All are attractive, but I fell in love with room 1, which has French doors opening onto the beautiful garden, which slopes down to a little stream. On a lower terrace a large swimming pool beckons guests after a day of sightseeing. Niels and David are charming hosts with a genuine talent for making guests feel at home. They are also excellent chefs and the delicious dinners are artistically presented. *Directions:* Exit the A6 at Chalon Sud and follow signs on N80 toward Le Creusot. After about 12 km, you see a sign for Moroges. Go into the village and follow signs to L'Orangerie.

L' ORANGERIE
Hosts: Niels Lierow & David Eades
Vingelles
71390 Moroges, France
Tel: 03.85.47.91.94, Fax: 03.85.47.98.49
5 Rooms, Double: €72–€102
Minimum Stay Required
Table d'hôte: €25–€40
Open: Mar to Nov, Credit cards: none
Other Languages: fluent English, German
Region: Burgundy, Michelin Map: 519

This lovely old merchant's house in a quiet and peaceful French village has been lovingly restored by Annemarie and John Williams. Since every home on the street sports the name "Les Bordes," name of the residential hamlet, look for the name La Chouette qui Chante or you might find yourself knocking on a private home. A handsome Yorkshire clock dominates the tiled entry and fresh flowers are found throughout the house. The family kitchen is just off the wide front hallway opposite the wide oak staircase that climbs to the two spacious guestrooms. Overlooking the front is the Armancon room with a king bed in a very modern décor of ivory and black with red accents whose private bathroom is accessed off the landing. The back bedroom, Serein, is traditionally decorated in cream and blue with antique furniture; has large windows framing views of the back garden, the village church and surrounding hillsides. Serein enjoys an ensuite bathroom. Downstairs, the public rooms are the lovely large dining room and living room with sofas and fireplace. Across the street, the Williams have renovated a lovely old barn to serve as two one-bedroom apartments with garden for long-term rentals. *Directions:* Take the Bierre les Semur/Saulieu exit off A6 and exit onto D980 towards Saulieu. In Saulieu take D26 to the east for 10 km to La Motte Ternant. Take the second right on Dllc before the road starts its climb from the village.

LA CHOUETTE QUI CHANTE
Hosts: John & Annemarie Williams
Les Bordes
La Motte Ternant, 21210 Saulieu, France
Tel: 03.80.84.33.78
2 Rooms, Double: €70–€80
1 Cottage: €385 weekly
Table d'hôte: €25
Open: all year, Credit cards: none
Other Languages: fluent English
Region: Burgundy, Michelin Map: 519

This 400 year-old, all-stone Provencal house became, thanks to Kilperick, a B&B after two years of renovation. He found all the fine antique decoration in the Provence area. This is a perfect blend of authenticity and elegance offering three exquisitely decorated, spacious suites. Each has silk curtains, a marble bath, linen sheets, cashmere blankets, king beds, and private safe. No TV disturbs the quiet ambience. The cozy St. Honorat suite has an 18th century feeling with a lovely sitting area. The Isadora, in brown colors complimenting beams on the ceiling, features a glass-house sitting area so you can enjoy the view. My favorite, the St. Exupery, has several surprises: the front door is like opening a closet and a glass roof is above the stairs. It is contemporary with gray walls, all wooden ceilings, and in the bathroom an opening so you can enjoy the fire while taking a bath! In the morning your host will prepare a delicious organic breakfast that you can enjoy inside or outside and then, visit the pool surrounded by olive trees and end your day with a massage. Kilperick has succeeded in making you feel a blend of energy, tranquility and serenity. As he said, "This house is my baby. I love the place and the area, so I will talk about them with all my heart." *Directions:* From the A8 going toward Grasse, exit Mougins-Valbonne, turn left, go straight and pass the roundabout following Mougins village; take Chemin de Font Neuve on your right, up to number 238.

LES ROSÉES
Host: Kilperick Lhobet
238 Chemin de Font Neuve
06250 Mougins, France
Tel: 04.92.92.29.64, Fax: 04.92.92.29.88
4 Rooms, Double: €270–€300
Open: all year, Credit cards: all major
Region: Provence-Alps-Côte d'Azur, Michelin Map: 527

The Château de la Grande Noë is truly a gem—the idyllic setting, the superb decor, and the genuine warmth of welcome are just what you've always dreamed of finding. The castle, dating back to medieval times, has been in the same family since 1393. You enter through stately gates into a manicured front garden overlooked by the handsome two-story château with intricate brick trim decorating the windows, a steep, gray-slate roof punctuated with gabled windows, and a profusion of tall chimneys. Behind the château horses frolic in the meadow. As you walk up the steps into the reception hall, you feel you have entered into the exquisite home of a friend. Throughout there are beautiful draperies, family portraits, English-style slipcovered sofas, and heirloom antiques. A staircase leads to the guestrooms. All are lovely but my favorite of the three is a large room decorated in tones of pale peach, soft green, and yellow. Pascale de Longcamp is a woman of amazing talents: not only did she decorate the rooms, sew all the drapes, make the bedspreads, and wallpaper the rooms, but she also tiled the bathrooms herself. The most exquisite room in the house is the gorgeous 18th-century oak-paneled dining room, where breakfast is served. *Directions:* Take N12 from Paris towards Alençon. At Carrefour/Saint Anne go south on D918 towards Longny au Perche for 4.5 km then turn left towards Moulicent. The château is on your right in less than 1 km.

🍺 🚲 @ P 🚭 👖 👫 🐎

CHÂTEAU DE LA GRANDE NOË
Hosts: Pascale & Jacques de Longcamp
61290 Moulicent, France
Tel: 02.33.73.63.30, Fax: 02.33.83.62.92
3 Rooms, Double: €100–€120
Open: Mar 1 to Nov 30, Credit cards: none
Other Languages: good English, Spanish
Region: Lower Normandy, Michelin Map: 513

Moustiers Sainte Marie is an absolute jewel and we were pleased to find a place to stay that immediately captivated our hearts. In 1999 Nicole and her husband, Stéphane, opened L'Escalo, which is located in the heart of the village, convenient to all the charming boutiques, quaint restaurants, and sights. When Nicole inherited the property from her grandmother, she and Stéphane moved from Marseille and renovated the home, transforming it into a sweet and simple bed and breakfast. The house is painted orange set off by white trim and brown shutters. From the street you enter immediately onto a staircase that leads to a small reception area on the upper floor, where your charming hostess will check you in. The house is tall and narrow, so the guestrooms are tucked onto various levels off the main staircase. They are simply but tastefully decorated and all as neat as a pin. A couple of them are especially spacious and will accommodate a family with a child. Throughout are a few antiques that Nicole also inherited from her grandmother, including some chests of drawers and handsome antique beds. A few pieces of furniture came from Madagascar where her parents once lived. When the weather is warm, breakfast is served on a cozy terrace up on the roof, while on chilly days, guests eat breakfast at a table in the kitchen. *Directions:* In the center of town, fifty meters from the post office.

L' ESCALO
Host: Nicole Alliaume
Rue de la Bourgade
04360 Moustiers Sainte Marie, France
Tel & Fax: 04.92.74.69.93
4 Rooms, Double: €54–€59
Studio with kitchenette: €59 daily, €399 weekly
Open: Mar to Nov, Credit cards: none
Other Languages: some English, German
Region: Provence-Alps-Côte d'Azur, Michelin Map: 527

The Château des Ormeaux is a spectacular, cream-stone castle nestled on the hills above the Loire. Long-abandoned, it was restored by the owners to create a luxurious bed and breakfast, while lavishing detail to achieve the home of their dreams. Off the handsome entry the salon is set with comfortable sofas and chairs round a wood-burning fire. Continuing on, the dining room is gorgeous in blues and golds, with a lovely cabinet displaying a wealth of silver and a dramatic, deep-red chair, which brings out the reds in the wonderful Oriental carpets. Climb the elegant staircase to the bed chambers, each named for a French composer. On the second floor are three spectacular rooms. At the front, each enjoying a sitting area in the turret round, are Lully, in pretty colors of red and gold, and Couperin, a dramatic room in black and gold contrasting with the blues and creams of the bathroom. At the back, Rameau is a lovely room richly painted in warm yellow with complementing green and rose. On the third floor, Ravel is the smallest guestroom, but quite intimate under the eaves, and both Debussy, in lovely rose and cream, and Poulenc, with its display of blue-and-cream checks on plaids, enjoy the turret round. Endless trails, tennis courts, a gorgeous pool, and wonderful table d'hôte dinners make a stay here a delight. *Directions:* Located 20 km east of Tours via RN152 following signs to Blois. At Vouvray take the D1 towards Noizay. La Bardouillère is to the east.

CHÂTEAU DES ORMEAUX
Owner: Emmanuel Guenot
Hosts: Emmanuel, Eric & Dominique
Route de Noizay, La Bardouillère, D1
Nazelles, 37350 Amboise, France
Tel: 02.47.23.26.51, Fax: 02.47.23.19.31
5 Rooms, Double: €115–€165, 1 Suite: €115–€245
Minimum Stay Required, Table d'hôte: €48
Open: Feb 15 to Jan 15, Credit cards: MC, VS
Other Languages: good English, Italian, Spanish
Region: Center, Michelin Map: 518

The enchantingly intimate and informal Château de Nazelles is snuggled on a hillside across the River Loire from Amboise. Dating back to 1518, the château was built by Thomas Bohier, who about the same time constructed his dramatic castle at Chenonceau. Château de Nazelles was originally a wine estate and hints of its heritage are still about, including a very large press and caves in the hillside where the wine was stored. Wine is still produced from grapes grown on the property. The ivy-laced building has a fairy-tale quality with its steeply pitched roof, tiny dormer windows, jutting chimneys, gables, and pretty white shutters. A side door leads into a spacious, lovely lounge for guests. The lounge and the guestrooms all present a fresh, uncluttered, airy look, with light pouring in through large windows, soft pastel colors, and lovely antiques. A narrow staircase leads up to two delightful bedrooms. My very favorite, the Viele-Griffin, is an especially spacious room with yellow walls, beautiful parquet floor, king-sized bed, large bathroom, and windows on two sides. Another really sweet bedroom is located in a separate cottage. A series of romantic little gardens surrounds the château, each a jewel. Another bonus is a large swimming pool tucked on an upper terrace. *Directions:* On a hill above Nazelles-Négron, a village located across the bridge from Amboise. Ask for directions when making your reservation.

CHÂTEAU DE NAZELLES
Hosts: Véronique & Olivier Fructus
16, Rue Tue la Soif
Nazelles–Négron, 37530 Amboise, France
Tel & Fax: 02.47.30.53.79
5 Rooms, Double: €110–€150
Open: all year, Credit cards: MC, VS
Other Languages: good English, Italian
Region: Center, Michelin Map: 518

Madame Gourlaouen's property enjoys a tranquil location near the spectacular coastline and beaches of southern Brittany and the artist community of Pont Aven. This picturesque port town is the former home of many French impressionist painters, as well as Paul Gauguin. Madame Gourlaouen is a young, capable hostess who offers bed and breakfast as well as apartment accommodation in her pretty stone farmhouse. Dating from 1730, the long, low house is built from the golden-hued stones that are typical of the Concarneau, Pont Aven region. An independent entrance leads to the guest bedrooms, which are furnished with antique reproductions. Rooms are small but charming and all have private WC and shower—a great bargain for the money—and a salon is available for guests' use and comfort. The intimate breakfast room is full of charm with a low, beamed ceiling, old stone hearth, country antiques, and fresh garden flowers. *Directions:* Located about 30 km southeast of Quimper. Leave Pont Aven on D70 towards Concarneau, turn left just outside town, and follow signs to Nevez. In Nevez, continue past the church, then take the left fork in the road onto D77 towards Port Manech. After about 4 km, just before Port Manech, turn right at the Chambres d'Hôtes sign. Continue following signs, turning at the first left, and you arrive at the farmhouse (300 meters from the sea).

CHEZ GOURLAOUEN
Host: Yveline Gourlaouen
Port Manech
29920 Nevez, France
Tel & Fax: 02.98.06.83.82
4 Rooms, Double: €46
1 Cottage: €240 weekly
Open: mid-Mar to mid-Nov, Credit cards: none
Other Languages: some English
Region: Brittany, Michelin Map: 512

This place totally captivated my heart. Going down the driveway you see an immense landscape with an stone house and blue shutters surrounded by olive and pine trees and lavender bushes. Fabienne bought this 17th century sheepfold fully renovated and converted it to a B&B to open in 2005. She has preserved the authentic architectural features while adding all the amenities. The ground floor still has stones, a little watering place which belongs to the reception area, and an awesome volute gives atmosphere to the dining room with wooden tables and chairs covered with a light beige fabric in contemporary style. On the side a fireplace invites you to a cozy area. An ancient stone staircase leads to the rooms: three suites, three standard rooms and two superior rooms. None of the rooms are alike, each with different colors, fabrics and furniture. Almost all the rooms have stone floors, beamed ceilings, some with a terrace or a small private garden. And after having a bountiful breakfast, why not work out by playing tennis or golf, ride a bike around the seventy-five acre grounds, or just lay by the large natural pool and Jacuzzi and relax in the shade of the trees. The bonus is the table d'hôte with fresh local products of the day. This treasure is definitely a place to experience! *Directions:* From St. Remy, go toward Orgon, to the roundabout and turn right, following D24, Chapelle St. Sixte, and Le Mas will be on your right.

❄ ⚡ 💳 🍽 ☎ @ W P 🚭 ≋ 🏃 🏠 🔔 ⛱ 🍴 🐎 🍇

LE MAS DE LA ROSE
Host: Fabienne Luron-Huppert
Route d' Eygalières
13660 Orgon, France
Tel: (04) 90 73 08 91, Fax: (04) 90 73 31 03
5 Rooms, Double: €150–€320, 2 Suites: €210–€320*
1 Apartment: €550 daily*
*Breakfast not included: €15–€18, Table d'hôte: €45
Open: Mar 1 to Jan 4, Credit cards: all major
Châteaux & Hôtels Collection
Region: Provence-Alps-Côte d'Azur, Michelin Map: 527

La Doucinière is an enchanting inn, conveniently located just 30 minutes from the Paris, CDG airport—a heavenly spot to begin or end your holiday in France. Relax in total luxury for a fraction of the cost of a hotel in Paris. La Doucinière is an adorable, ivy-covered, 13th-century stone cottage, accented by white shutters and a walled garden with a lush lawn and beautifully manicured flower beds. In the main house there is one large bedroom elegantly decorated in a color scheme of peach. But splurge and request the deluxe room across the courtyard. This gorgeous room sets all standards for luxury and refinement. The room is decorated in pretty tones of pink and rose—a color scheme repeated from the beautiful fabric on the headboards to the sofa, lampshades, drapes, and carpet. The bathroom is incredibly splendid, with fixtures of superb quality. Although the town of Beaumarchais offers little charm, the location of this lovely inn is ideal. *Directions:* From Paris or the Charles de Gaulle airport, take N2 toward "Soissons" to Othis. Then go straight in Othis and watch for the Chambres d'Hôtes sign on the right. Ask for a map when making reservations.

LA DOUCINIÈRE
Hosts: Philippe & Marianne Clement
12, Rue des Suisses
77280 Othis–Beaumarchais, France
Tel: 01.60.03.33.98
2 Rooms, Double: €130–€150
Breakfast served in the privacy of guestrooms
Table d'hôte: €30
Open: all year, Credit cards: none
Other Languages: English
Region: Île-de-France, Michelin Map: 514

This lovely bed and breakfast with its wood shutters cut with hearts is draped in season with so many geraniums that the owner, Madame Maurer, spends two hours each day watering them! Although set on gorgeous acreage, this is no longer a true working farm—Monsieur Maurer works in town while Madame offers bed and breakfast accommodation in one wing of the complex in five guestrooms with their own entrance off the courtyard. Room 5 is the largest room, with twin beds and a bunk bed, making it perfect for a family. A mirrored staircase leads in one direction to two rooms in the oldest section of the building: room 1 is lovely with cornered windows, while room 2, smaller but very charming, is a favorite with its wonderful old exposed-beam walls. In the other direction, room 3 (with a double bed) and room 4 (three twin beds) are just a little larger. All the simply decorated rooms are comfortable and enjoy the quiet setting and the warm welcome of the Maurer family. Born and raised in the area, Madame is a true Alsatian and would love to share with you her knowledge of the region. Her English is limited but if you have questions, wait until her oldest daughter returns from school—her English is quite good. Breakfast is included in the already ridiculously low price and includes fresh baguettes, juice, and homemade jams. *Directions:* Located just on the outskirts of town on the road from Obernai (the D426).

CHEZ MAURER
Host: Marie-Dominique Maurer
11, Rue Obernai-Roedel
67530 Ottrott, France
Tel: 03.88.95.80.12
5 Rooms, Double: €46–€51
Open: Mar to Dec, Credit cards: none
Other Languages: some English
Region: Alsace, Michelin Map: 516

Set center stage in an attractive complex of weathered stone and ivy-covered buildings is the Château de Beaufer. It is a lovely château on an intimate scale dressed with white shutters and complete with end turrets and a gorgeous setting of lawn and surrounding forest. Doorways are framed by climbing roses and geraniums hang heavy from wrought-iron balconies. Six attractive, large guestrooms are found in the various buildings and enjoy pretty details such as stencil paintings, old furnishings, decorative plates, and lovely art. I particularly liked one that shared a climbing stair—dressed in colors of red and cream, it was beautiful, decorated with antiques set on handsome tile floors. The sitting room, next to the pool, with its exposed loft beams and massive rock fireplace, offers guests a spot to gather and watch television. The pool is gorgeous, set in the old stone walls with vistas out to the surrounding countryside. Breakfast is served on the terrace patio or indoors in the library or in the cozy turret room. Very friendly dogs shadow the owners, kittens frolic, and on a recent visit, we felt fortunate to observe endearing colts testing their legs, born just days before. *Directions:* Take the Tournus exit off A6, then travel east on the D14 to Ozenay.

CHÂTEAU DE BEAUFER
Host: Roggen Family
Route d'Ozenay, Col de Beaufer
71700 Ozenay, France
Tel: 03.85.51.18.24, Fax: 03.85.51.25.04
6 Rooms, Double: €140–€170
Minimum Stay Required
Open: Apr 1 to Oct 31, Credit cards: MC, VS
Other Languages: fluent English
Region: Burgundy, Michelin Map: 519

Château de Messey is one of the best bed and breakfasts in our guide. To begin with, the region is gorgeous—especially fascinating for wine buffs as this is the heart of the Chardonnay wine-producing district. Also, the bed and breakfast's setting is of fairy-tale quality—the adorable stone house, banked by flowers and accented with green shutters, nestles on the edge of a tiny mill stream where a weeping willow shades a rowboat beckoning guests for a lazy excursion. Breakfast and dinner are usually served outside in this hopelessly romantic setting. To add icing to the cake, the spacious guestrooms are all beautifully decorated in antiques and have excellent tiled bathrooms. (For longer stays there are cottages, rented by the week.) Even if the above did not entice you to visit, the extraordinary hospitality of the Schaefer family would alone suffice as reason to come. As an added bonus, Delphine is a superb cook. Although, termed a château, the bed and breakfast is located in a pretty building below the château where the workers used to live (some rooms in the château are available for rent). The charming Dumont family owns the château (and the bed and breakfast) and can arrange a visit to their winery, which produces a superb Chardonnay. *Directions:* Take A6 south from Beaune to the Tournus exit, then go west on D14 to Ozenay. Go through Ozenay, continue 2 km to Messey, and the bed and breakfast is on the left.

CHÂTEAU DE MESSEY   ***Cover painting***
Hosts: Delphine & Markus Schaefer
Messey, 71700 Ozenay, France
Tel: 03.85.51.16.11, Fax: 03.85.51.33.82
5 Rooms, Double: €75–€100*
3 Cottages, €220–€660 weekly*
*Breakfast not included: €7,50
Table d'hôte: €30
Closed: Jan, Credit cards: MC, VS
Other Languages: good English
Region: Burgundy, Michelin Map: 519

The lovely Chauveau home enjoys an idyllic setting on a hillside overlooking the family vineyards and the distant River Vienne. The fine art of relaxing is easy to master in these luxurious and scenic surroundings where each day begins with fresh croissants and coffee or tea on the terrace overlooking the lush valley. Impeccable taste prevails in the furnishings and decor, creating an elegant country-home ambiance. Madame Chauveau offers one suite with two bedrooms in her home and two more bedrooms in Tourelle, located poolside. Each guestroom enjoys its own private entrance and I was especially charmed by Tourelle Haute with its lovely views of the surrounding vineyards. The decor throughout is very handsome, with stone walls, slate-tile floors, and charming country antique furniture. Pretty print curtains and matching upholstery complete the pleasing ensemble. The Chauveaus' pool and sunbathing terrace are inviting—perfect for a dip in the early morning or late afternoon after a day of wine tasting. A stay at Domaine de Beauséjour is truly an experience to be savored. Those on a longer stay might want to consider the spacious two-bedroom, one-bath self-catering unit. *Directions:* Panzoult is approximately 12 km east of Chinon. From Chinon, take D21 to Cravant les Côteaux and continue towards Panzoult. The Domaine de Beauséjour is on the left after 2 km—the pretty, light-stone house is on the edge of the woods.

DOMAINE DE BEAUSÉJOUR
Hosts: Marie-Claude & Gérard Chauveau
Panzoult, 37220 L'Île Bouchard, France
Tel: 02.47.58.64.64, Fax: 02.47.95.27.13
3 Rooms, Double: €70–€90
1 Suite: €120
1 Cottage: €100 daily, €650 weekly
Open: all year, Credit cards: none
Other Languages: good English
Region: Center, Michelin Map: 517

Eric Gaucheron, a third-generation hôtelier, aims to offer charming, affordable, welcoming accommodations and certainly seems to succeed. He and his parents, Bernard and Colette, along with wife, Sylvie, see to it that each guest is looked after like family. Eric is proud to carry on this tradition in the Familia with its red-geranium-covered balconies in the colorful Latin Quarter. The walls of the hotel's lobby are decorated with custom murals of street scenes from the neighborhood and the small sitting room and halls are adorned with tapestries over original stone walls and Oriental carpets. Very small, clean rooms have modern marble-tiled baths, TVs, phones, small refrigerators, and double-paned windows, and some have tiny balconies overlooking the street (the highest floor has a view of the towers of Nôtre Dame). Some of the rooms also have sepia-colored murals of Paris scenes or landmarks. Bedspreads are of nice quality. All in all, a welcoming family hotel at a very affordable cost. This hotel has many American guests who rave in the comment books about the warm and caring service from a hôtelier who believes that small details make the difference.

FAMILIA HÔTEL
Hosts: Eric Gaucheron & Family
Fifth Arrondissement, 11, Rue des Écoles
75005 Paris, France
Tel: 01.43.54.55.27, Fax: 01.43.29.61.77
30 Rooms, Double: €106–€136
Open: all year, Credit cards: all major
Other Languages: good English
Located between the Panthéon & Nôtre Dame
Métro: Cardinal Lemoine
Region: Île-de-France

Your charming hosts, Robert and Stuart, were on holiday from England when they discovered Le Moulin Neuf and they bought it on the spot. They have since poured their love and immense talent into creating a dream. Robert and Stuart live in an enchanting stone house on the property. Next door, a cozy cottage (dedicated to guests) has an ever-so-appealing lounge with grey painted walls and soft cream drapes, accenting comfortable sofas grouped around an enormous walk-in fireplace. There are six prettily and newly decorated bedrooms, each with a tranquil view of the parklike grounds. Meticulously tended flowerbeds abound and the old millstream loops lazily through lush grass dappled with shade from large trees. Completing this idyllic scene is a romantic pond. Dotting the lawn are lounge chairs where guests relax, only occasionally disturbed by a duck waddling by, or perhaps a nuzzle from Benji and Sammy, the adorable dogs. Le Moulin Neuf is truly a very special bed and breakfast and the price is remarkably low for such fine quality and outstanding charm. If you are going to arrive after 6 pm, please call to make special arrangements. *Directions:* From Limeuil, take the D31 for the Cingle de Limeuil. After passing the Cingle de Limeuil, continue down the hill then at the crossroads go straight on D2 towards Saint-Alvère. Fork left after 100 meters and continue about 2 km. The sign for Le Moulin Neuf is on the left at the small crossroads.

LE MOULIN NEUF
Hosts: Robert Chappell & Stuart Shippey
Paunat, 24510 Sainte Alvère, France
Tel: 05.53.63.30.18, Fax: 05.53.63.30.55
6 Rooms, Double: €85–€89
Minimum Stay Required: 3 nights in winter
Open: all year (in winter by reservation)
Credit cards: none
Other Languages: fluent English, German
Region: Aquitaine, Michelin Map: 524

Le Lavandin is the fruit of one woman's passion for Provence and the French savoir-vivre. Georgia, an American, has created a space that is a breathtaking combination of traditional Provencal architecture and contemporary French design and furnishings. In doing so, she offers her guests a piece of heaven. She loves flowers, books, music and cooking. You will be captivated by her garden: a lavender field, a rose garden with 257 bushes, Olive trees, fruits trees, a flower garden, and a vegetable/fruit area. The garden, surrounding the pool, also includes six little salons in which to relax. On the property are the main house, home to your host, and a separate guest house to insure privacy and independence. The guests' house enjoys an outside "summer kitchen;" a contemporary living-room with a library that faces the terrace with all wooden furniture, and four beautiful bedrooms each with its own bath and terrace. All rooms have terracotta floors, handmade doors, contemporary décor and a library. If you prefer a larger space, ask for the studio with kitchenette—a large room with miniature sofas and a big library. This place will capture your heart. *Directions:* From Avignon take the D28 east to Pernes-les-Fontaines. Travel south on D938, toward L'Isle sur la Sorgue. Travel a short distance and at the intersection with a Motocross sign, turn left, follow roads marked Motocross and arrive at Le Lavandin.

❄ ☕ ✂ 🍲 🔔@ W Ⴠ P 🚭 ≈ ♿ ⚓ 🚶 🚶‍♀️ 🏇 ⚓ 🍇

LE LAVANDIN
Host: Georgia Perrin
1830 Chemin du Val de Guilhaud
Pernes-les-Fontaines, France
Tel: 04.90.61.26.95, Fax: 04.90.61.26.98
4 Rooms, Double: €175–€205
1 Suite: €215 daily, €1400 weekly
Table d'hôte: €50
Open: Apr 15 to Oct 31, Credit cards: none
Region: Provence-Alps-Côte d'Azur, Michelin Map: 527

The Manoir de Kergrec'h, located on the northern coast of Brittany, is a superb 17th-century manor, impressively large, yet tremendously inviting—especially in early summer when a profusion of old-fashioned pink roses lace and soften the stern gray-stone exterior. This is truly a gorgeous home filled with fine antique furniture and with an added attribute of having a splendid setting in an enormous park that stretches to the sea, an absolute paradise for walking. When you enter into the large front hallway, to the right is a formal, beautiful living room. To the left is a handsome dining room with beautiful parquet floors in a herringbone pattern and a massive fireplace, which soars almost to the ceiling. A spiral stone staircase, worn with the footsteps of time, winds up through the tower to the bedrooms, which are most attractively appointed with color-coordinated fabrics and gorgeous antique furniture. All the bedrooms are beautifully decorated in an individual style. I loved them all, but I think my particular favorite is room 7, a lovely corner room decorated in tones of blue and cream and with windows on two sides looking out to the enchanting grounds. All of the bedrooms have exceptionally large, modern bathrooms. *Directions:* Exit the N12 at Guingamp and go north to Tréguier. From Tréguier take D8 to Plougrescant. Turn right after the church and follow signs for 600 meters to the manor.

MANOIR DE KERGREC'H
Hosts: Vicomte & Vicomtesse de Roquefeuil
Plougrescant, 22820 Kergrec'h, France
Tel: 02.96.92.59.13, Fax: 02.96.92.51.27
6 Rooms, Double: €110
Open: all year, Credit cards: none
Other Languages: some English
Region: Brittany, Michelin Map: 513

A lane through the woods leads to the Château de Kermezen, one of those wonderful old châteaux that is totally unpretentious and abounds with the kind of authenticity that you find only in a property that has been in the same family for many, many years. This stately 17th-century castle, made of the typical beige Breton stone, has been in the de Kermel family for over 600 years and is furnished with their personal belongings, which have been collected over many generations and give the place a family, lived-in ambiance. Your hostess, Comtesse de Kermel, was a pioneer in the bed and breakfast business, being one of the very first owners of a château to open her doors to paying guests. There are two small loft bedrooms, but I would recommend asking for either the Coqs room (with roosters on the design of the fabrics) or the pretty twin-bedded room decorated with a sweet rose-patterned Laura Ashley fabric. Breakfast is served at one large table in a marvelous old room with a stone floor, beamed ceiling, large armoire, and collection of antique plates on the wall above a huge open stone fireplace. A family of nobility, the de Kermels are as unpretentious and friendly as their château. Comtesse de Kermel's hearty laugh, no-nonsense manner, and great sense of humor will make you feel instantly at home. *Directions:* From Tréguier take D8 to Pommerit-Jaudy and turn right at the roundabout, following signs to the château.

CHÂTEAU DE KERMEZEN
Hosts: Comte & Comtesse de Kermel
22450 Pommerit–Jaudy, France
Tel & Fax: 02.96.91.35.75
5 Rooms, Double: €90–€110
Open: all year, Credit cards: AX
Other Languages: good English
Region: Brittany, Michelin Map: 512

Les Tuillières is a rare find. This gem of a 17th-century stone farmhouse has everything—superb hosts with boundless warmth of welcome, lovely flower gardens, spacious bedrooms, appealing decor, a gorgeous setting, large swimming pool, and delicious meals served with produce straight from the garden. With Les Tuillières being located a bit off the beaten path, a stay here affords an introduction to a breathtakingly beautiful niche of northern Provence. Although within easy reach of Avignon, Montélimar, and Orange, this is a sunny, quiet area of lavender, sunflowers, vineyards, and sleepy villages. From the moment you walk into Les Tuillières' courtyard, your heart will be won. Ivy laces the honey-toned stone home with its white trim and green shutters, roses and geraniums add a dash of color, while lavender scents the air. Hermann Jenny (who is Swiss) was formerly a top executive in hotel management, so knowing how to please guests is second nature to him. Susan (who is American) has a natural gift of hospitality and pampers her guests like cherished friends. Hermann is your superb chef and on most days dinner is served under the stars in the romantic garden. *Directions:* From the south take the A7 to Montélimar Sud exit. Follow signs to Dieulefit, go through the village of La Batie Rolland and into La Bégude de Mazenc where you turn left on D9 to Charols. Turn right in Charols on D128 for about 2 km. Les Tuillières is on the right.

LES TUILLIÈRES
Hosts: Susan & Hermann Jenny
26160 Pont de Barret, France
Tel & Fax: 04.75.90.43.91
5 Rooms, Double: €85–€105, 1 Suite: €600–€900
1 Studio: €500–€750 weekly
Table d'hôte
Minimum Stay Required
Open: May to Sep, Credit cards: MC, VS
Other Languages: fluent English, German, Italian
Region: Rhône-Alpes, Michelin Map: 527

After being a horticulturist for many years, Pierre Ducruet decided to switch careers. He bought this 19th-century house in 2002 and after an extensive four-year renovation (which preserved many original elements, such as stone walls, fireplaces, and beamed ceilings), Pierre's dream was realized: once you enter this exquisite four-star bed and breakfast conveniently situated on a quiet square in the historical district of Remoulins, you'll feel transported back in time. All the rooms are decorated with antique furniture and Provençal fabrics. On the first floor the Louis XIII guestroom has an impressive canopy bed, beautiful fireplace, and a giant bathroom with a corner bathtub and a shower. Pierre kept as many original elements in the rooms as possible. For example, in the Louis XIII guestroom the closet doors were crafted from the home's original shutters. If you come with your family be sure to ask for the largest room, the apartment Nilla. The master bedroom is Louis XV style, with a spacious wood and marble-detailed bathroom; a stairway leads up to a cozy sitting area. There's also a nice balcony with gorgeous views. Breakfast is served on a terrace inside a 12th-century tower, which is attached to the main property. *Directions:* From Avignon, follow Nimes (N100), then follow Remoulins to "centre ville." About 100 meters in front of the church is Place du Portail. Bize de la Tour is at number 2.

BIZE DE LA TOUR   *New*
Host: Pierre Ducruet
2, Place Du Portail
30210 Remoulins, France
Tel: 04 66 22 39 33, Fax: 04.66.63.97.25
3 Rooms, Double: €75–€80
1 Suite: €90–€160
Open: all year, Credit cards: all major
Region: Provence-Alps-Côte d'Azur, Michelin Map: 527

Pont du Gard, the ancient, three-tiered stone aqueduct spanning the Le Gardon river, is one of France's star attractions and La Terre des Lauriers offers bed and breakfast within walking distance of this impressive sight. The house, beautifully situated in 13 acres of parkland, is typical of the region, with a tan stucco exterior, tiled roof, and lavender-blue shutters. Although, described as homelike in earlier editions, when the Langlois took over residence they spent time and money beautifully redecorating the guestrooms and concentrating on improvements in the garden. Readers have confirmed how lovely the property now is! Each of the bedrooms has its own personality and the benefit of a small balcony looking over the large swimming pool and out to the forest. On the same floor as the bedrooms there is an intimate parlor, which is solely for the use of the guests. One of the delights of staying at La Terre des Lauriers is its location: from the garden you can wander down a path through a dense forest of poplar, laurel, bamboo, and oak trees to the river. *Directions:* From the A9 (north of Nîmes) take exit 23 following signs to Remoulins and Pont du Gard. Go through Remoulins, cross the river, and turn right to Pont du Gard–Rive Droite. Before you reach Pont du Gard, watch for a sign to La Terre des Lauriers on your right.

LA TERRE DES LAURIERS
Hosts: Marianick & Gérard Langlois
30210 Remoulins (Pont du Gard), France
Tel & Fax: 04.66.37.19.45
5 Rooms, Double: €89–€99
1 Cottage: €600–€1050 weekly
Table d'hôte: €20
Open: Mar to Oct, off season by reservation
Credit cards: none
Other Languages: good English
Region: Provence-Alps-Côte d'Azur, Michelin Map: 527

Years ago, your charming hosts, Joelle and Gérard Dru-Sauer, decided to leave Paris and move to the countryside for a less hectic life, so they bought a small property near Chinon and started farming, which they found they loved. Soon they discovered they needed more land and in their search for a new home came across La Varenne, an abandoned, 17th-century farmhouse. They purchased the home, totally renovated it and made three bedrooms for bed and breakfast guests. They also added a large swimming pool in the enclosed courtyard in front of the house and enhanced the area with a lawn and colorful flowers. There is a wonderful parklike lawn behind the house where one can relax under a huge shade tree. It is obvious that Joelle is a meticulous, hard-working woman because the gardens are all well kept and the interior of the house is sparkling clean and as tidy as can be. There are three guestrooms, two upstairs and one downstairs, all spacious and filled with sunlight. If you want to economize, the best bargain is the Garden Room. It is the least expensive, but very large and with the added bonus of a private door into the garden. Joelle and Gérard continue to farm the land, producing walnuts and honey, which they serve to guests each morning. *Directions:* Take the D58 toward Richelieu. One km before Richelieu, turn left at the roundabout on D20 toward Braslou and go 2 km. The entrance to La Varenne is on your left, just after the hamlet of Chizeray.

🍽 🤽 P 🏊 🎿 🚶 👭 🐎 🍇

LA VARENNE
Hosts: Joelle & Gérard Dru-Sauer
37120 Richelieu, France
Tel: 02.47.58.26.31, Fax: 02.47.58.27.47
3 Rooms, Double: €85–€110
Open: all year, Credit cards: none
Other Languages: good English
Region: Center, Michelin Map: 517

Riquewihr is a beguiling walled town with cobbled streets, timbered facades, and steeply pitched slate-and-tile roofs—all set against a backdrop of green vineyards. The town is an ideal base from which to explore the Alsatian wine route and we are pleased to recommend the family-run Hotel Saint Nicholas. We were escorted on a tour of the rooms by the daughter and, overseeing the dining room, the father was ever-present to attend to our needs. Be sure to ask about the future innkeeper, Charlotte, the absolutely adorable granddaughter. The restaurant is quite handsome with high-back chairs upholstered in a regal green-and-rust stripe. Local specialties are featured on the menu as well as wines from local vintners—the village of Riquewihr boasts 100 winemakers. Guestrooms are found in the building across from the restaurant, which is where, typically, inquiries about rooms and reservations need to be addressed. In the hotel wing we climbed an attractive staircase whose wall was painted with murals of regional scenes and found the guestrooms to be comfortable, but quite basic in their amenities and decor. The Hotel Saint Nicholas also has plans to convert the historic, neighboring building into a true B&B. *Directions:* Riquewihr is located on the D3 just west of the D10, south of Ribeauvillé. The town is closed to vehicles, so you have to park outside the town wall. The Hotel Saint Nicholas is accessed most easily from the tower gate.

HOTEL SAINT NICHOLAS & RESTAURANT
Host: André Schneider
2, Rue St. Nicholas
68340 Riquewihr, France
Tel: 03.89.49.01.51, Fax: 03.89.49.04.36
33 Rooms, Double: €54–€58*
*Breakfast not included: €8
Open: Apr to Jan, Credit cards: VS
Other Languages: some English
Region: Alsace, Michelin Map: 516

The medieval town of Rochefort en Terre, with its fortified château, cobbled streets, and antique shops, is enchanting. Nestled on 20 acres of park just minutes away is the gorgeous Château de Talhouet. A beautiful forested drive leads to a handsome entry with an absolutely spectacular salon beyond. This striking, wood-paneled room was the place where the judge once held court—the spot where he sat and passed judgment is now enclosed by glass and the fireplace is now a deep, arched doorway into a beautiful dining room where tables are set intimately for two. Beyond the billiard room is a beautiful guest living room with gorgeous fabrics draping the full-length windows and lovely hand-painted beams. Most guestrooms are found up a stone stairway with a dramatic 16th-century wood gate. Chambre d'Honneur is a twin-bedded room with a large armoire and a view of the stunning grounds. Louis XV is a smaller room with a draped canopy over a queen bed and a table set at the window. Louis XIII has twin beds and a table with high-backed chairs at the fireplace. The Montgolfière has gold stripes with dark furnishings. The Directoire, a twin under lowered ceilings, is not in keeping with the ambiance of the château, while Les Oiseux is pretty with recent redecoration. Up a back staircase are a few more simple rooms. *Directions:* Leave Rochefort en Terre in the direction of Pleucadeuc on the D774. The château is signposted 2 km from town.

CHÂTEAU DE TALHOUET
Host: Jean Pol Soulaine
56220 Rochefort en Terre, France
Tel: 02.97.43.34.72, Fax: 02.97.43.35.04
8 Rooms, Double: €140–€225
Table d'hôte: €46
Open: all year, Credit cards: MC, VS
Other Languages: some English
Region: Brittany, Michelin Map: 512

Everything about La Bastide de Cassiopee is outstanding: the architecture of the beautiful 18th-century stone farmhouse, the stunning setting, the convenient location for exploring the Luberon, the tasteful decor in all the rooms, the inviting swimming pool, the beautiful gardens, the cherry trees, the vineyards. The previous owners discovered this abandoned farmhouse in Provence and spent ten years creating the jewel you see today. Each of the pretty, individually styled bedrooms has beamed ceilings, handmade tiles, delightful views from the windows, and excellent bathrooms. The guest lounge is a very cheerful room with furniture upholstered in yellow-and-blue material. There is also a dining room, but usually breakfast is served outside on the terrace, shaded by a hundred-year-old plane tree. Jean-Pierre Dupré is the property's new owner and your charming host. *Directions:* From Avignon, take N100 toward Apt. At Coustellet, take D2 toward Gordes. At the foot of Gordes continue on D2 toward St. Saturnin d'Apt. After the D2 crosses the D4, continue on about 200 meters and on the right is the hamlet, Les Yves and La Bastide.

LA BASTIDE DE CASSIOPEE
Host: Jean-Pierre Dupré
Hameau Les Yves, D2
84220 Roussillon, France
Tel & Fax: 04.90.04.65.35
5 Rooms, Double: €100–€110
Open: Feb 1 to Nov 30, Credit cards: none
Other Languages: good English
Region: Provence-Alps-Côte d'Azur, Michelin Map: 527

Saint Clar's market place is enclosed by charming arcaded buildings. In the center of the square stands a wonderful 13th-century covered market, officially designated as a historic monument. Also on the plaza is the old town hall: hence its name, Place de la Mairie. Nicole and Jean-Francois Cournot are a gracious, artistic couple who live in one of the buildings facing the square and when they renovated the house, they converted part of it into a bed and breakfast. You enter through an arched stone doorway into a wide hall, formerly horse stables, and ascend a stone stairway to the next floor. Nicole has tastefully decorated the guestrooms (which are in a separate wing of the house) in a charming, attractive style, using pretty Laura Ashley fabrics and wallpapers throughout. Guests are welcome to relax in a lovely salon with a marble fireplace flanked by comfortable chairs and couch. There is also a large garden in back where guests can relax. Breakfast is served in the cozy kitchen with a blue-and-white-tiled floor and country antique furnishings. *Directions:* Saint Clar is located about 40 km south of Agen. From the A62, take exit 8, marked Valence d'Agen. Go south on D953 following signs to Saint Clar. In Saint Clar, look for Place de la Mairie, the square with the medieval market in the center. The house faces the square.

LA GARLANDE
Hosts: Nicole & Jean-Francois Cournot
12, Place de la Mairie
32380 Saint Clar, France
Tel: 05.62.66.47.31, Fax: 05.62.66.47.70
3 Rooms, Double: €57–€68
Open: Apr to Nov, Credit cards: none
Other Languages: some English
Region: Midi-Pyrénées, Michelin Map: 525

In the fertile wine district of Saint Émilion you can stay in the château of one of the grand wine estates. Château Franc Mayne (Grand Cru Classé) nestles in 7 hectares of vineyards planted on the famous stone quarries in the Côte de Franc, within walking distance of Saint Émilion. The ambiance in the public rooms is elegant, but relaxed and informal, like a private home. Off the entry is a pretty salon with a sitting area, a billiard table, and a well-stocked honor bar. Table d'hôte dinners can be arranged for groups of eight or more and are served in the elegant dining room. There are also many restaurants in Saint Émilion. Breakfast is enjoyed with other guests in the dining room at one long table set before a large open fireplace. The guestrooms, which look out over the grounds and enjoy the quiet setting, are of the standard of a luxury hotel—spacious, beautifully decorated, with comfortable table and seating arrangements, and large modern bathrooms with amenities such as robes, shampoos, and hairdryers. The price is more consistent with a hotel, too, but included in the rate is a guided tour of the winery, the old Relais de la Poste, and the network of caves and tunnels that connect the Relais with the cellars. For those who don't mind commuting back for breakfast, there are also four other rooms, just ten minutes away. *Directions:* From St. Émilion follow the D243 in the direction of Libourne. The château is signed shortly after town on the left.

CHÂTEAU FRANC MAYNE
Hosts: M & Mme Hervé & Griet Laviale
La Gomerie
33330 Saint Emilion, France
Tel: 05.57.24.62.61, Fax: 05.57.24.68.25
9 Rooms, Double: €150–€220*
*Breakfast not included: €10
Table d'hôte: €75
Open: all year, Credit cards: MC, VS
Other Languages: good English, Spanish, German
Region: Aquitaine, Michelin Maps: 521, 524

St. Etienne de Baïgorry is in that glorious part of the Basque country at the base of the Pyrénées alongside the River Nive. With its many timbered homes, the village is rich in character and tradition. On its outskirts, in complete contrast to the timbered village, sits the absolutely regal Château d'Etxauz, dramatic with its four corner turrets. The château dates from the 11th and 16th centuries and is truly a historical monument—staying here gives guests the opportunity to "live" history. The bedchambers, each recently renovated are large, well-lit and enjoy modern bathrooms. All decorated for an historical character and period, the guestrooms are all luxuriously appointed and incredible in their historical details. The Bertrand d'Etchauz has a handsome four poster bed. The King Navarre suite has a lovely but standard-size bedroom, but an enormous living room where the king used to hold court when he was in residence. One guestroom is named in honor of a more contemporary, distinguished guest—Charlie Chaplin. While the bedchambers are spectacular, my favorite room is the dining room where a handsome hutch takes up an entire wall opposite a large open fireplace and a beautiful trestle table runs the length of the room in between. A grandfather clock takes command of one corner of the room and copper pots cover the walls. *Directions:* Located just above St. Etienne de Baïgorry, the château is well signed from the village center.

CHÂTEAU D'ETXAUZ
Hosts: Ajit Asrani & Maria Alicia Urrutia
64430 Saint Etienne de Baïgorry, France
Tel: 05.59.37.48.58, Fax: 05.59.37.42.30
6 Rooms, Double: €169–€250
Open: all year, Credit cards: all major
Other Languages: fluent English, Spanish
Region: Aquitaine, Michelin Map: 524

Chalet Rémy is an adorable 18th-century stone-and-wood farmhouse perched way up in the mountains with a view over the valley to the extraordinary summit of Mont Blanc. A profusion of flowers surrounds the house and geraniums grace the balconies. Chalet Rémy is particularly famous as a restaurant and on sunny days the terrace is brimming with families who have come to enjoy a wonderful meal there, surrounded by nature at its finest. The guestrooms all open onto a gallery, which looks down upon the floor below. Be forewarned: the accommodations are tiny and quite basic—staying here is a bit like camping out in a mountain lodge. Each room has a sink, but all share showers and toilets down the hall. Rooms 1 through 6 peek up at Mont Blanc. If luxury is important to you, this would not be an appropriate choice, but this rustic restaurant with rooms has a lovely location and plenty of old-fashioned natural charm. In winter, you can leave your car at St. Gervais, take the tram up to Bettex, take advantage of the shuttle between the chalet and the lifts, and at day's end ski right to the front garden. *Directions:* Take D909 from Mègeve towards Saint Gervais. Just before coming to Saint Gervais, turn right on D43 signposted to Saint Nicholas and Le Bettex. Continue winding up the road, following signs for Le Bettex where you will see signs for Chalet Rémy.

CHALET RÉMY
Host: Mme Micheline Didier
Le Bettex
74170 Saint Gervais, France
Tel: 04.50.93.11.85, Fax: 04.50.93.14.45
14 Rooms, Double: €45*
*Breakfast not included: €8
Open: all year, Credit cards: MC, VS
Other Languages: good English
Region: Rhône-Alpes, Michelin Map: 527

This lovely home sitting on a grassy knoll above a gorgeous stretch of beach to the north of St. Jean de Luz was originally built as a family retreat. La Maison Tamarin is built like a traditional Basque farmhouse, with old weathered beams, windows with stone trim set in cream stucco, and a wonderful sun-washed tiled roof. The interior is beautifully designed, with an open and airy floor plan, gorgeous Spanish floor tiles, and windows looking out to the ocean. I loved the spacious main room, open to the kitchen, whose French doors lead to the surrounding terrace with its view of the ocean, Pyrénées, and swimming pool. An inviting end living room would be a nice place to settle with a book or quiet conversation. There are seven guestrooms, all prettily decorated and some with balconies. The most dramatic room is the one intended as the master suite. It is a large room with a wall of windows and enjoys its own private balcony, an enormous bathroom, and absolutely spectacular views of the sea. *Directions:* From the A63 take the St. Jean de Luz–Nord exit, going north on the N10. Take the first road to the right then turn back under the N10 on Chemin de Chibau, which weaves under the train tracks, and at the bottom, turn right on Ave de la Ferme de Kokotia. Drive past four buildings to La Maison Tamarin's entry gates. Just a small sign identifies the residence and there is an intercom to request entry. Ask for a map to aid directions.

LA MAISON TAMARIN
Host: Carmen Murcia
Chemin de la Ferme de Kokotia, Quartier Acotz
64500 Saint Jean de Luz, France
Tel: 05.59.47.59.60, Fax: 05.59.47.59.69
5 Rooms, Double: €120–€200, 2 Suites: €220–€250
Entire house: €8000–€13000 weekly
Table d'hôte €30
Open: all year, Credit cards: all major
Other Languages: fluent English, Spanish
Region: Aquitaine, Michelin Map: 524

Mas Vacquières is a secluded jewel, truly a rare find for the traveler seeking decorator-perfect decor, stunning architectural design, award-winning gardens, a swimming pool hidden in a romantic walled garden, memorable dining, and genuine warmth of welcome. Miriam's great passions are gardening and cooking. Several times a week she prepares a superb dinner for her guests, which is served on the terrace with its gorgeous views. The bed and breakfast is located in a cluster of centuries-old stone farmhouses, romantically nestled in a wooded hamlet. Guests have their own charming stone cottage with artistically decorated bedrooms which are not large, but do not need to be since they share a spacious living room which is as comfortable as it is beautiful, along with a flower-laden terrace. Owners Miriam and Thomas are committed to making their guests welcome and comfortable. *Directions:* From Ales take D981 southeast towards Uzès. After about 15 km, turn left on D7, then right on D339 towards Vacquières. Turn right again at the first asphalt road and continue down the hill. After you pass under a stone archway, Mas Vacquieres is the first house on your right, with yellow shutters and a discreet sign.

MAS VACQUIÈRES
Hosts: Miriam & Thomas van Dijke-Küchler
Hameau de Vacquières
30580 Saint Just et Vacquières, France
Tel: 04.66.83.70.75
5 Rooms, Double: €75–€125
Table d'hôte: €25
Open: all year, Credit cards: VS
Other Languages: fluent English, Dutch, German
Region: Languedoc-Roussillon, Michelin Map: 526

The pretty, old complex of La Croix de la Voulte is built of white regional stone and dates from the 15th and 17th centuries. All the guest bedrooms are found in an independent wing and were renovated with much attention to detail. A high level of comfort prevails: each room has a private bathroom, soft Pakistani carpets covering the stone floors, and luxurious bedding to assure a good night's sleep. Each room has a private entry and a special character all its own. Anjou, the largest bedroom, is very regal, with a massive old stone fireplace, four-poster bed, old armoire, and tapestry chairs. I adored Périgord, painted in a warm yellow and enjoying the advantage of an end/corner location. Low, beamed ceilings, light-stone walls, and lovely antique furniture add historical character to all the bedrooms. There is a tranquil courtyard, a park with a pond, and a sunny terrace in front of the swimming pool-a pleasant place to enjoy a leisurely breakfast. Guests may also elect to pamper themselves by bringing ice buckets and glasses that they find in their rooms to the side of the pool to enjoy a drink. This is a gem. *Directions:* Saint Lambert des Levées is located about 5 km west of Saumur on the north bank of the Loire. Take D229 in the direction of Saint Lambert des Levées and Château de Boumois. Pass the Saumur train station and continue 4 km until the sign "La Croix de la Voulte" directs you to turn into a driveway on the right.

❧ 🏠@ W P ≈ ⚕ 🏃 🐎 🛶 🍇

LA CROIX DE LA VOULTE
Hosts: Helga & Jean Pierre Minder
Rue de Boumois
Saint Lambert des Levées, 49400 Saumur, France
Tel & Fax: 02.41.38.46.66
4 Rooms, Double: €74–€88*
*Breakfast not included: €8
Open: Easter to Oct, Credit cards: none
Other Languages: fluent English, German
Region: Center, Michelin Map: 517

Le Moulin de Linthe, hugging the banks of the River Sarthe, has an idyllic setting. While the mill dates back several hundred years, most of what you see today is an ingenious reconstruction by Claude Rollini. For three months he hauled stones from the riverbed, which he used (along with old beams, bricks, and antique paneling) to rebuild the mill. The result is a charming cottage-style bed and breakfast with gabled windows accented by a red-tiled roof. Within there is a cozy parlor with a large window looking out to the slowly turning waterwheel. Most of the bedrooms overlook the old millpond and an enchanting scene of the meandering river. Ask for the corner bedroom decorated in soft pinks and greens, for it has captivating views in two directions. Jackie prepares a breakfast with homemade jams (don't be surprised if several ducks waddle by the dining-room window). You might choose to dine at the mill or check out Claude's latest venture, his own restaurant, L'Auberge des Peintres, just 5 km away. In addition to sweet accommodations and ever-so-friendly hosts, there is another bonus—fishing along the Sarthe where trout and pike abound. *Directions:* Head southwest from Paris on A10/A11 to Le Mans, then turn north on N138 in the direction of Alençon. At Beaumont-sur-Sarthe, take the D39 to Fresnay-sur-Sarthe, and the D15 to Saint Leonard des Bois. As you enter the village, take the first road on your left to the mill.

LE MOULIN DE LINTHE
Hosts: Jackie & Claude Rollini
72130 Saint Leonard des Bois, France
Tel & Fax: 02.43.33.79.22
5 Rooms, Double: €60–€70
Open: all year, Credit cards: none
Other Languages: good English
Region: Loire Valley, Michelin Map: 513

La Pastourelle is a low, stone farmhouse whose style is typical of the Brittany region. A pleasing construction is formed by gray stones of varying sizes mortared together in a seemingly haphazard manner: in fact it is easy to pick out one large boulder that was simply left in place and incorporated into the front wall of the house. The Lédés live in a separate wing of their pretty farmhouse, offering guests an independent entry, salon, dining room, and six guest bedrooms. In charge of the gîtes in her region, Madame Lédé displays great warmth and charm. An appealing, country ambiance is felt throughout, created by Madame's collection of lovely antiques and special touches such as wildflower bouquets. The bedrooms are spotlessly clean and tastefully decorated with dainty flower-print wallpaper, softly colored carpets, and crocheted bedspreads. Delicious table d'hôte dinners are served downstairs in the cozy dining room and often include local fish or grilled meats and regional specialties such as crêpes. *Directions:* Saint Lormel is located approximately 66 km northwest of Rennes, near the town of Plancoët. From Plancoët, travel north on D768 for 1 km, then turn left onto D19 towards Saint Lormel. At the T-junction, turn left (away from the village sign) then turn right at the Chambres d'Hôtes signs indicating La Pastourelle, which will lead to the Lédés' Breton farmhouse.

LA PASTOURELLE
Host: Mme Lédé
Saint Lormel, 22130 Plancoët, France
Tel & Fax: 02.96.84.03.77
6 Rooms, Double: €45–€47
1 Suite: €90–€94
1 Cottage: €350–€450 weekly
Table d'hôte €20
Open: Mar to Nov 15, Credit cards: none
Other Languages: some English
Region: Brittany, Michelin Map: 512

The Domaine d'Aurouze, a handsome stone farmhouse dating from the 17th century, is secreted in the glorious countryside of the Luberon with its lovely scenery and fascinating perched villages. Do not think because the rate is so very reasonable that you are in any way compromising on value—quite the contrary. Domaine d'Aurouze is an outstanding place to stay, and would be a bargain at any price. Viviane runs the bed and breakfast in a most professional manner complimented with her gracious welcome and hospitality. All the guestrooms are spacious, pleasantly decorated, and have fine bathrooms. My favorite room in the house is the dining room. The walls of the room are exposed stone, a beautiful antique clock hangs on the wall, and a lovely antique cabinet is tucked into one corner. The room is as cozy as can be. However, when the weather is mild, breakfast is served outside on the terrace beside the lovely swimming pool. Although, Viviane does not provide evening meals she does, graciously make a kitchen available to guests for their own culinary attempts! *Directions:* From Avignon, take the N100 east toward Apt. Turn right on D105 following signs to Saint Martin les Eaux. Continue toward Dauphin. Domaine d'Aurouze is on your left about 2.5 km after leaving Saint Martin les Eaux.

DOMAINE D'AUROUZE   **New**
Host: Viviane Noël-Schreiber
04300 Saint Martin Les Eaux, France
Tel: 04.92.87.66.51
4 Rooms, Double: €90
Minimum Stay Required: 3 nights
Open: May 15 to Sep 15, Credit cards: none
Other Languages: fluent English
Region: Provence-Alps-Côte d'Azur, Michelin Map: 528

Leonard and Esther (both from the Netherlands) transformed this 1800 former farmhouse into a jewel with a complete renovation then opened it up to guests. This young, energetic couple do their best to make your stay unforgettable and it is great fun to be around such a happy pair. Situated on the edge of Languedoc-Roussillon and Provence, about 5 kilometers from Uzès, Mas d'Oléandre has a lot to surprise you. As soon as you enter through the blue gate, you feel you're in a hamlet of peace. You are surrounded by all types of plants and this natural decoration gives an aura of authenticity and simplicity. The stone house with blue shutters offers four spacious bedrooms all with their own private terrace and bathroom, brightly decorated in a Provençal style, and two two-story apartments with well-equipped kitchens. The swimming pool, surrounded by lavender and other plants, looks out to a breathtaking view of the valley—as Leonard said, this view is like a movie that is playing all the time, like a never-ending story! During the high season Esther cooks dinner, her Provençal specialties including trout, salmon, rabbit, and chicken à l'estragon. *Directions:* From Avignon leave the A9 at exit 23 for Remoulins, In Remoulins take the D981 towards Uzes/Ales then continue on to Montaren. In Montaren turn right at the light onto the D337 in the direction of Saint-Mediérs. Mas d'Oléandre is at the end of the hamlet (you will see a blue sign).

MAS D'OLÉANDRE
Hosts: Leonard & Esther Robberts-Kuchler
Hameau Saint-Médiers, Montaren/Uzes
30700 Saint Médiers, France
Tel: 04.66.22.63.43
4 Rooms, Double: €70–€105
2 Apartments: €99–€126 daily, €645–€819 weekly*
*Breakfast not included with apartments, Table d'hôte: €25
Open: Mar 1 to Nov 15, Credit cards: MC, VS
Other Languages: English, Dutch, German
Region: Provence-Alps-Côte d'Azur, Michelin Map: 526

Old mills are almost always extremely appealing, and the pretty, 17th-century Petit Moulin du Rouvre is no exception. The picturesque stone building with steeply pitched, dark slate roof nestles in a lush grassy garden next to a small millpond that is backdropped by a dense green forest. You enter directly into the dining room, which is as cozy as can be with a cradle in front of a large fireplace. Stone walls, tiled floors, country-French table and chairs in the middle of the room, a wonderful antique armoire, and colorful plates on the walls make the room very warm and appealing. An adjacent parlor, with beamed ceiling and open fireplace, is somewhat more formally decorated and has windows opening onto the pond. There are five bedrooms, which are quite small and basic in decor, but immaculately clean. The choice bedroom is Les Amis, also referred to as Marine, decorated in blues and with an opening where you can look below and see the old water wheel. *Directions:* From Rennes take N137 for 40 km north towards Saint Malo. Take the Saint Pierre de Plesguen exit, then take the D10 towards Lanhelin. Before you reach Lanhelin, you see the road leading to Le Petit Moulin du Rouvre well signposted on the right side of the road. (Along the way you will see another bed and breakfast sign with another name.)

LE PETIT MOULIN DU ROUVRE
Host: Régis Maillard
35720 Saint Pierre de Plesguen, France
Tel: 02.99.73.85.84, Fax: 02.99.73.71.06
8 Rooms, Double: €65–€78
Table d'hôte: €20–€60
Open: all year, Credit cards: MC, VS
Other Languages: good English
Region: Brittany, Michelin Map: 512

Far off the beaten path, Le Moulinage Chabriol is a bed and breakfast made in heaven for those who enjoy walking through quiet woodlands with only the song of the birds and the music of rushing water to interrupt the absolute quiet. Lize and Edouard de Lang wearied of their demanding careers in Holland and moved to France to enjoy a less harried life. They discovered a wonderful 18th-century silk mill high in the hills, nestled on the banks of the rushing La Glueyre river, which they renovated and remodeled to accommodate six guestrooms, five of which have a stunning view of the river below. The rooms are fairly small, but big enough for twin beds (which can be joined to make kings), a writing desk, and a chair. There is nothing contrived or "country-cozy" here—although there are some antiques used as accents, there is a pleasing austerity to the decor, with freshly painted white walls, modern blue chairs, and track lighting. Handsomely displayed on the walls is a museum-quality exhibit of very old photographs of men and women working in the silk factory. The terraced gardens surrounding the home are exceptionally beautiful. *Directions:* Leave the A7 at the Loriol exit (just south of Valence). Cross the Rhône, following signs to La Voulte, take D120 to St. Sauveur de Montagut, then D102 toward Albon. Stay on the D102. In 20 minutes (15 km) you will see the blue "Chabriol" sign on your left.

LE MOULINAGE CHABRIOL
Hosts: Kim & Gerben Boogaard
Chabriol Bas
07190 Saint Pierreville, France
Tel: 04.75.66.62.08, Fax: 04.75.66.65.99
5 Rooms, Double: €70
1 Cottage: €730 weekly
Minimum Stay Required
Open: May to Oct, Credit cards: none
Other Languages: good English
Region: Rhône-Alpes, Michelin Map: 527

Mas de Cornud, in the charming village of Saint Rémy de Provence, provides a one-of-a-kind vacation: it's a lovely country inn and also the location of the Seasons of Provence cooking school. Guests can either take classes with Nito Carpita, the Director and principal instructor of the cooking school, who is a Certified Culinary Professional (CCP) under the auspices of the International Association of Culinary Professionals (IACP), or just enjoy her delicious cooking at the family-style meals the inn offers. Wine classes are also available, where you'll learn the art of pairing food and wine. Nito runs the inn with her husband David, and they are excellent hosts, attending to guests' needs while also affording them privacy. The property is gorgeous, with a lush garden, large pool, and outdoor Jacuzzi. You can also enjoy the use of the Pétanque court and then why not have a drink at the bar near the pool, or inside the spacious living room? The six guestrooms are quite pleasant; each has its own bathroom, wireless internet access, and all the modern conveniences you'd expect from an upscale inn. They're decorated in a Provençal style with some delightful touches from Istanbul—where Nito and David lived for few years. Our favorite room was the Alpilles, which has a fantastic view over les Alpilles and the orchards. *Directions:* From Saint Remy, take D27 in direction of Les Baux; after 1 km turn left. Mas de Cornud will be on your left.

MAS DE CORNUD   **New**
Hosts: David Carpita & Nitockrees Tadros
Petite Route des Baux
13210 Saint Rémy de Provence, France
Tel: 04.90.92.39.32, Fax: 04.90.92.55.99
6 Rooms, Double: €150–€240
Minimum Stay Required: 2 nights
Table d'hôte & Cooking School
Open: Mar to Nov, Credit cards: none
Region: Provence-Alps-Côte d'Azur, Michelin Map: 527

The Auberge du Moulin de Labique sits on the rise of a hill overlooking a little creek that flows into a picture-perfect pond with lazily swimming ducks. Christine and Patrick Hendricx, the gracious, hard-working owners, operate the property as a farm, bed and breakfast, and table d'hôtes where Patrick is the chef. The oldest part of their beige-stone home dates back to the 15th century. The building is typical of the area except for an amazing, two-story, columned verandah stretching across the front, giving the effect of an ante-bellum mansion. No one can remember who added such a fanciful embellishment, but it is very old. One of the guestrooms is in the main house while the rest are found in the old stone hay barn above the dining room. The bedrooms are attractively decorated with pretty wallpapers, excellent country antiques, and color-coordinating fabrics—the front-facing bedroom is particularly appealing, with cheerful flower-sprigged wallpaper. In the meadow behind the house is a swimming pool. *Directions:* From Périgueux go south on N21 to Bergerac. From Bergerac take the N21 south to Castillonnès, the D2 east to Villeréral, then south towards Monflanquin for 2 km. Turn right on the D153 for 2 km to Born and south towards Saint Vivien for 2 km. Domaine du Moulin de Labique is on your left, before Saint Vivien.

DOMAINE DU MOULIN DE LABIQUE
Hosts: Christine & Patrick Hendricx
Saint Eutrope de Born, St Vivien, 47210 Villeréral, France
Tel: 05.53.01.63.90, Fax: 05.53.01.73.17
5 Rooms, Double: €90–€115, 1 Suite: €150*
1 Apartment: €140 daily*
*Breakfast not included: €10
Table d'hôte (Nov to May): €30, Restaurant (Jun to Oct)
Open: all year, Credit cards: MC, VS
Other Languages: good English
Region: Aquitaine, Michelin Map: 524

The Maison Dominxenea is very special. Located about a kilometer from the center of Sare, the bed and breakfast is a picture-perfect, 16th-century cottage with cute red picket fence in front and red shutters accenting a white façade. Your enter into a cozy parlor dominated by a large fireplace. Just beyond is a second lounge that looks out onto a back garden with a lush lawn stretching back to 300 rose bushes. In the garden is a flagstone terrace, a favorite spot for guests to lounge and enjoy the idyllic scene. A handsome, centuries-old, spiral wooden staircase leads from the front parlor up to the three bedrooms, each of which is individually decorated with great taste and abounds with antiques. Fresh bouquets of flowers lend the final note of perfection. Two of the guestrooms (which are slightly more expensive) are extremely spacious. In the morning freshly baked croissants, rolls, and homemade jams are left in the pantry so guests can enjoy breakfast at their leisure. For dinner, stroll to the family's other property, the Hôtel Arraya, where the meals are absolutely fantastic. When making reservations, since the telephone and fax numbers are the same as at the Hôtel Arraya, be sure to be specific as to where you want to stay. *Directions:* Leave the A63 at Saint Jean de Luz (Nord, exit 3). Take the D918 through Ascain to Sare. Go to the Hôtel Arraya in the center of the village and they will take you to their bed and breakfast.

MAISON DOMINXENEA
Hosts: Laurence & Jean Baptiste Fagoaga
Quartier Ihalar
64310 Sare, France
Tel: 05.59.54.20.46, Fax: 05.59.54.27.04
3 Rooms, Double: €50–€60
Open: end-Mar to end-Oct, Credit cards: none
Other Languages: good English
Region: Aquitaine, Michelin Map: 524

Near the Spanish border, the rolling green foothills of the Pyrénées are filled with picturebook villages, including Sare. Here you find an outstanding bed and breakfast, the Olhabidea. Use this perfect hideaway as your base to explore this enticing area and to venture to the coastal resorts of Biarritz and Saint Jean de Luz. This lovingly restored farmhouse captures the tradition and rustic flavor of the Basque region. You will be captivated by the delightful ambiance of this charming home—an old wooden settle beside the fireplace whose mantle is trimmed with fabric, a rustic polished table laid with blue-and-white dishes, bouquets of fresh flowers, and comfortable sofas. The snug farmhouse atmosphere is further enhanced by the Basque blue-and-white color scheme and the polished flagstone floor set beneath the low, beamed ceiling. Every spacious bedroom has its own bathroom. A delicious breakfast is the only meal served by the effervescent Anne Marie. For dinner, guests often sample traditional Basque fare at the Hotel Arraya in Sare, owned by Anne Marie's sister-in-law. The hotel is a handy place for asking directions if you have difficulty finding Olhabidea. *Directions:* Exit the N2 autoroute at junction 3 signposted Saint Jean de Luz (Nord). Take the D918 through Ascain to Saint Pée sous Nivelle and the D3 towards Sare. 2 km before Sare, turn left at the old church on the right. The bed and breakfast is signposted from here.

OLHABIDEA
Hosts: Anne Marie & Jean Fagoaga
64310 Sare, France
Tel & Fax: 05.59.54.21.85
3 Rooms, Double: €75
Table d'hôte €35
Open: Mar to Nov, Credit cards: none
Other Languages: English
Region: Aquitaine, Michelin Map: 524

Located just up the river from Saumur and its castle, the Château de Beaulieu is impressive and has its own claim to history: Jean Drapeau, architect of Louis XV, was commissioned to build this romantic château in 1727. Guests will enjoy its beautiful setting embraced by a park, gardens, and a wonderful new pool. Inside, the large living room with fireplace, the handsome billiards and breakfast rooms, all have a warm and light ambiance. The bed chambers (accessed by the central main staircase or the creaking backstairs) are all decorated in a style befitting the home's origins. Choices include the dramatic La Louis XIII Suite with a four-poster bed and an expanse of corner windows; the La Vallière (named for one of Louis XIV's mistresses) with its pretty rose and cream décor; and the more cozy third floor Cendrillon (Cinderella), intimate with twin beds. The home's delightful grounds are populated by centuries-old trees, and enhanced by a charming pond and well-kept flowerbeds. Dr. and Mrs. Coady-Maguire love to talk with guests and introduce them to the history-filled Loire region. *Directions:* Located just outside Saumur on the D947 toward Chinon. A large sign just opposite the gate highlights the entrance.

CHÂTEAU DE BEAULIEU
Hosts: Dr. Conor & Mary Coady-Maguire
Route de Montsoreau
49400 Saumur, France
Tel: 02.41.50.83.52, Fax: 02.41.51.19.01
5 Rooms, Double: €90–€130*
2 Suites: €140–€160*
*Breakfast not included: €9
Open: Easter to Nov, Credit cards: MC, VS
Other Languages: fluent English, German
Region: Center, Michelin Map: 517

Parisians Jacques and Maïté wanted to retire in the South of France so they bought this 18th-century stone house surrounded by vineyards, lavender, and olive trees at the foot of Séguret, ""the most beautiful village in France,"" entirely renovated it at great expense, and opened it as a unique bed and breakfast. When you enter through the heavy wooden front door, you find a wonderful contrast of antique and modern, with an enormous chandelier, a very old tapestry, an automatic glass door, white walls, and ceiling beams painted light blue. All the paintings and furniture—including a Louis XIII mirror, a Louis XIV table, and furniture from Russia—are authentic. The three superior large double bedrooms upstairs are decorated with treasures collected from the Reys' world travels and have every imaginable amenity including motion-sensitive lights, electrical shutters, and showers with multiple jets. All are very nicely decorated and have pretty views either of Séguret or Sablet villages, vineyards, or the large swimming pool. Jacques, with his passion for flowers, has fashioned a garden like a painting and is now creating a park with all different kinds of trees. A bountiful breakfast is served every morning including juices, cereals, yogurts, breads, cheeses, homemade marmalades, and cake. *Directions:* From Orange, take D975 to Cameret, then D23 and D977 to the D7. One km after the D7/D977 intersection turn left and follow signs to Le Vieux Figuier.

■ ✣ @ W P 🚭 ≈ 🎿 🚶 🏇 ⛷ 🍇

LE VIEUX FIGUIER
Hosts: Jacques & Maïté Rey
Les Pres
84110 Séguret, France
Tel & Fax: 04.90.46.84.38
3 Rooms, Double: €120
Open: all year, Credit cards: none
Other Languages: some English
Region: Provence-Alps-Côte d'Azur, Michelin Map: 527

Old mills are usually delightfully romantic, with the bonus of a picturesque setting, and Le Moulin de Choiseaux is no exception. Your very gracious hosts, Marie-Françoise and André Seguin, bought this charming 18th-century water mill in the heart of the Loire Valley and meticulously restored it, retaining its wonderful old character. Many mills are quaint and tiny, but Le Moulin de Choiseaux is a large, cheerful, two-story, creamy-beige stone building with perky dormer windows accenting the roof. Flanking one side is a still-functioning waterwheel, powered by a small stream. The home is sweetly decorated in a simple, tasteful style, most appropriate for the heritage of the building. The fabulous stone floor in the entrance hall is many centuries old. Also very antique is the beautiful circular wooden staircase, which winds up to two of the bedrooms (three additional bedrooms are in the adjacent house where the miller lived). All are very nice, but because of its beautiful garden views, my favorite bedroom is the Vieux Livres. Marie-Françoise has decorated each of the rooms individually and since she is an artist, many of the walls are decorated with her paintings. Two pretty ponds enhance the parklike grounds and several romantic streams wind their way through the gardens. Only the song of birds disturbs the blissful silence. *Directions:* Located off the N152, between Mer and Suevres. The turn is signposted Diziers, 3 km on the right after Mer.

LE MOULIN DE CHOISEAUX
Hosts: Marie-Françoise & André Seguin
8, Rue des Choiseaux, Diziers
41500 Suevres, France
Tel: 02.54.87.85.01, Fax: 02.54.87.86.44
5 Rooms, Double: €59–€90
Open: all year, Credit cards: MC, VS
Other Languages: some English
Region: Center, Michelin Map: 518

Distanced from the river Lot by lush fields, across from the silhouette of St. Cirq Lapopie, this handsome, ivy-clad bourgeois home is an incredible bed & breakfast. Past the stone gates, I was impressed immediately by the meticulous grounds; weathered barn, garden with sitting areas and beautiful flowers, back terrace, and outdoor pool. Enter the home and the warmth, ambiance, and sense of family are enchanting. Originally purchased by Patrice's father (inventor of a surgical clamp known internationally as the "Redon"), raised his family in Paris; but Patrice remembers family vacations at Redon and knew he was destined to return. He married Denise and they now share their beautiful home with fortunate travelers. Handsome antiques and family treasures decorate the rooms—including samplers made by Patrice's grandmothers. The dining room, with a large, open, working fireplace, is the heart of the home. A gorgeous, spiral staircase winds upstairs; where five appealing guestrooms reside under cozy angled beams, overlooking the garden or a combination garden and canyon view. I favored Jaune, a creamy-yellow corner room with queen bed, and sofa tucked under a fan of beams. Pigonnier enjoys a small salon and bedroom with curtains cleverly made of beautifully embroidered sheets. *Directions:* Travel D662 on the north banks of Le Lot, east of Cahors. After the bridge, in Tour de Faure, turn north at the town hall.

LA MAISON REDON
Hosts: Denise & Patrice Redon
La Combe
46330 Tour de Faure, France
Tel: 05.65.30.24.13
5 Rooms, Double: €64–€74
Open: all year, Credit cards: none
Other Languages: good English
Region: Midi-Pyrénées, Michelin Map: 525

Bed & Breakfast Descriptions

297

La Tour du Trésorier is located on the outskirts of the beautiful city of Tournus, in front of the imposing Roman Abbey Saint Philibert. A charming couple, French Michel and Swiss Lotti, did a remarkable job remodeling this former house of the monk-treasurer. While renovating they tried to keep as many original 17th century attributes as possible. Inside, you are treated to the beautiful view of the Saone river and feel incredibly distanced from the bustle of town. Climb the original tower to three bedrooms. On the first floor is a superb Art Deco suite with a huge bathroom, where you can take a bath facing the roof of the abbey. The second floor winds up to "La Saone" room, a very spacious beamed-ceiling suite with two bedrooms, facing the abbey or the Saone river. Then the most incredible room is "La Tour"—the only one actually embraced by the walls of the tower. This was originally the monk's chapel and has breathtaking 360-degree views. You can still observe the fresco on the walls, the beamed ceiling and paving stones. One other guestroom is located on the main floor of the adjoining house. Dating from the 14th century it enjoys a private entrance and faces the abbey. A bountiful breakfast is served on the expanse of terrace facing their park and overlooking the river. La Tour du Trésorier is a wonderful place to stay. *Directions:* From Beaune, take A6, direction Lyon, exit N°27 Tournus, follow sign to "L'Abbaye". La tour du Tresorier is right in front.

LA TOUR DU TRÉSORIER   *New*
Hosts: Lotti & Michel Vialle
9 Place de l'Abbaye
71700 Tournus, France
Tel: 03.85.27.00.47, Fax: 03.85.27.00.48
4 Rooms, Double: €130–€180
Closed: Jan, Credit cards: all major
Other Languages: fluent English, German, French, Italian
Region: Burgundy, Michelin Map: 519

The Villa Rosa is a wonderful old family home, located in a forested region of Alsace, in the hills above Colmar, offering eight rooms for overnight guests. You will be charmed by the owners whose dedication, gracious hospitality and artistic talents (evident both in the kitchen and in the garden), make this a very special place to stay. The inn is a mélange of artistic and whimsical—a theme staged by the two yellow-painted bikes set by the driveway as if ready to take off for a country picnic. The guestroom decor, while always simple, includes some distinctive touches: teddy bears are often nestled on the beds, and many are adorned with lovely Alsatian stenciling, very Bavarian in appearance. The rooms can only be described as intimate in size and many are up some very narrow, steep stairs or almost ladders (although a few are also accessible by outside entrances)—definitely pack light if you plan to stay here. While rooms vary dramatically, they are all clean and all are named for the rose featured in the print that hangs on their wall. Ask to see the book that shows the Villa Rosa, a rose created and named for the inn! Please note there is a strict non-smoking policy in the guestrooms and the dining room—the guest salon is the one smoking area in the house. We agree with our readers—it is the owners, Francis and Anne Rose who make the Villa Rosa so special. *Directions:* Located 12 km east of Colmar following the D11.

VILLA ROSA
Host: Anne Rose Denis
4, Rue Thierry Schoerré, 68410 Trois Epis, France
Tel: 03.89.49.81.19, Fax: 03.89.78.90.45
8 Rooms, Double: €60–€65*
1 Cottage: €80 daily, €400 weekly*
*Breakfast not included: €8–€10
Table d'hôte: €25
Open: all year, Credit cards: MC, VS
Other Languages: good English
Region: Alsace, Michelin Map: 516

Bed & Breakfast Descriptions

Les Volets Bleus is an old ochre-colored stone farmhouse with cheerful blue shutters that enjoys a setting of great natural beauty. In a separate, centuries-old stone farmhouse of great charm, six lovely guestrooms are offered. Although simple, this bed and breakfast is exceptionally inviting, the hospitality outstanding, and the scenery breathtaking. The bedrooms and bathrooms are fairly small but very attractive, extremely comfortable, decorated with taste, and as clean as new pennies. Four of the rooms have doors opening onto private terraces. The meals are delicious, with most of the produce coming from the organic garden. Complete with chickens and donkeys, Les Volets Bleus is typical of the large farmhouses of Provence and while guest facilities have been completely modernized, great care has been taken to preserve the ambiance and charm of old. *Directions:* Exit the A7 at Montélimar Sud. Follow white signs to Dieulefit. In Dieulefit, turn north on D538 toward Bourdeaux. Before you reach Bourdeaux, take a small road on your left marked to Truinas. Before Truinas, Les Volets Bleus is signposted on your right.

LES VOLETS BLEUS
Hosts: Sophie & Serge Gaubert
26460 Truinas, France
Tel: 04.75.53.38.48
6 Rooms, Double: €65–€95
Table d'hôte €26
Open: all year, Credit cards: none
Other Languages: good English
Region: Rhône-Alpes, Michelin Map: 527

Vaison la Romaine, an unspoiled fortified village rising steeply from the banks of the Ouveze river, has a superb bed and breakfast owned by the Verdier family. Jean, an architect, and Aude, his pretty wife, moved from Paris to this ancient walled city in 1975 and worked together to transform the ruins of what was once a part of the bishop's palace into a gracious home for themselves and their three sons. There are three guest bedrooms and two suites with their own charmingly decorated lounge and a private entrance to the street. Of the guestrooms, my favorites are the twin-bedded rooms, which have more of an antique ambiance than the double-bedded room with its somewhat art-deco feel. Both suites have a view of the city and one has a terrace solarium. Aude serves breakfast on an enticing terrace snuggled amongst the rooftops or, when the weather is chilly, in the family dining room. Although Aude and Jean speak only a smattering of English, their absolutely genuine warmth will guarantee a very special stay in this highly recommended bed and breakfast. *Directions:* Vaison la Romaine is located 45 km northeast of Avignon. When you reach the town of Vaison la Romaine, cross the river and climb the narrow road to the Ville Médiévale (below the castel). L'Évêché is on the right side of the main street, Rue de l'Évêché.

🍴 🚴 @ W 🚭 ⬆ 🏃 🚶🚶 🏇 ⛵ 🍇

L' EVÊCHÉ
Hosts: Aude & Jean Loup Verdier
Rue de l'Évêché, Ville Médiévale
84110 Vaison la Romaine, France
Tel: 04.90.36.13.46, Fax: 04.90.36.32.43
3 Rooms, Double: €80–€88
2 Suites: €110–€135
Open: all year, Credit cards: none
Other Languages: some English
Region: Provence-Alps-Côte d'Azur, Michelin Map: 527

In the years before they opened Le Mas Samarcande, Mireille and Pierre Diot traveled all over the world in connection with their magazine jobs. When they decided to settle down, they chose the beautiful French Riviera and bought a recently constructed Mediterránean-style home in the hills above the sea, only a five-minute drive from the beaches of Cap d'Antibes. With guests in mind, the Diots renovated the house and made five lovely bedrooms. Two very large rooms face the front garden, while three slightly smaller rooms face the back garden and have French doors opening onto the terrace that captures a view over Vallauris and to the hills beyond. You can even see Picasso's home tucked amongst the trees, just across the valley. All of the guestrooms exude quality and have obviously been designed by experienced travelers. The rooms are spacious, have exceptionally large bathrooms that would rival the most deluxe hotel's, fine large towels, splendid linens, air conditioning, good lighting, and incredibly comfortable mattresses. Every detail reflects loving attention, such as tables set with pretty blue-and-yellow china and lovely silverware each morning for breakfast. *Directions:* From the A8, exit at Antibes. Follow signs to Vallauris and go through town, following signs to Golfe Juan. At the roundabout, take the road on the right to Boulevard des Horizons, then turn right at the first street, Grand Boulevard de Super Cannes. The house is on your right.

❄ ☕ � @ P 🚭 ⚓ 🚶 👫 🏇 🏄

LA MAS SAMARCANDE
Hosts: Mireille & Pierre Diot
138, Grand Boulevard de Super Cannes
06220 Vallauris, France
Tel & Fax: 04.93.63.97.73
5 Rooms, Double: €120–€130
Minimum Stay Required
Open: all year, Credit cards: none
Other Languages: good English
Region: Provence-Alps-Côte d'Azur, Michelin Map: 527

The Lady A is certainly not your typical bed and breakfast—it is a barge. But the quality is so high, the warmth of welcome so genuine, that it is a pleasure to recommend it. Nowadays the 100-foot barge moves no more but remains moored on a charming small canal in an absolutely beautiful setting—beneath Châteauneuf, an extremely picturesque walled village crowning the nearby hill. The colorful barge is lots of fun. You quickly become friends with the other guests in a house-party atmosphere. Each of the three staterooms has a small private bathroom. The bedrooms are just big enough for two beds (which can be made into a king-sized bed), a closet, and shelves for clothes. Although cozy, the rooms are actually surprisingly spacious for a boat. When not sleeping or exploring Burgundy, guests spend most of their time on the deck—a great place to enjoy a drink in the twilight and watch the action of the other boats on the waterway. Another diversion: Sami now offers bicycle rides along the canal and into the countryside. *Directions:* From the A6 take the Pouilly-en-Auxois exit through Créancy to Vandenesse (D18)—Lady A is moored in the basin.

LADY A
Hosts: Catherine & Sami Yazigi
Port du Canal, Cedex 45
21320 Vandenesse en Auxois, France
Tel: 03.80.49.26.96
3 Rooms, Double: €65–€80
Table d'hôte: €25
Open: all year, Credit cards: none
Other Languages: fluent English, German, Arabic, Spanish
Region: Burgundy, Michelin Map: 519

Villa Velleron had been abandoned for 40 years when the previous owners turned it into a bed and breakfast. During restoration, they discovered treasures such as a beautiful stone wall no one knew existed and clues to the building's varied heritage—an old olive press and racks used for the processing of silk. Your hosts, Claudia and Christian Hickl extend a warm welcome to individual travelers and families alike. There is a stunning swimming pool romantically nestled on a terrace bordered by picturesque stone walls, and an inner courtyard that simply oozes charm—potted geraniums, ivy-draped walls, fragrant roses, and lush lawn make every niche a dream. It is in this enclosed garden that guests enjoy both breakfast and dinner at small tables draped in pretty Provençal-print fabric. While the sitting and dining rooms have a decidedly Provençal charm, each of the bedrooms follows a specific theme, which varies all the way from Natural to Classy Elegant. Claudia prepares four- to six-course meals with fresh seasonal ingredients from the region. Christian, a frequent traveler, knows from experience what it takes to truly enjoy being a guest. *Directions:* Exit the A7 at no. 23, Avignon Nord/Centre. Follow D942 in the direction of Carpentras until you get to Monteux. In Monteux center turn right on D31 to Velleron Centre. Villa Velleron is in the center of town and well sign-posted.

VILLA VELLERON
Hosts: Claudia & Christian Hickl
15 rue Roquette
84740 Velleron, France
Tel: 04.90.20.12.31, Fax: 04.90.20.10.34
4 Rooms, Double: €105–€125, 1 Suite: €185–€195
1 Apartment: €126 daily, €880 weekly
Minimum Stay Required, Table d'hôte: €31
Closed: mid-Nov to weekend before Easter
Credit cards: none
Other Languages: fluent English, German, Italian
Region: Provence-Alps-Côte d'Azur, Michelin Map: 528

In French, La Maison aux Volets Bleus means The House of the Blue Shutters—indeed, the bright cobalt shutters of the Marets' charming home can be seen from far below the hilltop town of Venasque. Follow a winding road up from the plains to this ancient town, which is now a haven for painters and art lovers. An old stone archway leads to the Marets' romantic walled garden and their picturesque home filled with colorful dried-flower bouquets hanging from every available rafter. The cozy living room opens onto a balcony with a sensational panoramic view. Each bedroom is unique and decorated with Martine Maret's artistic flair for harmonious colors, Provençal prints, and simple, attractive furnishings. Martine and her husband Jerome are an energetic couple with many talents who enjoy welcoming guests into their home and to their table. Plan to stay for several days to enjoy genuine hospitality and delicious meals. *Directions:* From the A7 take the Avignon North exit following signs northeast to Carpentras. From Carpentras take the D4 towards Apt for 8 km and turn to Venasque. Look for the turnoff marked Venasque to the right up a hill. Continue to the fountain square (Place de la Fontaine) and look for a Chambres d'Hôtes sign down the road a little to the left indicating the arched entry to the Marets' home.

LA MAISON AUX VOLETS BLEUS
Hosts: Martine & Jerome Maret
Place des Bouviers, Le Village
84210 Venasque, France
Tel: 04.90.66.03.04, Fax: 04.90.66.16.14
6 Rooms, Double: €75–€95
1 Suite: €125
Table d'hôte: €26
Open: Mar to Nov, Credit cards: none
Other Languages: good English
Region: Provence-Alps-Côte d'Azur, Michelin Map: 527

Laurence and Claude searched for three years before finding this "perfect" property, a large, Mediterranean-style villa built in the 1980s, conveniently located about midway between the historic villages of Vence and St. Paul de Vence. As you approach the property along a nondescript road, it is difficult to imagine what awaits you, but when you drive through the gates, the splendor of the setting and a warm welcome become a reality. The home sits on a hillside with a sweeping, panoramic view out over the green, rolling hills of Provence. A lovely large swimming pool nestles on the terrace in front of the house, again facing the splendid view, and there is also a clay tennis court. The ground level of the house is the Oliviers' family home, the guest bedrooms being found upstairs. There is one deluxe suite, but my favorite rooms are the more simple ones: Olivia which has no balcony but has a pretty view from the window, or Emeline, a spacious room with balcony and a lovely view. In the central hallway sits a large table spread with information on what to see and do in this region so rich in beauty and culture. A plentiful breakfast is served in the large summer kitchen with its stone table. Stay here and you will appreciate the quiet ambiance, beautiful views and gracious welcome. *Directions:* From Vence, take the road signposted to Grasse. Soon after leaving Vence, at the roundabout, turn left on Chemin de la Sine. La Bastide is on your right after about 1 km.

BASTIDE AUX OLIVIERS AT VENCE
Hosts: Laurence & Claude Ollivier
1260, Chemin de la Sine
06140 Vence, France
Tel: 04.93.24.20.33, Fax: 04.93.58.55.78
4 Rooms, Double: €90–€175
1 Cottage: €450–€850 weekly
Table d'hôte: €30
Open: all year, Credit cards: none
Other Languages: good English
Region: Provence-Alps-Côte d'Azur, Michelin Map: 527

La Colline de Vence, a 200-year-old villa tucked in the hills above Vence, is an absolute jewel. You will be instantly captivated by its superb setting, stunning views, pretty bedrooms, lovely swimming pool, and, most of all, by your charming young hostess, Kristin. Kristin was born in East Berlin, moving to Burgundy after she married her French husband, Frédéric. They both dreamed of living near Vence and opening a bed and breakfast, so they bought an exceptionally large villa with enormous potential to use both as their own home and as a place to welcome guests. Each of the three bedrooms has its own private entrance opening off a sunny, flagstone terrace. The rooms are not especially large, but quite big enough, and each has a large window with a splendid view of the sea and mountains. They are tastefully decorated in a fresh, sweet, uncluttered style. Each is similar in decor, except for the color scheme: Amandiers is green, Orangers is a Provençal yellow, and Mimosas is a pastel lemon. There are also two junior suites: Bougainvilliers in handsome reds and yellows and Oliviers in a decor of soft cream and brown. The pool is gorgeous with a beautiful setting—on a lovely terrace with a breathtaking view over the picturesque landscape of Provence. *Directions:* From Vence, take D2 toward Coursegoules/Col de Vence. About 800 meters after leaving Vence, turn left, following signs.

❋ ☕ 🏌 ⛾ P 🚭 ≈ 🖼 ⛱ 🏃 👫 🐎 ⛵

LA COLLINE DE VENCE
Hosts: Kristin & Frédéric Bronchard
808, Chemin des Salles
06140 Vence, France
Tel & Fax: 04.93.24.03.66
5 Rooms, Double: €90–€135
Open: all year, Credit cards: none
Other Languages: good English
Region: Provence-Alps-Côte d'Azur, Michelin Map: 527

The Château de Boucéel, listed as a historical monument, is truly a treasure. Surrounded by a vast park, it sits proudly on the crest of a small hill, facing a lawn that rolls gently down to a small lake, complete with white swans and a little bridge. This handsome stone mansion was built in 1763, though it has roots in the 12th century. Since the very beginning it has been in the family of your charming host, Comte de Roquefeuil, who can enthrall you for hours with fascinating stories of the château's colorful past and of the role his ancestors played in various battles. The lovely Comtesse de Roquefeuil is equally charming and they both extend a genuinely warm welcome. The impeccably maintained interior is spectacular. All of the rooms are filled with astonishing antique furniture and the walls abound with family portraits. On the ground floor is a dramatic foyer with a sweeping staircase on one side, a cozy library, a billiard room, and an elegant dining room. The bedrooms display the same refined, elegant decor and perfect taste, decorated with family antiques. One of my favorites, Oncle François, is a very large room with windows overlooking the front garden. Mont Saint Michel and the landing beaches of Normandy are nearby. *Directions:* From Avranches, towards Mont St Michel, exit 34, travel 1 km on N175 and then take exit D40 towards Antrain. Follow the D40 for 6 km; turn left on D308 towards St. Senier de Beuvron. The château is 800 meters down the road.

CHÂTEAU DE BOUCÉEL
Hosts: Comte & Comtesse Régis de Roquefeuil-Cahuzac
50240 Vergoncey, France
Tel: 02.33.48.34.61, Fax: 02.33.48.16.26
5 Suites: €150–€170
1 Cottage: €160 daily, €480–€800 weekly
Closed: Jan 15 to Feb 15, Credit cards: all major
Other Languages: fluent English, Spanish
Region: Lower Normandy, Michelin Maps: 512, 513

Accolades for this discovery came from a couple who has used our recommendations and "found them always exactly as represented—and in many cases even better than described." Well, Mr and Mrs Doty, thank you for directing us to La Ferme—it is even better than you described! Located just south of Tournus, in a farm village just up from the River Saône, this wonderful complex is guarded by heavy doors. Framing the courtyard, the whitewashed walls of the main farmhouse are a showcase for protruding beams and exposed stone, while beautiful red tiles, weathered by the sun, add a splash of color. The five guestrooms, found up two mirroring stairways, are tucked under the steep pitch of the old roof. Low doorways, enormous beams, and exposed, thick nails are evidence of the age of this charming old complex. The spotlessly modern bathrooms, excellent plumbing and lighting, and comfortable beds topped with cozy down comforters are testament to the work and attention to detail that the Stahel-Zerlauths have lavished on their property. Their professional level of service is reflective of the finest Swiss hotels in which they both made a career for more than three decades. An accomplished chef, Ruedi prepares evening meals incorporating the farm's own produce. *Directions:* Exit the Lyon–Dijon motorway at Tournus and then take the N6 south in the direction of Mâcon. Le Villars is just south of Tournus to the east of N6.

LA FERME DU VILLARS
Hosts: Ilse & Ruedi Stahel-Zerlauth
71700 Le Villars, France
Tel: 03.85.32.51.85
5 Rooms, Double: €95–€130
Table d'hôte: €25
Open: Apr to Oct, Credit cards: MC, VS
Other Languages: fluent English & German
Region: Burgundy, Michelin Map: 519

Le Petit Romieu is situated in an intriguing part of France, a wild, open, unpopulated region of flatlands and marshes that stretch from Arles to the sea. You see some brilliant green rice fields, but this is also a region of vast estates where champion bulls are bred for the bullring and wild horses roam free. We love this open country and were happy to discover Le Petit Romieu. The home is very appealing—a two-story, creamy-toned stone building with tall French doors on the ground level and tall windows above, all attractively framed with light-blue shutters. A terrace dotted with white chairs and tables plus a green lawn bordered by rose bushes complete the attractive scene. There are a couple of guest lounges and a dining room on the first floor and then a staircase winds up to the bedrooms, each of which is individually decorated using pretty fabrics. The home operates as a bed and breakfast from April through August and at other times of the year serves as a hunting lodge. *Directions:* From A54, take the Arles exit 4, heading for Les Saintes Maries de la Mer on the D570. After about 3 km, turn left on D36 marked to Salin de Giraud. After about 3 km more, turn right on D36B marked to Gageron and on to Villeneuve. At the intersection, go towards Fielouse. Turn left on a lane signposted Le Petit Romieu. Continue past the large manor, an owner's home, and follow signs.

LE PETIT ROMIEU
Host: M. Blanchet Villeneuve
13200 Villeneuve (Arles), France
Tel: 04.90.97.00.27, Fax: 04.90.97.00.52
5 Rooms, Double: €70
Open: Apr to Aug, Credit cards: none
Other Languages: no English
Region: Provence-Alps-Côte d'Azur, Michelin Map: 527

The Château du Riau, although charmingly small, happily lacks none of the accoutrements of a proper castle. A bridge spans the ancient moat and leads through a whimsical, twin-towered keep (fashioned from bricks arranged in a fanciful diamond design) into the enclosed courtyard. Facing the courtyard, the two-story manor house with steep gray-slate roof reflects a harmonious blend of styles from the 15th, 16th, and 17th centuries. The Baron and Baronne Durye are descendants of the original owner, Charles Papillon, a goldsmith from Moulins, who received the property from Anne de Beaujeu, daughter of King Louis XI. Although a historical monument and at times open to the public for tours, the castle is definitely a family home, occupied by the Duryes and their three sons. Reached by an impressive circular stone staircase, the bedrooms are appointed in fine antiques, with museum-quality and museum-size beds and all look onto a tranquil forest. Victoria, a lovely room with pretty pink decor, offers the most modern comforts and has a small adjoining room set with twin beds, which would be perfect for children. Throughout the house, family portraits and memorabilia abound—one portrait is of a portly ancestor who fought in the American Revolution with Lafayette. *Directions:* From Moulins take the N7 north towards Nevers for 15 km. Just after the dual carriageway changes to two lanes, the lane to the château is on the right.

CHÂTEAU DU RIAU
Hosts: Baron & Baronne Durye
03460 Villeneuve sur Allier, France
Tel: 04.70.43.34.47, Fax: 04.70.43.30.74
2 Rooms, Double: €130
1 Suite: €160
Open: Mar to Dec, Credit cards: none
Other Languages: good English
Region: Auvergne, Michelin Map: 519

When Christine and Xavier Ferry bought Manoir de la Semoigne, 25 kilometers west of Reims, it looked absolutely hopeless: no water, no electricity, cows and pigs living in the house. However, with the help of family and friends, they transformed the derelict house back into a proper home. Christine and Xavier have boundless energy. He runs the farm and, when cows became unprofitable, he turned the grazing ground into an 18-hole golf course. (Energetic guests will also enjoy the tennis court on the grounds.) Christine is a busy woman, yet manages to offer four of her nicely decorated bedrooms to the public. Also at hand is the charming Sophie, who sees to guests' needs. There are three guestrooms in the main house, all named for their color scheme: Bleue, Jaune, and Beige. The largest and most dramatic room, Bibliothèque, is housed in a separate wing. Evening meals can be prepared with advance reservation. From the front, the building looks like a farmhouse flanked by stone barns but from the rear garden with its own little stream, the house looks quite different: more like a small, turreted castle. *Directions:* From the A4 (Paris to Reims road) take the Dormans exit 21. Turn right towards Dormans, right again back over the expressway towards Villers Agron, then right at the first road, which leads to the Manoir de la Semoigne.

MANOIR DE LA SEMOIGNE
Hosts: Christine & Xavier Ferry
Chemin de la Ferme
02130 Villers Agron, France
Tel: 03.23.71.60.67, Fax: 03.23.69.36.54
4 Rooms, Double: €73–€93
Table d'hôte: €42
Open: Apr to Oct, Credit cards: none
Other Languages: fluent English
Region: Champagne-Ardenne, Michelin Map: 515

The 13th-century Château de Villiers-le-Mahieu fulfills any childhood fantasy to live in a fairy-tale castle. The beautifully maintained castle sits in parklike grounds, manicured to perfection, on its own little island surrounded by a moat. The main access is over a narrow bridge leading into the inner courtyard-garden, framed on three sides by the ivy-covered stone walls of the château. The Château de Villiers-le-Mahieu is not an intimate bed and breakfast, but rather a commercial operation with 26 guestrooms in the château and 11 in the garden annex. Splurge and request room 1, a grand room in the original castle, wallpapered in a handsome blue print fabric, which repeats in the drapes at the three tall French windows looking out to the gardens. In the park surrounding the castle there are tennis courts and a superb swimming pool. You will also enjoy and delight in the comfort of 43 recently added guestrooms. Attractive in their Oriental furnishings, they enjoy the benefit of modern facilities such as Internet connections, air conditioning, and luxurious bathrooms. They also have a spa, described as "a haven of peace, harmony and relaxation". *Directions:* Located 40 km west of Paris. Take the A13 west from Paris; exit south on A12 toward Dreux-Bois d'Arcy. Follow signs to Dreux until Pontchartrain; then take D11 signposted to Thoiry. As the road leaves Thoiry, turn left on D45 toward Villiers le Mahieu; continue through town—the château is on the left.

CHÂTEAU DE VILLIERS-LE-MAHIEU
Host: Jean-Luc Chaufour
78770 Villiers le Mahieu, France
Tel: 01.34.87.44.25, Fax: 01.34.87.44.40
95 Rooms, Double: €199–€349*
*Breakfast not included: €16
Closed: Christmas, Credit cards: AX, VS
Other Languages: good English
Châteaux & Hôtels Collection
Region: Île-de-France, Michelin Map: 514

James and Marie-José Hamel are a charming couple who take great pleasure in welcoming guests to their magnificent manor home. Originally a fortress dating from the 12th century, the château was rebuilt in 1450 and again in 1750 and has a colorful history. The Hamels are fond of recounting the story of their most famous visitor, Andy Rooney of Sixty Minutes fame. Rooney worked here as a journalist during World War II when the château was inhabited by the American Press Corps and revisited in 1984. General Bradley was also stationed nearby. James, born three months after the end of the war, was a name his parents often saw in the press. Breakfast is served in the former press room complete with brass nameplate in English still intact on the door. A lofty ceiling, dark, pine-paneled walls, and a lovely old tile floor provide intimate surroundings to begin the day or enjoy an evening aperitif. Guest bedrooms are tastefully furnished and decorated with handsome antiques and harmonious color schemes. Les Jardins is a gorgeous room looking across the moat to the expanse of back garden. The rooms are found in a separate wing of the château, thus affording guests a convenient, private entry. *Directions:* Take the N13 to Cherbourg, exit at Vouilly, and continue on the D113. After entering Vouilly, look for the church (after Vouilly Marie) and the Chambres d'Hôtes sign directing you left onto a winding road and on to the manor.

CHÂTEAU DE VOUILLY
Hosts: Marie-José & James Hamel
Vouilly, 14230 Isigny-sur-Mer, France
Tel: 02.31.22.08.59
5 Rooms, Double: €75–€95
Open: Mar to Dec, Credit cards: MC, VS
Other Languages: some English
Region: Lower Normandy, Michelin Map: 513

Driving up to the Domaine de Bidaudières, we thought we must have made a wrong turn—this sensational château could not possibly be a bed and breakfast but rather a wine estate of a prestigious hotel! Happily, we were absolutely wrong. Indeed, the 18th-century Domaine de Bidaudières, which sits in majestic splendor looking over a manicured terrace with swimming pool and farther below to a small lake and woodlands, does receive guests. Another fabulous surprise is that your hosts are also not what you might expect at all. Instead of being well on in years, formal, and reserved, Sylvie and Pascal Suzanne are a young, attractive, friendly couple with three children. They purchased the property in a state of dereliction and totally renovated it, even adding an elevator, a new wing with guest lounge, and a glass-enclosed sun terrace overlooking the gardens for breakfast. The decor throughout reflects the young, informal spirit of the owners, with cheerful fabrics and stylish furniture. All of the attractive guestrooms are of excellent quality and very pretty. My favorite, Le Clos Bouchet, is an especially spacious room with two large windows capturing a view of the gardens. The day we arrived there was a wedding dinner being held in the beautiful old wine caverns—a marvelously romantic setting. *Directions:* From Vouvray, take D46 east toward Vernou. Just after leaving town, turn left at the second road after going under the railroad tracks.

※ ■ ☞ ☎ ⚱ ♈ @ W P ≈ ⚓ ⛷ 𐀃 ♁ 🏇 ♇

DOMAINE DE BIDAUDIÈRES
Hosts: Sylvie & Pascal Suzanne
Rue du Peu Morier
37210 Vouvray, France
Tel: 02.47.52.66.85, Fax: 02.47.52.62.17
5 Rooms, Double: €130–€160
1 Suite: €140–€160
1 Cottage: €160 daily, €1200 weekly
Open: all year, Credit cards: none
Other Languages: some English
Region: Center, Michelin Map: 518

316

Index

A

Abbaye de Fontenay (L'), 138
Abbaye de Montmajour, 99
Aiguines, 105
Aïnhoa, 74
Airfare, 5
Aix en Provence, 91
  Atelier Paul Cézanne, 92
  Cathedral Saint Sauveur, 92
  Cours Mirabeau, 92
  Domaine de la Brillane, 176
  Museum of Tapestries, 92
  Old Quarter, 92
Aix les Bains, 171
Albert Schweitzer, 153
Albertville, 171
Albi, 84
  Musée Toulouse Lautrec, 84
Alise Sainte Reine, 139
Aloxe Corton, 144
Amboise, 49
  Châteaux, 49
  Clos Lucé, 49
  Vieux Manoir, Le, 177
Ambonnay, 163
American Cemetery in Hamm, 132
Ammerschwihr, 154
Andelys (Les), 26
  Château Gaillard, 26
Andlau
  Château d'Haute Andlau, 156
Angers, 46
  Châteaux, 46
Annecy, 172
Antibes, 116
  Château de Grimaldi, 116

Musée Picasso, 116
Appeville-Annebault
  Aubépines aux Chauffourniers, Les, 178
Apt, 92
Arles, 99
  Amphithéâtre, 99
  Musée de l'Arles Antique, 99
  Muséon Arlaten, 99
  Théâtre Antique, 99
Arpaillargues
  Mas du Moulin, Le, 179
Ascain, 73
Aubèle, L', Lay-Lamidou, 235
Aubépines aux Chauffourniers, Les, Appeville–
  Annebault, 178
Auberge d'Inxent, Inxent, 227
Aubignan
  Vallon, Le, 180
Aubigny sur Nère
  Château de la Verrerie, 181
Audierne, 39
Aurifat, Cordes-sur-Ciel, 203
Autoire, 61
Auxey-Duresses
  Château de Melin, 182
Avallon, 140
Avignon, 81, 95
  Cathédral de Notre Dame des Doms, 96
  Église Saint Didier (L'), 96
  Musée Calvet, 96
  Palais des Papes, 96
  Pont Saint Bénezet, 96
Ay, 164
Azay-le-Rideau, 47
  Châteaux, 47
Azay-sur-Indre
  Bihourderie, La, 183

B

Balcons de la Mescla, 103
Banyuls, 86
    Cellier des Templiers, 86
    Musée Maillol, 86
Barr, 156
    Château de Landsberg, 156
Bastide aux Oliviers at Vence, Vence, 306
Bastide Clairence (La), 77
Bastide de Cassiopee, La, Roussillon, 276
Bastide Saint Mathieu, Grasse, 223
Bastide Sainte Agnes, Carpentras, 194
Baux de Provence (Les), 97
Bayeux, 30
    Musée Baron Gérard, 31
    Musée de la Tapisserie, 30
    Saint Patrice Square, 30
Bayonne, 77
    Basque Museum, 77
    Bonnat Museum, 77
    Medieval Cellars, 77
    Saint Mary's Cathedral, 77
Beaugency, 51
    Nôtre Dame, 51
Beaulieu sur Mer, 112
Beaune, 144
    Hôtel Dieu, 145
    Musée du Vin de Bourgogne, 145
Beausset, Le
    Cancades, Les, 184
Bed & Breakfast Travel
    General Information, 3
Beguinage, Le, Cour–Cheverny, 205
Belval, 165
Belvédère du Pas de Souci, 83
Benodet, 40
Bergheim, 155
Berzé le Ville & Châtel, 147
Beynac, 57
    Hôtel Bonnet, 57

Biarritz, 70
    Chocolate Museum, 70
    Côte des Basque, 71
    Historical Museum, 70
    Hôtel du Palais, 70
    Lighthouse, 71
    Marine Museum, 70
    Port Vieux, 71
    Villa Le Goëland, 185
Bidart, 72
Bihourderie, La, Azay-sur-Indre, 183
Biot, 116
Bize de la Tour, Remoulins, 271
Blienschwiller, 156
    Winzenberg, Hotel, 186
Bligny Les Beaune
    Clos des Saunières, Le, 187
Blois, 50
    Châteaux, 50
Bonnieux, 92
    Clos du Buis, Le, 188
    Trois Sources, Les, 189
Bosdarros
    Maison Trille, 190
Bourdeilles, 55
Bouzies, 64
Bouzy, 163
Brancion, 147
Brantôme, 55
Bretenoux, 61
Breuil-en-Bessin, Le
    Château de Goville, 191
Brittany, 35
    Itinerary & Map, 35

C

Caen, 30
    Memorial, 30
Cagnes sur Mer, 115
    Musée Renoir, 115

Cahors
  Pont Valentré, 63
Calvisson
  Chez Burckel de Tell, 192
Cambo les Bains, 75
  Arnaga, 75
Campagne, 57
Cancades, Les, Beausset, Le, 184
Cancale, 37
Cannes, 117
  Boulevard de la Croisette, 117
  Old Port, 117
  Suquet (Le), 117
Cap d'Antibes, 116
  Villa Panko, 193
Cap Ferrat, 111
Car Rental, 5
Carcassonne, 84
Carennac, 61
Carnac, 41
  Musée de la Préhistoire, 41
Carpentras
  Bastide Sainte Agnes, 194
Castelbouc, 82
Castellane, 103
  Nôtre Dame du Roc Chapel, 103
Castelnau de Médoc, 61
  Château du Foulon, 195
Cavaillon, 95
Cellphones, 6
Céret, 86
  Musée d'Art Moderne, 86
Chablis, 138
Chalet des Troncs, Le, Grand Bornand, Le, 221
Chalet Rémy, Saint Gervais, 280
Chambéry, 171
Chambolle–Musigny, 143
  Château-Hôtel André Ziltener, 143
Chambord, 51
  Châteaux, 51

Chambres d'Hôtes, 4
Chamonix, 169
Champigné
  Château des Briottières, 196
Chantonnay
  Manoir de Ponsay, 197
Chapelle de la Reconnaissance, 165
Chapelle des Moines, 147
Chartres, 45
  Cathedral, 45
Chasse sur Rhône
  Domaine de Gorneton, 198
Château Bazoches-du-Morvan, 141
Château de Beaufer, Ozenay, 262
Château de Beaulieu, Saumur, 294
Château de Boucéel, Vergoncey, 308
Château de Cormatin, 147
Château de Fuissé, 148
Château de Garrevaques, Garrevaques, 217
Château de Goville, Breuil-en-Bessin, Le, 191
Château de Grimaldi, Antibes, 116
Château de Kermezen, Pommerit–Jaudy, 269
Château de la Caze, Malène (La), 82
Château de la Flocellière, Flocellière, La, 215
Château de la Grande Noë, Moulicent, 254
Château de la Rue, Cour-sur-Loire, 204
Château de la Verrerie, Aubigny sur Nère, 181
Château de Larroque Toirac, 64
Château de Melin, Auxey-Duresses, 182
Château de Messey, Ozenay, 263
Château de Montfort, 58
Château de Nazelles, Nazelles–Négron, 257
Château de Talhouet, Rochefort en Terre, 275
Château de Villiers-le-Mahieu, Villiers le Mahieu, 313
Château de Vougeot, 143
Château de Vouilly, Vouilly, 314
Château des Briottières, Champigné, 196
Château des Ormeaux, Nazelles, 256
Château d'Etxauz, Saint Etienne de Baïgorry, 279
Château d'Ivoy, Ivoy le Pré, 229

Château du Foulon, Castelnau de Médoc, 195
Château du Guilguiffin, Landudec, 232
Château du Plessis, Jaille-Yvon, La, 230
Château du Riau, Villeneuve sur Allier, 311
Château Franc Mayne, Saint Emilion, 278
Château Hauterives, 82
Chateau les Roches, Mont-Saint-Jean, 249
Château Talaud, Loriol du Comtat, 241
Château Thierry, 165
Château-Hôtel André Ziltener, Chambolle-Musigny, 143
Châteauneuf De Gadagne
    Clos des Saumanes, Le, 199
Châteauneuf en Auxois
    Chez Bagatelle, 200
Châteaux Country, 43
    Itinerary & Map, 43
Chatenois, 156
Châtillon-sur-Marne, 165
Chaumont, 49
    Châteaux, 49
Chenonceaux, 48
    Châteaux, 48
Chevaliers du Tastevin, 143
Cheverny, 51
    Châteaux, 51
Chez Bagatelle, Châteauneuf en Auxois, 200
Chez Burckel de Tell, Calvisson, 192
Chez Gourlaouen, Nevez, 258
Chez Maurer, Ottrott, 261
Children
    Policies Concerning Welcome, 6
Chinon, 46
    Châteaux, 46
Chouette qui Chante, La, Motte Ternant, La, 252
Cingle de Montfort, 59
Cipières, 119
Citadel of Bitche, 131
Civray de Touraine
    Marmittière, La, 201
Clos de Vougeot, 143

Clos des Saumanes, Le, Châteauneuf de Gadagne, 199
Clos des Saunières, Le, Bligny Les Beaune, 187
Clos du Buis, Le, Bonnieux, 188
Closerie de Gilly, La, Gilly-les-Citeaux, 218
Cluny, 147
Col de Calvair, 153
Col de la Schlucht, 153
Colline de Vence, La, Vence, 307
Collioure
    Château Royal, 86
Collonges la Rouge, 62
Colmar, 152
    Petite Venise, 152
    Unterlinden Museum, 152
Concarneau, 41
    Musée de la Pêche, 41
    Ville Close, 41
Conques, 65
Contres
    Rabouillère, La, 202
Cordes-sur-Ciel, 84
    Aurifat, 203
Corniche des Cevennes, 81
Corniche Inférieure, 111
Corniche Sublime, 103
Cour–Cheverny
    Beguinage, Le, 205
Cour-sur-Loire
    Château de la Rue, 204
Coux, Le
    Manoir de la Brunie, 206
Credit Cards, 7
Crépon
    Manoir de Crépon, 207
Crillon le Brave
    Hostellerie de Crillon le Brave, 94
Croix Blanche (La), 147
Croix de la Voulte, La, Saint Lambert des Levées, 283
Croix d'Etain, La, Grez–Neuville, 224

Crouttes (Vimoutiers)
    Prieuré Saint Michel, Le, 208
Cumièrs, 165
Currency, 7

D

Dambach la Ville, 156
Damery, 165
Deauville, 28
Demi-Pension, 14
Détroits (Les), 82
Dieffenthal, 156
Dijon, 142
    Musée des Beaux Arts, 142
Dinan
    Logis du Jerzual, Le, 209
Dinard, 38
Dissay sous Courcillon
    Prieuré, Le, 210
Domaine D'Aurouze, Saint Martin Les Eaux, 286
Domaine de Beauséjour, Panzoult, 264
Domaine de Bidaudières, Vouvray, 315
Domaine de Gorneton, Chasse sur Rhône, 198
Domaine de la Brillane, Aix en Provence, 176
Domaine de Layaude Basse, Lacoste, 231
Domaine de Mestré, Le, Fontevraud l'Abbaye, 216
Domaine de Montgivroux, Le, Mondement-Montgivroux, 247
Domaine de Saint Géry, Lascabanes, 233
Domaine du Bois Vert, Grans, 222
Domaine du Haut Baran, Duravel par Puy l'Evêque, 212
Domaine du Moulin de Labique, Saint Vivien, 291
Domme, 58
    Terrasse de la Barre, 58
Dordogne & Lot River Valleys, 53
    Itinerary & Map, 53
Dormans, 165
Doucinière, La, Othis–Beaumarchais, 260
Drain
    Mésangeau, Le, 211

Driver's License, 8
Driving & Directions, 8
Duravel par Puy l'Evêque
    Domaine du Haut Baran, 212

E

Eguisheim, 152
Eichhoffen
    Feuilles d'Or, Les, 213
Electrical Current, 9
Enclos, L', Hautefort, 226
English
    Level of English Spoken, 11
Épernay, 163
Escalo, L', Moustiers Sainte Marie, 255
Esvres sur Indre
    Moulins des Vontes, Les, 214
Euro, 7
Evêché, L', Vaison la Romaine, 301
Evires Pottery, 173
Eyzies de Tayac (Les), 56
    Font de Gaume, 57
    Les Combarelles, 57
    Musée National de la Préhistoire, 56
Èze Bord de la Mer, 114
Èze Village, 114

F

Familia Hôtel, Paris, 265
Faux de Verzy, 163
Fayet Pass, 105
Ferme Auberge, 14
Ferme de la Tourelle, Longues-sur-Mer, 240
Ferme du Villars, La, Villars, Le, 309
Feuilles d'Or, Les, Eichhoffen, 213
Figeac, 65
Flavigny sur Ozerain, 140
Fleury, 165
Flocellière, La
    Château de la Flocellière, 215

Florac, 81
Fontaine de Vaucluse, 95
Fontenay Abbey, 138
Fontevraud l'Abbaye
    Domaine de Mestré, Le, 216
Fontvieille, 98
    Moulin de Daudet, 98
    Régalido (La), 98
    Roman Aqueduct, 98
Forêt Fouesnant (La), 41
Fort Carré, 116
Fouesnant, 41
Foundation Maeght, 120

G

Garlande, La, Saint Clar, 277
Garrevaques
    Château de Garrevaques, 217
Gasoline, 8
Geneva, 169
Gevrey Chambertin, 143
Gilly-les-Citeaux
    Closerie de Gilly, La, 218
Giverny, 25
    Monet's Home, 25
    Musée d'Art Américain, 26
    Réserve, La, 219
Gorbio, 113
Gordes, 93
Gorges de la Jonte, 83
Gorges du Loup, 119
Gorges du Tarn, 79
    Itinerary & Map, 79
Gorges du Verdon, 101
    Itinerary & Map, 101
Gouffre de Padirac, 60
Gourdon, 118
    Nid d'Aigle (Le), 118
Gramat
    Moulin de Fresquet, 220

Grand Bornand, Le
    Chalet des Troncs, Le, 221
Grande Corniche, 111
Grange de Jusalem, La, Mazan, 243
Grans
    Domaine du Bois Vert, 222
Grasse, 118
    Bastide Saint Mathieu, 223
    Fragonard, 118
    Gallimard, 118
    Molinard, 118
Grez–Neuville
    Croix d'Etain, La, 224
Gueberschwihr, 152
Guérande
    Tricot, Le, 225
Guéthary, 72

H

Hackenberg, 127
    Hackenberg Fortress, 124
Haut de Cagnes, 115
    Château Grimaldi, 115
Haut Koenigsbourg, 156
Haute Côte de Beaune, 145
Hautefort
    Enclos, L', 226
Hauterives, Château, 82
Hautvillers, 164
Hendaye, 73
Hilltowns of the French Riviera, 107
    Itinerary & Map, 107
Honfleur, 27
    Eugène Boudin Museum, 27
    Musée d'Art Populaire, 28
    Musée Marine, 28
Hostellerie de Crillon le Brave, Crillon le Brave, 94
Hostellerie le Phébus, Joucas, 94
Hunawihr, 154
    Center for the Reintroduction of Storks, 154

Husseren les Châteaux, 152

I

Icons, 10
Inxent
    Auberge d'Inxent, 227
Isle sur la Sorgue, L', 95
    Maison sur la Sorgue, La, 228
Ispagnac Basin, 82
Itineraries, 10
    Brittany, 35
    Châteaux Country, 43
    Dordogne & Lot River Valleys, 53
    Gorges du Tarn, 79
    Gorges du Verdon, 101
    Hilltowns of the French Riviera, 107
    Normandy, 23
    Pays Basque, 67
    Provence, 89
    The French Alps, 168
    The Maginot Line & Exploring Lorraine, 122
    Wine Country—Alsace, 149
    Wine Country—Burgundy, 135
    Wine Country—Champagne, 159
Itterswiller, 156
Ivoy le Pré
    Château d'Ivoy, 229

J

Jaille-Yvon, La
    Château du Plessis, 230
Jardin des Colombières, 113
Joan of Arc, 26
Joucas
    Hostellerie le Phébus, 94
Juan les Pins, 116

K

Kaysersberg, 153
Kientzheim, 153

L

Lac d'Annecy, 172
Lac de Sainte Croix, 105
Lac du Bourget, 171
Lacave
    Château de la Treyne, 59
Lacoste
    Domaine de Layaude Basse, 231
Lady A, Vandenesse en Auxois, 303
Lamballe, 38
Landudec
    Château du Guilguiffin, 232
Langeais, 45
    Châteaux, 45
Language
    Level of English Spoken, 11
Lannion, 38
Lascabanes
    Domaine de Saint Géry, 233
Lascaux Caves, 55
Lascaux II, 55
Lasseube
    Maison Rancèsamy, 234
Lavandin, Le, Pernes-les-Fontaines, 267
Lay-Lamidou
    Aubèle, L', 235
Legé
    Mozardière, La, 236
Letter in French and English for Making Reservations, 20
Levernois
    Parc, Hôtel le, 237
Ligré
    Manoir Le Clos de Ligré, 238
Lisieux, 29
Livarot, 30
    Musée de Fromage, 30
Loches, 47
    Châteaux, 47
Logis du Jerzual, Le, Dinan, 209

Longué
    Manoir Saint-Gilles de la Cirottière, 239
Longues-sur-Mer
    Ferme de la Tourelle, 240
Loriol du Comtat
    Château Talaud, 241
Lot River Valley, 63
Loubressac, 61
Loumarin, 92

M

Maginot Line (The), 124
Mailly Champagne, 163
Maison aux Volets Bleus, La, Venasque, 305
Maison Dominxenea, Sare, 292
Maison Rancèsamy, Lasseube, 234
Maison Redon, La, Tour de Faure, 297
Maison sur la Sorgue, La, Isle sur la Sorgue, L', 228
Maison Tamarin, La, Saint Jean de Luz, 281
Maison Trille, Bosdarros, 190
Malène, La, 82
    Château de la Caze, 82
    Relais des Monts, 242
Manoir de Clénord, Mont Près Chambord, 248
Manoir de Crépon, Crépon, 207
Manoir de Kergrec'h, Plougrescant, 268
Manoir de la Brunie, Coux, Le, 206
Manoir de la Semoigne, Villers Agron, 312
Manoir de Ponsay, Chantonnay, 197
Manoir Le Clos de Ligré, Ligré, 238
Manoir Saint-Gilles de la Cirottière, Longué, 239
Maps, 12
    Itineraries
        Brittany, 35
        Châteaux Country, 43
        Dordogne & Lot River Valleys, 53
        Gorges du Tarn, 79
        Gorges du Verdon, 101
        Hilltowns of the French Riviera, 107
        Maginot Line (The), 123

Normandy, 23
Overview Map, 21
Pays Basque, 67
Provence, 89
The French Alps, 167
Wine Country—Alsace Itinerary, 149
Wine Country—Burgundy, 135
Wine Country—Champagne, 159
    Michelin maps, 12
Marmittière, La, Civray de Touraine, 201
Marseille, 91
    Canebière (La), 91
    Musée Grobet-Labadie, 91
Mas Azemar, Le, Mercuès, 245
Mas de Cante-Perdrix, Le, Mazan, 244
Mas De Cornud, Saint Rémy de Provence, 290
Mas de la Rose, Le, Orgon, 259
Mas d'Oléandre, Saint Médiers, 287
Mas du Moulin, Le, Arpaillargues, 179
Mas Samarcande, La, Vallauris, 302
Mas Vacquières, Saint Just et Vacquières, 282
Mazan
    Grange de Jusalem, La, 243
    Mas de Cante-Perdrix, Le, 244
Meals, 12
Megève, 170
Membership Affiliations, 14
    Châteaux Hôtels de France, 15
Menthon St. Bernard, 172
Menton, 113
    Jardin des Colombières, 113
Mercier, 164
Mercuès
    Château de Mercuès, 63
    Mas Azemar, Le, 245
Mésangeau, Le, Drain, 211
Metz, 133
Meursault, 145
Meyrueis, 83
Millau, 84

Miolans, 171
Mittelbergheim, 156
Modène
    Villa Noria, La, 246
Möet et Chandon, 163
Molines, 82
Monaco, 112
    Monte Carlo, 112
    Palais du Casino, 113
Mondement-Montgivroux
    Domaine de Montgivroux, Le, 247
Monet's Home, 25
Money, 7
Mont Blanc, 170
Mont Près Chambord
    Manoir de Clénord, 248
Mont Saint Michel, 34, 37, 39
Montagne de Reims, 162
Montagne, La
    Terre d'Or, La, 250
Montbrun, 64, 82
    Saut de la Mounine, 64
Monte Carlo, 112
Montignac, 55
Mont-Saint-Jean
    Chateau les Roches, 249
Morey-Saint-Denis, 143
Morlaix, 38
Moroges
    Orangerie, L', 251
Motte Ternant, La
    Chouette qui Chante, La, 252
Mougins, 117
    Rosées, Les, 253
Moulicent
    Château de la Grande Noë, 254
Moulin de Choiseaux, Le, Suevres, 296
Moulin de Fresquet, Gramat, 220
Moulin de Linthe, Le, Saint Leonard des Bois, 284

Moulin Neuf, Le, Paunat, 266
Moulinage Chabriol, Le, Saint Pierreville, 289
Moulins des Vontes, Les, Esvres sur Indre, 214
Moustiers Sainte Marie, 105
    Escalo, L', 255
    Faience, 105
    Nôtre Dame de Beauvoir, 105
Moyenne Corniche, 111
Mozardière, La, Legé, 236
Mumm, 161
Munster, 153
Musée du Fromage, Livarot, 30

N

Nazelles
    Château des Ormeaux, 256
Nazelles–Négron
    Château de Nazelles, 257
Neuville aux Larris (La), 165
Nevez
    Chez Gourlaouen, 258
Nice, 109
    Cimiez, 110
    Hôtel Negresco, 110
    Musée Chagall, 111
    Musée d'Archéologie, 111
    Musée des Beaux-Arts Jules Cheret, 109
    Musée International d'Art Naïf, 109
    Musée Matisse, 111
    Place Masséna, 110
    Promenade des Anglais, 109
    Vieille Ville (La), 110
Nîmes, 81, 100
    Amphithéâtre, 100
    Arénas, 100
    Fountain Gardens, 100
    Maison Carrée, 100
Normandy, 23
    Itinerary & Map, 23

Normandy Invasion
  Arromanches, 32, 360
    D-Day Museum, 32
    Gold Beach, 32
  Bayeux
    1944 Battle of Normandy Museum, 32
    British Cemetery and Memorial, 32
  Caen
    Memorial, 30
  Colleville sur Mer
    American Cemetery, 33
  Grandcamp Maisy
    Musée des Rangers, 34
  Juno Beach, 33
  Longues sur Mer, 33
  Omaha Beach, 33
  Pointe du Hoc, 33
  Port en Bessin, 33
  Saint Laurent sur Mer
    Musée Omaha, 33
  Sword Beach, 33
  Utah Beach, 33
Noyers, 138
Nuits Saint Georges, 143

O

Obernai, 156
Olhabidea, Sare, 293
Orangerie, L', Moroges, 251
Orches, 145
Orgon
  Mas de la Rose, Le, 259
Orléans, 51
Othis–Beaumarchais
  Doucinière, La, 260
Ottrott
  Château d'Ottrott, 156
  Chez Maurer, 261
Ozenay
  Château de Beaufer, 262

Château de Messey, 263

P

Panzoult
  Domaine de Beauséjour, 264
Parc d'Amorique, 38
Parc, Hôtel le, Levernois, 237
Paris
  Familia Hôtel, 265
Parking, 9
Pas de Souci, Belvédère du, 83
Pastourelle, La, Saint Lormel, 285
Paunat
  Moulin Neuf, Le, 266
Pays Basque, 67
  Itinerary & Map, 67
  Route du Fromage, 76
Pays d'Auge, 29
Pension Complète, 14
Périgueux, 55
Pernes-les-Fontaines
  Lavandin, Le, 267
Pérouges, 148
Perpignan, 87
Petit Moulin du Rouvre, Le, St Pierre de Plesguen, 288
Petit Romieu, Le, Villeneuve (Arles), 310
Peyreleau, 83
Pfaffenheim, 152
Piper-Hiedsieck, 161
Plancoët, 38
Plougrescant
  Manoir de Kergrec'h, 268
Point Sublime, 83
Pointe de la Croisette, Cannes, 117
Pointe du Raz, 39
Pommard, 145
Pommerit–Jaudy
  Château de Kermezen, 269
Pommery, 162
Pont Aven, 41

Pont Croix, 39
Pont de Barret
    Tuillières, Les, 270
Pont de l'Artugy, 104
Pont du Gard, 100
Pont du Loup, 119
Pont l'Abbé, 40
    Musée Bigoudin, 40
Porte Saint Pierre, 165
Prades, 82
Prieuré Saint Michel, Le, Crouttes (Vimoutiers), 208
Prieuré, Le, Dissay sous Courcillon, 210
Provence, 89
    Itinerary & Map, 89

Q

Quimper, 39
    Musée de la Faïence, 39
Quimperlé, 41

R

Rabouillère, La, Contres, 202
Rates, 15
Régalido (La), Fontvieille, 98
Regional Parc d'Amorique, 38
Reims, 161
    Nôtre Dame Cathedral, 161
Relais des Monts, Malène, La, 242
Remoulins
    Bize de la Tour, 271
Remoulins (Pont du Gard)
    Terre des Lauriers, La, 272
Reservations
    Cancellations, 17
    Check In, 17
    Deposits, 16
    General Information, 15
    Making Reservations by E-mail, 16
    Making Reservations by Fax, 16
    Making Reservations by Mail, 16
    Making Reservations by Telephone, 16
    Reservation Letter in French and English, 20
Réserve, La, Giverny, 219
Restaurants, 13
Rhune (La), 73
Ribeauvillé, 155
Richelieu
    Varenne, La, 273
Rilly la Montagne, 163
Riquewihr, 154
    Dolder Gate, 154
    Saint Nicholas & Restaurant, Hotel, 274
    Tour des Voleurs, 154
Roads, 9
Rocamadour, 59
Rochefort en Terre
    Château de Talhouet, 275
Rochepot (La), 146
    Château de la Rochepot, 146
Roque Gageac (La), 58
Roque Saint Christophe (La), 56
Roquebrune, 113
Roquefort sur Soulzon, 84
Rosées, Les, Mougins, 253
Rouen, 26
    Cathedral, 27
    Musée des Beaux-Arts, 27
Rouffach, 151
Roussillon, 93
    Bastide de Cassiopee, La, 276
Route de Fromage, 29
Route des Crêtes, 153
Route des Grands Crus, 142
Route du Champagne, 162
Route du Vin, 152
Rozier (Le), 83

S

Saint Avold, 124
Saint Avold American Cemetery, 124, 131

Saint Céré, 61
    Atelier Musée Jean Lurçat, 61
    Tours de Saint Laurent (Le), 61
Saint Chély du Tarn, 82
Saint Cirq Lapopie, 64
Saint Clar
    Garlande, La, 277
Saint Cyprien, 57
Saint Emilion
    Château Franc Mayne, 278
Saint Étienne Cathedral, 133
Saint Etienne de Baïgorry, 75
    Château d'Etxauz, 279
Saint Germain de Livet, 29
    Château, 29
Saint Gervais
    Chalet Rémy, 280
Saint Hippolyte, 156
Saint Jean Cap Ferrat, 112
Saint Jean de Luz, 72
    Maison Tamarin, La, 281
Saint Jean du Gard, 81
Saint Jean Pied de Port, 75
Saint Just et Vacquières
    Mas Vacquières, 282
Saint Lambert des Levées
    Croix de la Voulte, La, 283
Saint Leonard des Bois
    Moulin de Linthe, Le, 284
Saint Lormel
    Pastourelle, La, 285
Saint Malo, 37
Saint Martin Les Eaux
    Domaine D'Aurouze, 286
Saint Médiers
    Mas d'Oléandre, 287
Saint Nicholas & Restaurant, Hotel, Riquewihr, 274
Saint Paul de Vence, 120
    Foundation Maeght, 120

Saint Pierre de Plesguen
    Petit Moulin du Rouvre, Le, 288
Saint Pierre Toirac, 64
Saint Pierreville
    Moulinage Chabriol, Le, 289
Saint Rémy de Provence, 97
    Antiques (Les), 97
    Clinique de Saint Paul, 97
    Glanum, 97
    Mas De Cornud, 290
Saint Rivoal, 39
    Maison Cornic, 39
Saint Romain, 145
Saint Vivien
    Domaine du Moulin de Labique, 291
Sainte Agnes, 113
Sainte Croix, Lac de, 105
Sainte Énimie, 82
Sare, 74
    Maison Dominxenea, 292
    Olhabidea, 293
Sarlat, 59
Saumane de Vaucluse, 95
Saumur, 46
    Château de Beaulieu, 294
    Châteaux, 46
    École Nationale d'Équitation (L'), 46
Saut du Loup, 119
Scherwiller, 156
Seat Belts, 8
Séguret
    Vieux Figuier, Le, 295
Semur en Auxois, 140
Senanque, 94
Simserhof, 129
Simserhof Fortress, 124
Souillac, 59
Speed Limits, 9

Strasbourg, 157
    Maison des Tanneurs, 157
    Nôtre Dame Cathedral, 157
    Petite France, 157
Suevres
    Moulin de Choiseaux, Le, 296

T

Table d'Hôte, 13
Taittinger, 162
Telephones-General Information, 17
Terre Catalane, 86
Terre des Lauriers, La, Remoulins (Pont du Gard), 272
Terre d'Or, La, Montagne, La, 250
The French Alps, 168
    Itinerary & Map, 168
Toulzanie (La), 64
Tour de Faure
    Maison Redon, La, 297
Tour du Trésorier, La, Tournus, 298
Tourist Information, 18
Tournus, 146
    Perrin-de-Puycousin Museum, 146
    Saint Philibert Abbey, 146
    Tour du Trésorier, La, 298
Tourrettes sur Loup, 119
Trains, 19
Trébeurden, 38
Trépail, 163
Tricot, Le, Guérande, 225
Trigance, 103
Trip Cancellation Insurance, 19
Trois Epis
    Villa Rosa, 299
Trois Sources, Les, Bonnieux, 189
Trouville, 28
Truinas
    Volets Bleus, Les, 300
Tuillières, Les, Pont de Barret, 270
Turbie (La), 113

Turckheim, 153
Turenne, 62

U

Urcy, 142
Ussé, 46
    Châteaux, 46

V

Vaison la Romaine
    Evêché, L', 301
Vallauris, 117
    Galerie Madoura, 117
    Mas Samarcande, La, 302
    Musée de Vallauris, 117
Vallée du Cousin, 140
Vallon, Le, Aubignan, 180
Vandenesse en Auxois
    Lady A, 303
Vannes, 42
    Saint Peter's Cathedral, 42
Varenne, La, Richelieu, 273
Vaucluse, Fontaine de, 95
Velleron
    Villa Velleron, 304
Vénasque, 94
    Chapelle Notre Dame de Vie, 94
    Église de Notre Dame, 94
    Maison aux Volets Bleus, La, 305
Vence, 119
    Bastide aux Oliviers at Vence, 306
    Chapelle du Rosaire, 120
    Colline de Vence, La, 307
Verdun, 125
Vergoncey
    Château de Boucéel, 308
Verneuil, 165
Verzy, 163
Vézelay
    Basilica Sainte Madeleine, 140

Vieux Figuier, Le, Séguret, 295
Vieux Manoir, Le, Amboise, 177
Vignes (Les), 83
Villa Le Goëland, Biarritz, 185
Villa Noria, La, Modène, 246
Villa Panko, Cap d'Antibes, 193
Villa Rosa, Trois Epis, 299
Villa Velleron, Velleron, 304
Villandry, 47
    Châteaux, 47
Villars, Le
    Ferme du Villars, La, 309
Villefranche sur Mer, 111
Villeneuve (Arles)
    Petit Romieu, Le, 310
Villeneuve les Avignon, 97
    Fort Saint André, 97
    Philippe le Bel Tower, 97
Villeneuve sur Allier
    Château du Riau, 311
Villers Agron
    Manoir de la Semoigne, 312
Villers Allerand, 163
Villers Marmery, 163
Villiers le Mahieu
    Château de Villiers-le-Mahieu, 313
Volets Bleus, Les, Truinas, 300
Vougeot
    Château de Vougeot, 143
Vouilly
    Château de Vouilly, 314
Vouvray
    Domaine de Bidaudières, 315

W

Wheelchair Accessibility, 19
Wine Country—Alsace, 149
    Itinerary & Map, 149
Wine Country—Burgundy
    Itinerary & Map, 135

Wine Country—Champagne, 159
    Itinerary & Map, 159
Winter Olympics, 170, 171
Winzenberg, Hotel, Blienschwiller, 186

Y

Yvoire, 173

Z

Zellenberg, 154

KAREN BROWN wrote her first travel guide in 1976. Her personalized travel series has grown to 17 titles, which Karen and her small staff work diligently to keep updated. Karen, her husband, Rick, and their children, Alexandra and Richard, live in a small town on the coast south of San Francisco.

CLARE BROWN was a travel consultant for many years, specializing in planning itineraries using charming small hotels in the countryside. Her expertise is now available to a larger audience—the readers of her daughter Karen's travel guides. When not traveling, Clare and her husband, Bill, divide their time between northern California, Colorado, and Mexico.

JUNE EVELEIGH BROWN hails from Sheffield, England and lived in Zambia and Canada before moving to northern California where she lives in San Mateo with her husband, Tony, their German Shepherd, and a Siamese cat.

MARIE NOTOT, a contributing editor, is French and joined the Karen Brown team when she worked for a few years in California. She has settled on the Riviera with her husband, Philippe, and beautiful daughters, Jessie and Chloé. She has a consulting company, Tresors of France, *www.tresorsoffrance.com*, and assists clients with their travel arrangements.

BARBARA MACLURCAN TAPP draws all of the delightful hotel sketches and illustrations in this guide. Barbara was raised in Sydney, Australia, where she studied interior design. Although she continues with architectural rendering and watercolor painting, she devotes much of her time to illustrating the Karen Brown guides. Barbara lives in Kensington, California, with her husband, Richard, and is Mum to Jono, Alex and Georgia. For more information about her work visit *www.barbaratapp.com*.

JANN POLLARD, the artist of all the beautiful cover paintings in the Karen Brown series, has studied art since childhood and is well known for her outstanding impressionistic-style watercolors. Jann has received numerous achievement awards and her works are in private and corporate collections internationally. She is also a popular workshop teacher in the United States, Mexico and Europe. *www.jannpollard.com*. Fine art giclée prints of her paintings are available at *www.karenbrown.com*.

Notes

Ben Kong
Photography

Explore the world through his award winning images
on the Karen Brown World of Travel.
www.karenbrown.com

Romantik Hotel La Ferme d'Augustin, Ramatuelle

Romantik Hotels & Restaurants – Arrive, Relax, Enjoy!

At Romantik Hotels & Restaurants we invite you to arrive, relax and enjoy. Among our more than 200 Romantik Hotels you can find historic country inns, opulent estates and elegant city mansions in 11 European countries. We invite you to indulge in regional cuisines, discover award-winning restaurants or simply relax in one of our beautiful spas. We offer true Romantik hospitality, outstanding cuisine and a historic environment steeped in tradition. In France 15 Romantik Hotels & Restaurants are awaiting you. For more information and availability go to www.romantikhotels.com.

Romantik Hotels & Restaurants are about personal service, attention to detail and true hospitality.

ROMANTIK
HOTELS & RESTAURANTS
INTERNATIONAL

We look forward to your visit.
Romantik Hotels & Restaurants GmbH & Co. KG
Hahnstraße 70, 60528 Frankfurt, Germany

Fon: +49 (0) 69/66 12 34-0
Fax: +49 (0) 69/66 12 34-56

info@romantikhotels.com

www.romantikhotels.com

Karen Brown's World of Travel

A FREE KAREN BROWN WEBSITE MEMBERSHIP
IS INCLUDED WITH THE PURCHASE OF THIS GUIDE

$20 Value – Equal to the cover price of this book!

In appreciation for purchasing our guide, we offer a free membership that includes:

- The ability to custom plan and build unlimited itineraries
- 15% discount on all purchases made in the Karen Brown website store
- One free downloadable Karen Brown Itinerary from over 100 choices
- Karen Brown's World of Travel Newsletter—includes special offers & updates
Membership valid through December 31, 2009

To take advantage of this free offer go to the Karen Brown website shown below and create a login profile so we can recognize you as a Preferred Customer; then you can utilize the unrestricted trip planning and take advantage of the 15% store discount. Once you set up an account you will receive by email a coupon code to order the free itinerary.

Go to *www.karenbrown.com/preferred.php* to create your profile!

Karen Brown's
2009 Readers' Choice Awards

Most Romantic
Les Mas Vacquières
Saint Just et Vacquières

Warmest Welcome
La Croix de la Voulte
Saint Lambert des Levées

Greatest Value
La Colline de Vence
Vence

Splendid Splurge
Château Talaud
Loriol du Comtat

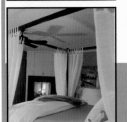

Be sure to vote for next year's winners by visiting
www.karenbrown.com